FENTANYL, INC.

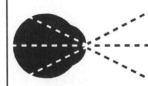

This Large Print Book carries the
Seal of Approval of N.A.V.H.

FENTANYL, INC.

HOW ROGUE CHEMISTS ARE CREATING THE DEADLIEST WAVE OF THE OPIOID EPIDEMIC

BEN WESTHOFF

THORNDIKE PRESS
A part of Gale, a Cengage Company

LIBRARY OF CONGRESS CIP DATA ON FILE.
CATALOGUING IN PUBLICATION FOR THIS BOOK
IS AVAILABLE FROM THE LIBRARY OF CONGRESS

ISBN-13: 978-1-4328-7619-7 (hardcover alk. paper)

Published in 2020 by arrangement with Grove Atlantic, Inc.

Printed in Mexico
Print Number: 01   Print Year: 2020

*In memory of
Michael "Helias" Schafermeyer,
inspired artist, generous soul*

CONTENTS

PART III: THE SOURCE

PART IV: A NEW APPROACH

INTRODUCTION

For Christmas vacation in 2014, Bailey Henke went on a road trip, driving west across the snowy plains of North Dakota. The recent high school graduate departed his apartment in Grand Forks with his roommate, Kain Schwandt. They passed the University of North Dakota, the lumber store, and the town landfill, before the city gave way to farmland. The sky began to open up.

Henke, who wore a chinstrap beard, put U2 on the stereo and watched the scenery speed by. Prone to goofy sarcasm, he had a way of putting others at ease, of putting on a brave face no matter how he felt inside. He and Schwandt knew that what lay ahead of them on this trip, that it wouldn't be easy, but they felt optimistic. They weren't just visiting family members for the holiday. They were traveling with a specific purpose: to get well.

The two eighteen-year-old friends had developed opioid addictions. In addition to nasty heroin habits, they had recently become consumed by an even more potent and destructive drug called fentanyl.

Most people, if they knew of fentanyl at all back then, knew of it as a medicine. Doctors had used it for decades, during surgeries, in epidurals for women during childbirth, and to help cancer patients and others in great pain. But around the time Henke and Schwandt started using it, fentanyl abuse was becoming increasingly common. Like heroin, fentanyl is a derivative of morphine, capable of producing both great pleasure and great suffering — except it can be fifty times stronger than heroin. Even a tiny amount can overwhelm the respiratory system, causing users to stop breathing.

Henke and Schwandt initially got their fentanyl from medical patches, bought on the black market. The prescription-grade patches were intended to be stuck onto one's chest or upper arm, to relieve pain, but Henke and Schwandt didn't use them that way. Instead, they cut them open with a knife and squeezed out the fentanyl gel onto tin foil, and smoked it through a tube. (They didn't shoot it up because they didn't like needles.) Later Henke acquired fentanyl in a white powder form that was made illicitly.

Fentanyl gave an incredibly powerful high — unlike anything the teens or their friends had ever experienced.

"I'd never tried it until Bailey brought some over one day," Henke's friend Tanner Gerszewski said. "He showed me a tiny little bit and said, 'That's $150 worth.' " Gerszewski thought it was a rip-off until they smoked some together. "I barely even got any smoke, but I was just blown away. I was sweating. I got a call, but couldn't see the phone well enough to answer it. Heroin is strong stuff, but fentanyl is just completely on another level."

Even though Henke had been smoking heroin for some time, fentanyl raised the stakes. He was experiencing a rough patch in his life. Not long before, he had split with his girlfriend after going through her text messages and discovering she was seeing someone else. And though he dreamed of becoming a cop, he had recently dropped out of community college in nearby Devil's Lake and started working at a local car dealership. Their drug habits were dragging them down, and so he and his close friend Schwandt resolved to get clean, to go through withdrawal on this road trip together, far away from their drug suppliers and their corrosive influences.

Opioid withdrawal is notoriously difficult, but the two young men had help in the form of Suboxone — a medication designed to help people beat these types of addictions. Perhaps just as important, they had each other.

Still, they expected roadblocks and soon encountered a literal one in the form of a massive blizzard. Before they could reach Minot, the western North Dakota town to which Bailey's parents had moved, the roads became almost impassable. Finally a local police officer, taking pity on the travelers, turned on his lights and led a caravan of cars slowly down the highway, and they safely arrived at their destination. While in Minot, they hung out with Henke's parents, went to the mall, and laughed a lot.

"We had a really nice Christmas," said Bailey's mom, Laura Henke.

Henke and Schwandt did their best to hide their withdrawal symptoms, which were beginning to kick in. "It was really uncomfortable," Schwandt said. After Henke's parents went to bed, they would stay up late and play video games, pilfering some beers or vodka from the liquor cabinet. The booze helped him sleep, Schwandt said, and

Henke's parents were none the wiser.

In fact, Laura Henke didn't notice anything out of the ordinary. "As far as I knew, they weren't using," she said. The truth is, she had absolutely no idea what her son was up against. She had never even heard of fentanyl.

"I was clueless," she told me.

Laura Henke wasn't alone. As recently as 2015, very few Americans were familiar with fentanyl.

After the heroin and prescription pill crisis took off in the 1990s and reached epidemic levels in the following decades, heartbreaking reports increasingly appeared about decimated communities, about young victims cut down in their prime.

Yet while civic leaders, law enforcement, and politicians struggled to find answers, fentanyl was quietly creating a brand-new drug epidemic, one that quickly outstripped the previous one and has become more destructive than any drug crisis in American history: worse than crack in the 1980s, worse than meth in the first decade of the 2000s, worse than heroin and prescription pills in the 2010s. "Fentanyl is the deadliest drug in America, CDC confirms," read a December 2018 CNN headline.

Because of its incredible potency, fentanyl is extremely difficult to dose properly. It can be lethal at only two milligrams, an amount barely visible to the eye and far smaller than a dose of heroin. Traffickers "cut" fentanyl into other drugs to give them more kick, unbeknownst to users. Thus, many fentanyl victims think they are taking heroin, cocaine, meth, or prescription pills. But when too much fentanyl is in the mix, it kills almost instantly.

Driven by fentanyl, overdose drug deaths are, by the time of this book's publication, for the first time killing more Americans under fifty-five than anything else — more than gun homicides and more than even AIDS during the peak years of the crisis. As of 2017, Americans were statistically more likely to die from an opioid overdose than a car accident. More than seventy thousand Americans died from drug overdoses in 2017 (the most recent year for which statistics were available), and synthetic opioids (mainly fentanyl and its analogues) were responsible for the greatest number of these deaths, more than twenty-eight thousand, compared to about sixteen thousand deaths from heroin overdose and about fifteen thousand from natural and synthetic opioids, including OxyContin (which contains the drug oxycodone). Compared to the previous year, the heroin and prescription opioid numbers were about flat, while synthetic-opioid deaths shot up more than 45 percent. Overdose death rates among African-Americans, middle-aged women, and young people continued to accelerate at alarming rates, with opioid deaths expected to increase 147 percent by 2025. Fentanyl has been cut into heroin for years, but now is often mixed into meth and cocaine, fueling rising death counts for those drugs, a troubling development, considering that Americans are much more likely to try meth and cocaine than heroin.

In Canada the numbers are similarly astronomical, and fentanyl deaths have marched upward in Puerto Rico, Australia, and many European countries as well. In 2015 fentanyl and its analogues overtook heroin to become the deadliest drug in Sweden.

"Today, we are facing the most deadly crisis in America's history," then US attorney general Jeff Sessions said during a 2018 press conference. "We've never seen anything like it."

"Fentanyl is the game changer," Special Agent in Charge James Hunt of the US Drug Enforcement Administration (DEA) told *Vice.* "It's the most dangerous substance in the history of drug trafficking. Heroin and cocaine pale in comparison to how dangerous fentanyl is."

In addition to fentanyl, a whole new generation of chemicals is radically changing the recreational drug landscape. These are known as novel psychoactive substances (NPS), and they include replacements for known drugs like ecstasy, LSD, and marijuana, as well as heroin. These new drugs aren't grown in a field — or grown at all. They are synthetic, made in a laboratory. There's nothing natural about them, and they are much more potent than traditional drugs. While the plants that yield the marijuana and heroin consumed in the United States have in recent times been grown in Mexico, these new drugs are most often manufactured in laboratories in China. According to Senate minority leader Chuck Schumer, China produces over 90 percent of the world's illicit fentanyl.

In 2018, a Brookings Institution report stated: "Replacing drugs derived from plants (e.g., heroin, cannabis) with synthetic analogues (e.g., fentanyl, Spice/K2), could be the most disruptive innovation in the history of the international drug trade."

These new drugs — fake heroin, fake

marijuana, fake LSD, and fake ecstasy — represent the harshest drug challenge in our history. And yet, ironically, most of them were "born" in legitimate laboratories, created by medical scientists. Long before they were hijacked by drug traffickers, they were designed to benefit society. It took decades before they landed in the hands of people looking to get high, people like Bailey Henke and Kain Schwandt.

Grand Forks is an unlikely place to be at the center of a new synthetic-drug wave. A purple dot in a red state — where the locals say "pop" instead of "soda" — it couldn't be further removed from the world's drug epicenters. Though it's one of North Dakota's biggest cities, Grand Forks is really a small college town at heart, located on the scenic banks of the Red River. Some money from the oil boom on the other side of the state has trickled in, but the town remains quiet. The University of North Dakota's Fighting Hawks (no longer known as the "Fighting Sioux") play at their slick hockey arena, and Charlotte's *lefse* stand at the farmers market offers a traditional Norwegian treat of mashed potatoes fried on a grill and served like flatbread.

It's the kind of place where locals would

sooner make cheerful pleasantries than burden someone with their struggles. Still, its residents have battled drug problems before. Like many Midwestern towns, it was hit hard by methamphetamines, starting in the late 1990s. Homemade labs were prevalent, until police crackdowns, and revised laws banning easy access to the cold medicines favored by crank cooks, drove the labs out. Yet the demand for meth and other hard drugs persisted. The beginning of the 2010s saw the local influx of the first NPS, a new designer chemical known as K2. Often called Spice or synthetic marijuana, K2 has little in common with traditional marijuana, which gives the user a mellow buzz, whereas K2 often makes people's hearts race, or makes them overdose. Ironically, however, K2 could be bought legally in many places at this time. In fact, a head shop in Grand Forks called Discontent sold it openly.

One day while Bailey Henke was in high school, his mother, Laura, found an empty packet of K2 in the house. He lied, denying he had been using it, and instead said it belonged to his buddy Tanner Gerszewski. Suspicious, Henke's mother forced him to sit down and watch videos of people freaking out while high on synthetic-marijuana strains like K2 — which are more accurately called synthetic cannabinoids. Bailey watched as the users screamed and ran around in circles, losing their minds.

Laura also paid a visit to Gerszewski's house, just around the corner. "I'm really scared the boys are using this," she told Tanner's mom, who seconded her concern and added that she was planning to have her son tested for marijuana.

Little did Tanner's mom know that the threat of these tests was what inspired her son to use K2 in the first place. Unlike traditional marijuana, synthetic cannabinoids don't show up on drug tests — not the kind parents give to their kids and not the kind instituted by employers. In fact, that's what made K2 so popular — plus the fact that US lawmakers, since they didn't yet know what it was, hadn't made it illegal.

There were other benefits too, at least in the eyes of Bailey and Tanner. K2 was potent — their other friends said it made them feel like they were dying — and they personally enjoyed the extra jolt. "That's what me and Bailey liked," Gerszewski said. "For us, it didn't stop at going to a party and drinking and smoking on the weekends. It was about getting fucked up."

But now that he was out of high school

and saddled with an opioid addiction, Henke resolved to get his life together. On the December 2014 road trip, after visiting Henke's parents in Minot, they drove out to see Kain Schwandt's family in Montana. It was a good time, and as they drove back eastward they congratulated themselves on accomplishing their goal. "We had both gotten clean," said Schwandt.

Around the same time in 2014, in Portland, Oregon, a woman named Channing Lacey was sliding into her stiletto heels. The twenty-seven-year-old mother of two worked as a dominatrix, controlling a stable of male slaves she had met on the Internet. Bespectacled and clad in black leather and fishnet stockings, she would beat them with whips, step on them with her high heels, or even apply clothespins — which were attached to a rope — all over their bodies and then rip them off with a flick of the rope. For the privilege, men would pay $150 to $200 an hour.

Lacey enjoyed her dominatrix alter ego. "I was into it," she said. "It got a bunch of my aggression out." This work was an escape from the rest of her life, which was becoming increasingly consumed by fentanyl. She was not only hooked on it but was assisting in what might have been, at the time, the country's biggest illicit fentanyl operation.

Growing up in Las Vegas, Lacey had dropped out of high school and gotten pregnant, in 2004, at age seventeen. After her son was born she was prescribed the opioid Vicodin and soon became addicted to pain pills. She began "doctor shopping" to get her fix. "I'd go to hospitals, I'd go to dentists, I'd get different prescriptions," she said, including those for OxyContin, an even stronger opioid. "I manipulated the system really bad." She even went so far as to marry a man in order to get on his health insurance.

Lacey moved to the Portland area around 2005, and a year or so later descended further into drug abuse, using meth and heroin. She got clean and had a second son but then went back to heroin in the early 2010s, using more heavily than before. Her habit led her to a dope house in Vancouver, Washington, just across the Columbia River from Portland, where she met an intriguing man named Brandon Hubbard. Though he was more than ten years her senior, Lacey found in him a kindred spirit. Short, with brown hair and a piercing stare, Hubbard also loved BDSM (bondage, domination, sadism, masochism) and possessed what

Lacey considered to be a fierce intelligence. "His IQ level is genius," she said.

Hubbard was also hooked on pain pills. His right arm was paralyzed from an injury sustained while riding a bike years earlier, and he had been prescribed heavy doses of OxyContin. Eventually he moved to street heroin, which was cheaper.

Caught up in a druggy, infatuated haze, Hubbard and Lacey became joined at the hip. "We were together every day after that," Lacey said, adding that her mother, who lived nearby, looked after her kids. "I was a really bad addict. I was out of control."

Despite her dexterity with a whip, Lacey didn't hold a steady job, and Hubbard wasn't really working either. To feed their heroin addictions, Hubbard sold his Oxy-Contin pills. It was a small-time drug hustle, and he soon shifted to selling black tar heroin, working with a local man who had a reliable connection and a good price.

Hubbard's business really took off, however, when he moved onto the Dark Web around 2013. This disguised Internet protocol was quickly helping local dealers like Hubbard become wealthy, international players. And it was enabling tech-savvy teenagers to get potent drugs delivered right to their front door by the mail carrier.

■ ■ ■ ■

In the past, to obtain illicit drugs, a buyer often had to meet up with a dealer in an alleyway or on a dangerous street corner. But as of the early 2010s one doesn't even have to leave the bedroom; it's as easy as booting up a smartphone or laptop. To access the Dark Web, one needs a special browser, such as Tor, which disguises one's location and identity and makes it possible to load Dark Web sites. Because these sites have hidden IP addresses, it's almost impossible to figure out who's running them.

Not everyone on the Dark Web is a criminal. Facebook even has a presence, to circumvent censors in countries where it's banned, like China. But the Dark Web is best known for its illegal emporiums, which run the gamut from extremely untrustworthy to quite professional, and sell almost every form of vice imaginable: credit card numbers, fake Rolexes, pornography passwords, weapons, and malware. "Make $3,000+ a Month as Fake Uber Driver," read one recent listing. It's stunningly easy to buy drugs — and not just traditional drugs like cocaine, ecstasy, and marijuana, but powerful NPS like fentanyl and K2.

The most famous of these markets, Silk Road, was founded by a Libertarian-leaning, magic-mushroom selling, tech autodidact named Ross Ulbricht and rapidly became a billion-dollar enterprise. Using sophisticated programming techniques to cover his tracks, Ulbricht established Silk Road in 2011 and eluded law enforcement for more than two years. (A rogue DEA agent, selling him tips for $50,000 each, helped him evade capture.) Growing increasingly paranoid and allegedly commissioning six murders, Ulbricht was finally arrested at a San Francisco library in 2013 and eventually sentenced to life in prison. In Silk Road's stead, another Dark Web behemoth called AlphaBay grew to be even bigger, until it too was shut down, in 2017.

But new markets keep sprouting up. They are really not much different from Amazon, right down to the reviews of sellers. Customers select their wares, give an address, and pay by Bitcoin — the cyber currency preferred by these markets because it's difficult to trace. Their discreetly wrapped items arrive soon after in the mail.

Brandon Hubbard utilized the Dark Web and got rich. At first he sold heroin. His vendor name on Dark Web sites such as Evolution and Agora was "PdxBlack," referencing Portland's airport code and his product — black tar heroin, a sticky strain known for its dark impurities and common on the West Coast. Channing Lacey helped him package up the product.

Hubbard prided himself on keeping prices low, and soon orders began pouring in from around the country. He touted his own success on Reddit, a forum commonly used by Internet drug traders, claiming to be on his way to becoming the "BTH King of the Dark Net!"

Fentanyl only upped the ante. Lacey said they first encountered the drug in 2014, when Hubbard received a package from someone he had been chatting with on the website Topix. The drug knocked Lacey and Hubbard on their backs. "I did a pinhead, or maybe a bit more, and I overdosed right away," she remembered, adding that this only increased its appeal. "In the drug addict's mindset you're like, 'This stuff is fucking amazing,' because it's so much stronger than heroin."

With longtime use, heroin doesn't continue to make users feel euphoric; it simply eases withdrawal symptoms. Many are drawn to fentanyl because it brings the euphoria back. "Heroin wouldn't even get me past sick anymore," said Bree, an addicted user from East Alton, Illinois, who prefers not to use her real name. "But fentanyl would always get me completely off sick, and high, and it always took less."

For dealers, the appeal of fentanyl is also clear: it is cheaper and more discreet, since it comes in smaller packages than heroin. And so Brandon Hubbard began ordering more. His main source was a distributor named Daniel Vivas Ceron. Originally from Colombia, Ceron had come to Canada as a child; the fact that he was currently locked up in a Quebec prison for attempted murder somehow didn't slow him down.

Allegedly working from prison with another incarcerated man, Ceron didn't touch the fentanyl himself, but since he somehow had access to the Dark Web in prison, he didn't have to. Using aliases, including Joe Bleau, and acting as a middleman, he ordered fentanyl from China and then paid someone on the outside to complete the transaction. Ceron's cut from a sale might be $10,000, while his co-conspirator on the outside might get $7,000.

Once the package from Ceron arrived, Lacey helped Hubbard bag up the portions and prepare the product for shipment. They cut it with mannitol, a diuretic and laxative that counters the constipation that often comes from opioid use. It also increased their profit margins. The product was a hit, and Hubbard and Ceron were in touch frequently, texting each other using encryption programs that scramble messages and make them harder for law enforcement to read.

Before long, Hubbard claimed to be the biggest illicit fentanyl dealer in the country — and Lacey believed him. "He was moving a lot of packages," she said, and his customers were paying huge quantities of Bitcoin, which he exchanged for hard cash. He was careful not to live too lavishly — he wanted to stay under the radar of law enforcement — but he splurged on some things, like a new Volkswagen GTI.

In November 2014, Hubbard placed an order with Ceron for 750 grams of fentanyl. Since that is less than a kilo, it might not sound like a lot, but considering a pinhead can cause an overdose, it was a colossal shipment, with a street value of $1.5 million. What Hubbard didn't realize was that law enforcement was on to him, having accessed the account of a boy who had purchased fentanyl from him on a Dark Web site called Evolution. Homeland Security was monitoring his activities.

Almost immediately after Bailey Henke and Kain Schwandt returned from their road trip they fell off the wagon. Despite their efforts to quit fentanyl, they couldn't stay clean long. It didn't help that the day of their return was New Year's Eve, and everyone was partying. Henke had some drinks that night and took some Xanax. On January 2, 2015 he went on an even bigger bender.

The new calendar brought brutally cold weather to Grand Forks. The temperature hit fifteen degrees Fahrenheit that day and the next day dropped a full thirty degrees farther. Henke and Schwandt stayed out of the cold and entertained themselves by doing drugs and playing video games. With another friend they went to the house of a local dealer named Ryan Jensen. In his bedroom, they played *Call of Duty* and smoked fentanyl.

Nineteen-year-old Jensen was under house arrest at the time, having been convicted of drunk driving. Formerly the neighborhood pot dealer, Jensen had become a Dark Web expert himself, procuring substances right off his computer. (To be safe, he had the packages sent to the address of a guy he knew in town.) Using the Dark Web site Evolution, Jensen ordered twelve grams of heroin and one gram of fentanyl from a dealer named PdxBlack — Brandon Hubbard. Of that one gram, he sold a quarter to Henke.

Yet this was different than the pharmaceutical-grade fentanyl Henke usually smoked, the kind extracted from medical patches. This was white powder fentanyl. Since it had been cut with mannitol, it was impossible to know exactly how potent it was. Nonetheless, while playing video games that January 2, Henke was hitting it hard.

Still, he seemed to be OK, and soon afterward Kain Schwandt agreed to drop him off at Tanner Gerszcwski's garden-level apartment, in a squat building with stained green carpeting by a trailer park. Since the days when the teens had smoked K2 together in high school, Gerszewski's drug habit had grown worse as well. Though he maintained a job as a plumber, he was hooked on heroin and had already smoked some by the time Henke arrived, in addition to drinking and dropping acid. Still, Henke seemed to be even more intoxicated than his friend, and he threw up immediately upon walking in the door.

Henke was clearly affected, but this didn't especially faze Gerszewski. "He seemed high, but he didn't seem in bad shape," he said. "Me and him had seen each other all through high school in very bad states — fucked up, throwing up."

They dipped into the fentanyl Henke had bought from Jensen, and powered up the Xbox to play a mixed martial arts video game. A few other people Gerszewski knew were there too, but they left at some point, leaving the two friends alone with their drugs. As midnight approached, Henke's energy flagged. In the midst of their game, Gerszewski noticed that Henke's avatar had stopped moving. His friend looked like he was nodding off.

Henke insisted he was fine. They continued playing until, again, Henke's avatar stopped moving. "I'm just a little tired," Henke said.

When his character froze again, Gerszewski saw that Henke's eyes were shut and he was growing pale. He tapped him, and then nudged him, getting no response. Gerszewski feared Henke had overdosed, but was so high himself that he had a hard time reading the situation. Was this a dream? Was

Henke faking it? He grabbed and shook him.

Now realizing the depth of the problem, Gerszewski made a mistake. Instead of immediately calling 911, he called Schwandt, who came over and attempted CPR. When an ambulance finally arrived, it was too late.

Just after midnight, Bailey Henke was pronounced dead. About three hours later a police officer knocked on his parents' door in Minot. He told them the bad news, but Laura and Jason Henke couldn't get to Grand Forks until the next evening to begin the mourning process. Another big snowstorm had closed down the highway.

Bailey Henke's death triggered the widest-ranging fentanyl investigation in history. Known as Operation Denial, it's an international endeavor begun in 2015 and still ongoing at the time this book went to print, involving agencies from the local Grand Forks police department to the Royal Canadian Mounted Police to the US Border Patrol and the DEA. It has tracked down people from every step in the fentanyl supply chain that killed Henke and charged thirty-two.

These include Ryan Jensen, who in 2016 received a prison sentence of twenty years for charges including drug distribution resulting in death; Brandon Hubbard, who that year received life in prison; and Daniel Vivas Ceron, who was still awaiting trial. Investigators believe Hubbard earned millions from his Dark Web sales of fentanyl and heroin, and that his collaboration with Ceron was responsible for twelve fentanyl overdose victims and four deaths around the country, including Bailey Henke and another Grand Forks teenager, nineteen-year-old Evan Poitra, who died in July 2014. Others on the periphery of the wide-ranging case were convicted as well, including Kain Schwandt, who spent about a year and a half behind bars, for conspiracy to possess illicit drugs with intent to distribute, and Channing Lacey, who snuck in fentanyl when she went to jail and distributed it there, causing a fatal overdose. She received eleven years for drug distribution resulting in death. For its efforts, in November 2018, Operation Denial received special recognition from the White House's Office of National Drug Control Policy.

Yet for all of Operation Denial's convictions, it has not been able to snag the person at the very top of the drug pyramid, Jian Zhang, the Chinese man who is believed to have manufactured the fentanyl that killed

Henke and others. Zhang is a chemical manufacturer born in 1978 and operating out of Shanghai. His company claims to make benign food additives, including spices and soy products, but in April, 2018, Attorney General Jeff Sessions traveled to Fargo to unseal an indictment against Zhang, accusing him of leading a drug ring that manufactured fentanyl sold throughout the United States. The indictment listed eleven states, including North Dakota and Oregon.

Zhang has been pursued with the full weight of not just the US Department of Justice but also the Treasury, which designated him a kingpin under the Foreign Narcotics Kingpin Designation Act, blocking his US financial assets and those of his company, Zaron Bio-Tech (Asia) Limited. "Combating the flow of fentanyl into the United States is a top priority of this administration," Sigal Mandelker, under secretary for terrorism and financial intelligence, said in a statement. "This action will disrupt the flow of fentanyl and other synthetic opioids into the United States."

Yet the United States couldn't jail Jian Zhang, because China refused to turn him over. The country has no extradition treaty with the United States, and China does not believe Zhang to be a criminal. Yu Haibin, director of precursor chemical control at China's Narcotics Control Commission, said that although the country's police were investigating Zhang, they did not have "solid evidence" that he broke Chinese law. Further, Chinese officials are quick to note, most NPS were invented in labs in Europe and the United States. And this isn't just a problem of production — it's one of consumption. China believes America needs to control its drug problem.

Considering that fentanyl has been banned (except for medical use) in China for decades, it's unclear why China could not, or simply did not, prosecute Zhang. But there's an even bigger problem. Many of the other NPS killing Americans, Europeans, and others are still 100 percent legal in China, even while banned in the West. In recent years, some of the biggest new drug kingpins can't be successfully prosecuted. The Pablo Escobars of today are coming out of China, and they don't have to worry about being imprisoned by their government. They can often operate free and in the clear, within the boundaries of their country's own laws. Whenever a deadly new drug is made illegal in China, manufacturers simply tweak its chemical structure and start producing a new drug that is still legal. Many fentanyl analogues and synthetic cannabinoids have been made this way. Though Chinese authorities have pledged to crack down — and in April, 2019, said they would ban all fentanyl analogues — their efforts so far have barely dented the country's clandestine international trade.

The rise of fentanyl and NPS happened quickly. When I started investigating these new drugs in 2013, fentanyl wasn't on the public radar at all. I had never heard of it. In fact, I only came to this story by accident.

Living in Los Angeles at the time, as the music editor at *LA Weekly,* I was investigating why so many people were dying at raves. Electronic dance music (EDM) had recently exploded in popularity, and with its rise came increasing deaths, mostly young kids experimenting with ecstasy.

I wasn't new to the scene. In the late 1990s I partied in abandoned San Francisco warehouses and deserted beach spots as part of the first wave of American electronic dance music — people then called it electronica. These events were usually populated only by those who had garnered a personal invitation from a friend of the organizer; to get directions one had to call a secret phone line. On the scene, maybe a few dozen people would dance to cutting-edge, drum-machine-driven beats. The drugs, ecstasy and LSD, made participants especially appreciate exotic rhythms. These ravers and club kids wore fluorescent colors and giant goggles and chewed on pacifiers or breathed Vicks VapoRub beneath surgical masks to enhance the sensation of ecstasy.

I, along with most Americans, dropped out of the scene by the middle of the first decade of the 2000s. EDM's popularity continued unabated in Europe, while in the United States many stars saw their music fall off the charts. But by the 2010s electronic dance music was back and bigger than ever, drawing tens of thousands of neon-clad kids to raves. The new raves couldn't have been more different from the underground parties I had attended. No longer secret affairs featuring obscure sounds, today's EDM events feature celebrity DJs spinning in mammoth venues such as stadiums and racetracks. Electric Daisy Carnival, now held every spring in Las Vegas, draws some four hundred thousand attendees. In the music industry, which had been decimated by audio-sharing services and still hadn't recovered in the early 2010s,

EDM was a shining star, awash in profits and adored by millions of young fans. And Los Angeles was the center of its universe. EDM was being celebrated in the national media as a big neon party that never ended.

And then I heard about the deaths.

In 2010, fifteen-year-old Sasha Rodriguez fatally overdosed at Electric Daisy Carnival at the LA Coliseum, reportedly from ecstasy. Local politicians revolted, and the event was forced to relocate to Las Vegas. A Plymouth State University student named Brittany Flannigan overdosed and died in late August 2013 after attending a Boston EDM concert featuring the popular DJ Zedd, and just days later a University of Virginia student named Mary "Shelley" Goldsmith passed away as well. Both were nineteen, and reports said they had taken "Molly."

At the time, many believed Molly was pure MDMA, the drug found in ecstasy, also known as 3,4-methylenedioxymethamphetamine. But this didn't seem right. The Molly users I witnessed dipped their fingers into a plastic bag of white powder and then licked it off, repeating the process every ten minutes or so. Some would snort it. This was different from my heyday on the rave scene. Back then, the ravers I knew simply took a pill and would be happily rolling for the whole night.

With mega-raves came increasing numbers of casualties. At New York's Electric Zoo over Labor Day weekend in 2013, a twenty-year-old University of New Hampshire student named Olivia Rotondo and a twenty-three-year-old recent graduate of Syracuse University named Jeffrey Russ both collapsed and died, reportedly after taking Molly. At the Hard Summer festival in August 2015, outside Los Angeles, two young women fatally overdosed and forty-nine people had to be taken to emergency rooms. The event sparked a *Los Angeles Times* article quoting emergency-room doctors as saying that raves on LA-county-owned property should be banned, at least temporarily. "If the county wants to make money while people are dying and medically compromised," said Dr. Philip Fagan Jr., emergency department director at Los Angeles's Good Samaritan Hospital, "they should come out and say it."

These weren't just freak accidents. The more I covered the EDM scene, the more I realized how widespread the fatalities were. Six people overdosed and died at a single EDM festival in Malaysia in 2014, while just about every major US EDM concert —

including Electric Daisy Carnival, Nocturnal Wonderland, Together as One, Monster Massive, Coachella, Ultra, and Electric Forest — saw festival-goers die from drug use. No statistics were available about the number of deaths at EDM festivals. But no one could dispute a disturbing fact: the number was growing.

Officials blamed ecstasy — a word many used synonymously with Molly — but that contradicts the relatively benign nature of the chemical. "You don't see many ecstasy overdose deaths," confirmed Emanuel Sferios, the founder of DanceSafe, a Denver-based organization dedicated to harm reduction at music festivals and other events. He estimates that MDMA deaths per year in the United States number around twenty — not just kids at raves, but everyone — which is a tiny fraction of total drug deaths. Further, large numbers of the MDMA deaths weren't brought about because users' dosages were too high, he adds, but because they suffered from heatstroke, from dancing continuously without drinking water or wearing themselves out beneath the hot sun.

Molly, however, is not ecstasy as it has been known. "Molly means, like, anything now," a Dallas toxicologist named Ashley

Haynes warned. It might contain a small amount of MDMA but most likely contains a hodgepodge of bizarre drugs with complicated chemical names users have never heard of, including so-called "bath salts." It turns out, she added, that there are hundreds of these new drugs. Almost every traditional drug — be it marijuana, cocaine, ecstasy, LSD, or heroin — is being replaced by new, sinister versions made in laboratories.

Further, as I discovered, they were being distributed in new ways, like the Dark Web, leading to an entirely upended drug landscape that nobody seemed to understand — not the parents of children who had lost their lives, not first responders, not cops, and certainly not politicians. The people consuming many of these bastardized types of speed, psychedelics, and other substances are not traditional hard-drug users. They are high school kids, college students, and recreational enthusiasts best described as drug nerds. Some know what they are doing, using sophisticated Internet forums to expand their minds and explore intellectual pursuits. A great many, however, have no idea just how potent and dangerous these new drugs can be.

NPS are hard to spot, as they can come as

powders, crystals, pills, or liquids, resembling traditional drugs, or even sprayed onto dried sage to be smoked like marijuana. Sometimes they are even professionally packaged and sold in stores, mislabeled as "bath salts" or "potpourri."

These new drugs aren't just confounding users. In recent years, law enforcement agencies have seized exponentially larger quantities of NPS, but this is a drop in the bucket. By the time police get wise to these chemicals, rogue manufacturers have already moved on to new formulas, because when it comes to creating synthetic drugs, the mathematical possibilities are endless. By varying a molecule just slightly, rogue chemists can come up with a whole new drug, one that is still legal because it hasn't yet been scheduled (controlled and restricted). After the chemicals sold as K2 and Spice were banned, for example, a whole new set of fake marijuana blends immediately popped up in their place.

"Over the past several years, the DEA has identified hundreds of designer drugs from at least eight different drug classes," DEA special agent Elaine Cesare observed. "There are a seemingly infinite number of possible new chemical compounds that are on the horizon."

41

Many law enforcement officers use the same expression when describing their attempts to stop these drugs: a game of whack-a-mole. Whenever one new drug is contained, another simply pops up in its place. The UN Office on Drugs and Crime (UNODC) has called the synthetics industry "hydra-headed." "When you control one derivative of fentanyl, another derivative comes out, which is not on the control list. Criminals are always one step ahead of law enforcement," said Tun Nay Soe, of the UNODC.

This book is the result of my interviews with 160 people, visits to drug sites and laboratories all over the world, and research drawn from hundreds of source materials. In some cases, often to preserve their own safety, subjects have requested I use pseudonyms; they are identified as such in the text.

While reporting the story of NPS, I met people suffering from fentanyl and other drug addictions, some destitute and living on the streets, others functioning in well-paid jobs. I spent time with psychonauts, thrill seekers who try brand-new drugs that have never been taken before. I learned how these chemicals are marketed and sold, from the factories to the streets to the search engine. I spent months on every step of the drug-distribution ladder, with everyone from low-level dealers to big-time traffickers, from the industrial manufacturers to the inventors of the drugs themselves. I went back over the details of my close friend Michael "Helias" Schafermeyer's death in Baltimore, from fentanyl combined with alcohol, in 2010 — long before I knew what fentanyl was.

I consulted politicians, police, DEA agents, and international drug policy makers, who would like to put these traffickers away forever; and I spoke with counselors, doctors, activists, and policy wonks, some of whom believe these drugs should be legal. I corresponded with two infamous, now-imprisoned LSD kingpins who worked together out of an abandoned missile silo in Kansas; the demise of their operation in 2000 may have inadvertently fueled the rise of a new hallucinogen whose effects are far worse than LSD.

I learned how a brilliant Belgian chemist created a multibillion dollar pharmaceutical company from scratch but in the process unleashed a horror like nothing ever seen before. I prowled dangerous St. Louis streets with an armed former fentanyl dealer to understand how the epidemic started,

43

tracing the history to Mexican cartel affiliates who traveled north to spread what had originated in China into inner cities all over the United States.

Finally, I infiltrated a pair of Chinese drug operations, one a sophisticated laboratory operation distilling outsize quantities of the world's most dangerous chemicals in industrial-size glassware, and the other an office of young, cheery salespeople, who sat in rows of cubicles and sold fentanyl ingredients to American dealers and Mexican cartels.

The latter company didn't even bother operating clandestinely, instead doing its business out in the open. That's because, as I soon learned, the Chinese government offers subsidies and tax rebates to chemical companies that are making these drugs. It's a case of financial incentives gone horribly wrong — one that seems likely to drive a further wedge between two powerful countries that are already extremely wary of each other.

"We need to make very clear to the Chinese, that this is an act of war. You are sending this into our country to kill our people," said former New Jersey governor Chris Christie, who headed President Trump's opioid epidemic commission, in the fall of

2017, speaking about fentanyl. China is "sending that garbage and killing our people," added President Trump, at an August 2018 cabinet meeting. "It's almost a form of warfare."

The former director of the DEA's Special Operations Division, Derek Maltz, used stark terms to describe the fentanyl-driven opioid epidemic. "Where it becomes a national security emergency is the connectivity between the drug traffickers and the terrorists that are out there that are trying to destroy our way of life," he said in November 2018.

Such rhetoric aside, America's problem with fentanyl and other new drugs undermines its national security as much as — perhaps more than — any other issue in the headlines, with the wrecking of families and relationships, the massive casualty toll, and the billions needed to fight the scourge. Many American political and thought leaders have castigated China's negligence; some even believe it is purposeful.

Addressing the problem is extremely complicated, however, because this is a story that goes well beyond drugs. It's a political story about the clashing of the world's biggest superpowers. It's an economics story about the deception of giant pharmaceutical companies. It's a higher-education story about how university science can go horribly wrong. It's a tech story about incredible innovation happening in real time, a business story about marketing genius. It's a physiological and philosophical story about the human body in conflict with the human mind.

And it's forcing us to rethink our assumptions. The drug economy no longer just benefits the producers and dealers. Nowadays it involves the otherwise innocent people who deliver our mail, who program Internet algorithms, who design medicine in chemistry labs, who scrub toilets at drug companies.

More than anything, this is a story of global capitalism run amok. The new-drugs trade is growing for the same reasons the world economy is growing — increasing speed of communications, Internet technology, and shipping; relaxed barriers to trade; and, of course, the ever-present pressure for higher profit margins. And if global capitalism is hard to control, the new-drugs trade is nearly impossible, given that it is peopled by local actors in jurisdictions with no overlap interacting with far-flung markets and supply chains.

PART I:
THE NEW DRUGS

ONE

Americans have used and abused opiates*
for as long as America has existed. Opium
was administered to Revolutionary War
soldiers, and for much of our history it was
one of the only medicines available, given
to colicky babies, the dying elderly, and
everyone in between. Misuse may even have
been more common in previous centuries
than now, and the problem grew particularly
acute after the Civil War, during which
morphine was used to soothe the injured.
In fact, the term *soldier's disease* was
coined to describe opiate addiction. At the
dawn of the twentieth century, one could
buy opium from the Sears, Roebuck catalog,
yet addiction was so widespread that Presi-

* *Opiates* generally refers to drugs derived naturally from the opium poppy, like morphine, while
opioids generally means similar chemicals made
synthetically in labs, like fentanyl.

dent Theodore Roosevelt appointed an opium commissioner in 1908. During the industrial revolution the problem ravaged the United Kingdom as well, and the country sought to balance its trade deficit by using its British East India Company to ply opium in tremendous quantities to the Chinese, causing a pair of wars.

Never, however, has an opiate — or any other drug, for that matter — killed so many annually as the fentanyl epidemic. It is the next phase in the opioid crisis that began with the overprescription of opioid painkillers, which was catalyzed by a short letter published in a 1980 issue of the *New England Journal of Medicine.* Written by a doctor named Hershel Jick and his graduate student, Jane Porter, the letter discussed the thousands of cases they had examined in which patients received opioid narcotics. In only four cases had anyone become addicted, they claimed, and only one of those was troubling. "We conclude that despite widespread use of narcotic drugs in hospitals, the development of addiction is rare in medical patients with no history of addiction."

The above sentence was one of only five in Jick and Porter's letter, which was far from comprehensive. It referenced only patients who received small doses and were closely monitored by their doctors, not outpatients taking home bottles of ultra-strong prescription drugs. Nonetheless, the letter had great influence; academics cited it in more than six hundred studies, and doctors and pharmaceutical companies pitching their products deferred to it as well.

During the 1990s another sea change swept American medicine: the desire to treat patients more humanely. Traditionally, doctors focused on four "vital signs" when caring for patients: their temperature, breathing rate, blood pressure, and pulse rate. But in the mid-1990s the American Pain Society called for pain to be considered a new "fifth vital sign." Whereas doctors were previously reticent to prescribe opioids because they considered them addictive, the ramifications of the Jick-Porter letter caused their thinking to shift: if opioids were, in fact, safe, patients should not be consigned to agony. "It was not only okay, but it was our holy mission, to cure the world of its pain by waking people up to the fact that opiates were safe," Boston pain specialist Dr. Nathaniel Katz told journalist Sam Quinones for his book *Dreamland: The True Tale Of America's Opiate Epidemic,* describing the new conventional wisdom that took hold.

51

"All those rumors of addiction were misguided. . . . My fellowship director even told me, 'If you have pain, you can't get addicted to opiates because the pain soaks up the euphoria.' "

The Sackler family, the owners of the company responsible for OxyContin, became billionaires many times over thanks to this new perspective. Long before the drug's creation, Arthur Sackler, a physician by training, had been a pioneer in the field of pharmaceutical advertising. In 1952, Arthur and his brothers, Raymond and Mortimer, purchased the company that became Purdue Pharma. With the inherent conflict of advertising and pharmaceuticals in its DNA, Purdue brought OxyContin to market in 1996, touting its benefits as a slow-release pill that contained high doses of the opioid oxycodone — *contin* means "continuous." Since the pills lasted twelve hours, the company claimed, patients would need only two per day, fewer than comparable medicines. Addiction, it promised, was extremely rare.

Purdue launched a huge marketing blitz, deploying hundreds of salespeople to sway doctors and dispense free promotional items, including pedometers, headgear, and even an OxyContin-branded music CD,

Swing Is Alive, with a pair of dancing geriatrics on the cover. Purdue sent doctors to tropical locations for "pain management seminars;" those who attended these events in 1996 were more than twice as likely to write OxyContin prescriptions as doctors who did not. Although originally OxyContin was promoted for use by cancer patients, according to internal reports, the company saw that market as too small. Annual sales might top out around $260 million, whereas if Purdue was able to sell to patients with a host of chronic conditions, the annual market was closer to $1.3 billion. Sales rose from just under $50 million in 1996 to more than $1 billion by 2000. Oxycodone became the most prescribed drug in the United States.

Yet for many patients, the dosages didn't last an entire half day, and they began experiencing withdrawal symptoms when the pills wore off hours early. And while Purdue salespeople told doctors that less than 1 percent of OxyContin patients would become addicted, Purdue's own study from 1999 found the rate to be 13 percent.

Misuse became rampant. Many users crushed the pills, known by some as "hillbilly heroin," into powder form to snort or make into an injectable solution, so they could get high faster. Others fashioned themselves into drug dealers and sold them; the going rate on the street for OxyContin was one dollar per milligram, meaning that an eighty-milligram pill sold for eighty dollars.

For some, using OxyContin as directed caused anguish. Patients recovering from knee surgery or a root canal, or experiencing chronic pain from a condition like rheumatoid arthritis, gained temporary relief but soon confronted a new problem: when their prescription ran out, they were addicted. Many tried to "doctor shop" for more pills, but some who couldn't do that, or couldn't afford the pills, turned to heroin, which is cheaper — as low as five dollars a dose in some places — and satisfied their opioid cravings. Before they knew it, they were regularly visiting dangerous parts of town to meet heroin dealers.

This is a complex problem. The vast majority of legitimate users of OxyContin and other opioid medicines receive the intended benefit. For the most part, people dying from oxycodone overdoses tend to get the pills on the black market, not their doctors. Nonetheless, Purdue bears "the lion's share" of the blame for America's opioid crisis, according to Andrew Kolodny, the codirector of the Opioid Policy Research Collaborative at Brandeis University. "If you look at the prescribing trends for all the different opioids, it's in 1996 that prescribing really takes off," Kolodny said, referencing the year OxyContin debuted. "It's not a coincidence. That was the year Purdue launched a multifaceted campaign that misinformed the medical community about the risks." The company, found guilty of playing down OxyContin's abuse potential, paid $600 million in fines in 2007. Considering the billions it had earned, and would continue to earn, this seemed a pittance. No one from the company received jail time, causing then US senator Arlen Specter, from Pennsylvania, to take issue with the sentence. "I see fines with some frequency and think that they are expensive licenses for criminal misconduct," he said at a Senate hearing. "I do not know whether that applies in this case, but a jail sentence is a deterrent and a fine is not."

In 2010 Purdue released a new version of OxyContin that couldn't be crushed up and injected, which the company believed would help stymie abuse. The FDA agreed. However, this new pill may have worsened the opioid crisis. In a 2015 study, psychiatrists at Washington University in St. Louis interviewed 244 people who had sought treatment for addiction to the new version of OxyContin. The study showed that while many were able to kick their OxyContin habit, about one-third of the subjects migrated to other drugs. Seven out of ten in this group started taking heroin. Further, in the early 2010s, prescription narcotics became harder to obtain. This, along with heroin shortages, likely accelerated fentanyl use in the United States, concluded a 2018 study at the University of California, San Francisco. (Fentanyl is an odd case, the UC San Francisco researchers noted, since its rise wasn't driven because people wanted it — they just feared withdrawal and didn't have access to other opioids. As one indication of this, unlike most drugs, which develop street names — smack, weed, Molly — fentanyl doesn't have much in the way of nicknames.)

Charges have also mounted against Insys Therapeutics, makers of the prescription fentanyl spray Subsys. The company has been sued by many parties, including state governments and individual patients, and its executives have been indicted (and in some cases pled guilty) of bribing doctors to prescribe Subsys. The spray is approved only for cancer patients, but individual doctors have been accused of prescribing it for lesser ailments and accepting gratuitous kickbacks. A former Insys sales rep named Maria Guzman detailed in her 2013 whistleblower lawsuit that the company provided doctors with stock options, trips to a gun range, fancy dinners, and even hired a woman specifically "to have sexual relations with doctors in exchange for Subsys prescriptions." The FDA had information about doctors prescribing Subsys and other fentanyl medications for noncancer patients but did little to stop it, according to documents obtained by Johns Hopkins public-health researchers.

Operating under the public radar as the crisis ramped up were drug distributors like Cardinal Health, AmerisourceBergen, and McKesson, which filled gigantic opioid prescription orders from corrupt doctors operating pill mills. For example, a drugstore in the small West Virginia town of Kermit (population: four hundred) received nine million hydrocodone pills in only two years. A 2017 investigation by television news program *60 Minutes* and the *Washington Post* outlined this practice and helped expose how Congress allowed it — and even encouraged it. As laid out by whistleblower Joe Rannazzisi, the former head of the

DEA's Office of Diversion Control, a 2016 law called the Ensuring Patient Access and Effective Drug Enforcement Act, signed by President Barack Obama, made it harder for the DEA to freeze suspicious opioid shipments by these drug distributors. The law had been sponsored by Pennsylvania representative Tom Marino, who, at the time of the investigation's publication, was President Trump's nominee for drug czar. He was forced to withdraw.

Did Obama realize the law — which Congress quickly green-lighted, without debate — would have such devastating consequences? No, concluded an October 2017 *Washington Post* story: "Few lawmakers knew the true impact the law would have," it reads, adding that the White House was also unaware. Nonetheless, according to a 2019 *Washington Post* analysis, the Obama administration did not take sufficient measures to stem the fentanyl crisis as it developed.

Pharmaceutical companies making opioids, among them Purdue, as well as others along the supply chain, including distributors, find themselves facing major lawsuits from states, cities, and other groups, supported by the US Justice Department. The groups seek something similar to the big tobacco settlement of 1998, which required cigarette companies to pay billions annually to the states, and limited the industry's marketing, to compensate for the heavy costs of dealing with the health effects of smoking.

The state of Florida has also included the country's biggest chain pharmacies — Walgreens and CVS — in its lawsuit, because of their roles in selling opioids, and Oklahoma is targeting Johnson & Johnson for its role in the crisis, including selling fentanyl through its Janssen subsidiary.

By the mid-2010s prescription pill deaths in the United States began leveling off, but "for every life we save from a prescription overdose," said Joel Bomgar, vice chairman of the House Medicaid Committee in the Mississippi House of Representatives, "four more are dying from switching to heroin and fentanyl."

Fentanyl is frequently cut into heroin but, increasingly, fentanyl is also being pressed into pills that look exactly like name-brand prescription tablets. Raids across the United States have turned up operations in houses and apartments that turn fentanyl powder into tablets using specialized presses. Both the drugs and the machines are bought from

China. These operations can make thousands of pills per hour. They stamp the pills with the OxyContin or Percocet logo, making them indistinguishable. This trend has quickly gained steam. In Arizona alone, the DEA reported seizing more than 120,000 fentanyl pills in 2017. And in May 2018, three twenty-one-year-old brothers from Raleigh, North Carolina — identical triplets named Atsouste, Etse, and Atsou Dossou — were arrested, accused of running a vast drug operation, which included making and selling thousands of fake Xanax bars cut with fentanyl. "The issue of counterfeit drugs is more complex and extensive than what can be seen on the surface," retired Phoenix detective sergeant David Lake said at a roundtable discussion on the opioid crisis held in August 2018. "The constant threat from online sales, illegal pharmacies and street sales is stretching the limited law enforcement resources dedicated to this issue in many states and communities to the breaking point."

The dosages of these fake pills vary greatly. One might have ten times as much fentanyl as the next. Investigators believe such counterfeit pills were responsible for the death of music star Prince; about one hundred white pills found on his property looked exactly like Vicodin but actually contained fentanyl. It's not clear how he obtained them; he may not have realized he was taking counterfeit medication. (Michael Todd Schulenberg, a Minnesota doctor who investigators believe prescribed opioids for Prince under another person's name, paid $30,000 to settle a Controlled Substances Act violation and is being sued by relatives of Prince, but he is not being charged criminally in the musician's death.)

Cocaine can also be spiked with fentanyl. American cocaine overdose deaths remained fairly steady throughout the first decade of the 2000s — ranging from roughly four thousand to seven thousand — but in the second decade began to surge, exceeding fourteen thousand in 2017. Fentanyl is part of the reason for this. Cocaine production is at an all-time high, and the product is flooding the market, but it's far from pure. Because they are both white powders, cocaine and fentanyl can be mixed easily, and fentanyl sometimes "contaminates" cocaine parcels, where the drugs are prepared in the same space. Fentanyl was involved in two of five cocaine overdose deaths in 2016, the most recent year for which such statistics are available. This trend disproportionately affects African

Americans, who are nearly twice as likely to die from cocaine overdoses as white people.

In New York City in 2016, more than one-third of all fatal drug overdose victims had both fentanyl and cocaine in their systems. By the end of 2017, in Massachusetts, cocaine used in conjunction with fentanyl was killing more people than heroin spiked with fentanyl, and in Ohio, cocaine was often mixed with carfentanil, a tranquilizer used to subdue rhinos and elephants (sometimes shot from dart guns) that can be one hundred times more potent than fentanyl. In July 2018 the director of the Centers for Disease Control and Prevention, Robert Redfield Jr., revealed that his thirty-seven-year-old son had nearly died from cocaine laced with fentanyl. Two months later, the popular rapper Mac Miller died in his Studio City, California, home — with fentanyl and cocaine in his system, and in December, 2018, Vine and HQ Trivia co-founder Colin Kroll was found dead with heroin, cocaine, fentanyl, and an analogue called fluoroisobutyryl fentanyl in his system. Fentanyl's rapid growth in the drug economy is putting users, from recreational to deeply addicted, at risk of grave consequences.

TWO

Humanity has long mined psychoactive chemicals from the natural world to worship gods, to feel bliss, to commune with the dead, to heal, to avoid problems, to escape ennui, to make art, or to just go on a little adventure of the mind. At first, people ingested these chemicals directly from living things, eating mushrooms, cactus buttons, and morning glory seeds; chewing coca and khat leaves; inhaling tree snuff; smoking cannabis, opium, or even the venom of toads; fermenting grapes and barley; curing tobacco; steeping leaves; and roasting beans.

Historically, only a few handfuls of different compounds have been used reliably to get people high, but over the past hundred years or so, humankind has learned to synthesize the active chemicals in laboratories and to manipulate chemical structures to invent new drugs — the numbers of which began growing exponentially in the 2010s. Anyone with computer acumen can acquire hundreds of psychoactive compounds that didn't exist even a few years ago.

According to the European Monitoring Centre for Drugs and Drug Addiction, 150 new illicit drugs were bought and sold between 1997 and 2010. Another 150 appeared in just the next three years, and since then, in some years as many as 100 new chemicals have appeared, with synthetic cannabinoids especially common.

Though they can be incredibly potent and affect the body in new ways, these latest drugs aren't conceived out of thin air. In fact, many are derived from the same naturally occurring chemicals our ancestors have been using for thousands of years. Fentanyl, for example, is a new plague, but its natural predecessor, the opium poppy, has been used (and abused) since at least the Mesopotamian era.

The story of fentanyl, however, can be traced to one man: Paul Janssen.

A Belgian chemist, Janssen was undoubtedly a genius. He could quote Homer in the Ancient Greek. During World War II he studied chemistry and other sciences at university in Namur, Belgium — enrolling secretly, despite the Nazi occupation — and in 1948, when he was twenty-two, he funded a trip to America in part by beating opponents in chess, at venues including the Manhattan Chess Club. What Janssen was best known for was creating medicines. Over his lifetime, he was responsible for some eighty new medical drugs, including fentanyl. One biographer called him "the most prolific drug inventor of all time." His brilliance wasn't just in coming up with new medicines but in realizing that new medicines could be created in the first place.

Janssen was born in 1926 in the small Belgian town of Turnhout. When she was four, Janssen's younger sister died of tubercular meningitis, a then untreatable condition that can now be controlled with antibiotics. Janssen was in high school at the time, and his sorrow over his sister's death inspired his journey into medicine. He was mentored by his father, a family doctor in Turnhout, who would operate on patients in their own homes. In these first decades of the twentieth century, rather than give patients the available medicines — organ extracts and tonics that are nowadays discredited — Janssen's father gave them placebos. "And he was absolutely right to do so," Paul Janssen later wrote. "Naturally, there was insulin, cardiac glycosides, aspirin and morphine, but where most of the other medicines were concerned, one could safely say they did more harm than good." Janssen's father nonetheless started his own medicine company. After the discovery of penicillin, his company sold the antibiotic and also produced its own products, which mainly were combinations of existing drugs. The enterprise's success did little to impress the younger Janssen, at the time a precocious chemistry and medical student.

"Come up with something better yourself, then," his father challenged him.

At age twenty-six, Janssen began pursuing new chemicals, with some help from his father, who fronted him money and lab space. But Janssen wasn't interested in slapping new labels on old chemicals. He wanted to create new drugs that actually made people feel better — and that he could patent. The key to this, he learned, was playing around with chemical structures. Based on the work of Nobel Prize–winning German medical scientist Paul Ehrlich, Janssen knew that adjusting the chemical makeup of a known drug, even just slightly, could create something that could affect the human body in dramatically new ways.

A year later, in 1953, Paul Janssen founded

his company, Janssen Pharmaceutica, initially working out of the third floor of his father's building. "We didn't even have a calculator, let alone a computer for the simplest calculations," Janssen wrote in 2000. "To reduce expenditure we economized by performing simple tests on pieces of gut from newly slaughtered rabbits, which I collected early in the morning from a butcher in Turnhout."

Despite its modest beginnings, the company hit the ground running with its discovery of a drug called ambucetamide, used to alleviate menstrual pain. Janssen would also invent loperamide (Imodium), for diarrhea, as well as chemicals that became critical to the fields of psychiatry, mycology, and parasitology. To spur his company's ascent, he recruited star Belgian scientists from the Belgian Congo, after the political upheaval there that would lead to the country's independence and the end of colonial rule. He was soon managing a large staff — its members called him Dr. Paul — but still closely involved with creating new chemicals. He literally daydreamed about molecules. "I often watched him at meetings," wrote Sir James Black, a physiology and medicine Nobel laureate of King's College London, "when bored with the proceedings, finding solace inside his head as he doodled new chemical compounds!"

One of these new chemicals was fentanyl, which Janssen and his team first synthesized in 1959 by experimenting with the chemical structure of morphine.

Derived naturally from the resin of the opium poppy, morphine was chemically isolated at the dawn of the nineteenth century by German pharmacist Friedrich Sertürner, who named it for Morpheus, the Greek god of dreams. By Janssen's time it was the reigning pain reliever. Janssen began subtly altering parts of its chemical structure to create new compounds. He tested the effectiveness of these creations, including fentanyl, on lab mice, placing the mice on hot plates and slowly turning up the heat to gauge their reactions.

He developed many morphine derivatives, but fentanyl was particularly profitable for Janssen Pharmaceutica. Doctors found it superior to morphine because of the way it acted. Like morphine, it bound with a receptor in the brain (which we now call the "mu" receptor) to cause pain relief. But fentanyl came on faster, was much more powerful, and wasn't as likely to cause nausea. "Fentanyl," Janssen later wrote, "made it possible for the first time to perform lengthy operations and, together with its successors, heralded a revolution in the operating theatre. Without this compound and its analogue, sufentanil, open-heart surgery [as performed today] would not be possible."

The drug was a revelation, and it went on to become the world's most widely used anesthetic. Janssen Pharmaceutica was purchased by American behemoth Johnson & Johnson in 1961, and Paul Janssen continued working for the company, tasked with developing other types of fentanyl, referred to as analogues. But almost from the start, fentanyl's potential addictive dangers were recognized, and it was placed under international control by a United Nations agreement in 1964. This led countries including the United States and the United Kingdom, in 1971, to schedule it — that is, to ban its recreational use. Indeed, its euphoric qualities would prove too much for many users to resist. "Fentanyl is a good medicine but a bad drug," Justice Tettey, chief of the Laboratory and Scientific Section at the United Nations Office on Drugs and Crime, summed up later. "It has excellent pain relieving properties, but is liable to abuse and can rapidly lead to dependency."

Despite fentanyl's quick success as a

painkiller in Europe, during the 1960s it was almost blocked for sale in the United States by the Food and Drug Administration. One vocal opponent to the drug's approval was University of Pennsylvania anesthesiology professor Robert Dripps. A rare outlier who believed fentanyl's high potency could lead to abuse, he eventually agreed to a compromise after being lobbied by Paul Janssen himself: fentanyl would be available, but only when diluted with another drug called droperidol, a sedative — also patented by Janssen — that was believed to mitigate fentanyl's detrimental effects. A ratio of fifty parts droperidol to one part fentanyl produced a "bad high" when taken recreationally, Dripps and Janssen agreed, and thus was unlikely to be abused. The FDA approved this combination in 1968. Fentanyl's success boosted Janssen's bottom line, which drove Paul Janssen and his colleagues to develop many other fentanyl analogues. Some, like alpha-methylfentanyl, were never turned into medicines that were sold. Others, however, made it to market, including sufentanil, used in long-lasting surgeries, and carfentanil, a veterinary medicine that is the strongest fentanyl analogue ever made commercially.

At the very end of the 1970s, a pair of overdose deaths in Orange County, California, stumped authorities. A few bits of information were known about the victims. They seemed likely to have both used heroin, as shown by the telltale scarring (tracks) on their bodies and the heroin paraphernalia discovered with their bodies. But toxicology reports bizarrely didn't turn up any known drugs in their system. Soon, a half dozen more people in the county had died under similar circumstances, and then twice as many.

Around the same time, police began discovering a new drug on the street, China White. Traditionally, dealers of China White touted their product as the finest heroin available — pale in color and originating in East or Southeast Asia. "To get connected with China White is a sort of fantasy for [opiate] addicts," Darryl Inaba, director of the Haight-Ashbury Free Clinic of San Francisco, said in a report in *US Navy Medicine.* This new China White had no heroin in it, however, and rather than a fantasy it was a nightmare. Instead of pure heroin from Asia, laboratory analysis determined that it contained something called alpha-methylfentanyl — a fentanyl analogue.

Though this particular chemical had been synthesized by Janssen Pharmaceutica, it was never developed into a medical product. The source of the China White remained a mystery. Presumably, the recipe had been stolen from scientific literature published by Janssen scientists, and then the drug had been cooked up by rogue chemists. But no China White lab was ever seized, and no one was arrested. There were plenty of guesses, however, including some wild speculation from a famed psychedelic chemist and drug expert named Alexander "Sasha" Shulgin. "Had China been developing some super-potent fentanyl analogues as potential warfare agents? Let the fantasy roll," he wrote in 1997. "Maybe the Chinese were using second class citizens (the drug-using population of California) as guinea pigs for the initial human trials of their new drugs." Also suspected were scientists in Russia, which had developed fentanyl problems of its own.

China White represented a fish-crawling-onto-land moment: it was the first popular, illicit drug synthesized by a rogue chemist that was new, rather than simply a copy of something already on the medical market.

And thus, alpha-methylfentanyl was the first in a long line of new psychoactive substances that came to include K2, Spice, "bath salts," and all the other substances this book is about. Back before they were called novel psychoactive substances, or NPS, they were known by another name: designer drugs.

Calling alpha-methylfentanyl China White was smart marketing, as it evoked a desirable type of heroin. What truly helped the product stand apart, however, was the fact that it was legal. Fentanyl itself had been illegal for recreational use since 1971, as a schedule II drug with a high potential for abuse.* And chemically alpha-methylfentanyl was almost identical. But the key word is *almost.* It wasn't identical. It had a unique molecular design. And therefore the police were powerless. "You could walk around with a shopping bag full of it and nobody could do anything to you," observed Robert J. Roberton, chief of the state of Califor-

---

* Schedule I drugs have "no currently accepted medical use and a high potential for abuse," while Schedule II drugs have "a high potential for abuse, with use potentially leading to severe psychological or physical dependence," according to the DEA.

nia's Division of Drug Programs.

Other fentanyl variations followed on alpha-methylfentanyl's heels. In the early 1980s, more troubling reports about users injecting drugs that weren't quite heroin emerged from California. In 1982 a man named George Carillo was brought to a San José hospital practically immobile, and his girlfriend, Juanita Lopez, came in a week later, also suffering from stiffness, paralysis, and other symptoms similar to Parkinson's, except Carillo and Lopez were too young to have the disease. A handful of other victims with similar symptoms were soon identified. Eventually their condition was traced back to a new opioid they had injected called MPPP, which was intended to imitate heroin but had been synthesized incorrectly, inadvertently creating a different substance, MPTP, with disastrous side effects. This story at least has a silver lining, as research on the victims catalyzed new discoveries leading to advancement in Parkinson's research.

Soon afterward, the US government began regulating drugs that didn't yet exist. The DEA needed six months to schedule a new drug, and by that time new analogues were already popular on the streets. So in 1984 Congress granted the DEA emergency scheduling powers, so the agency could ban drugs immediately. But even this was insufficient to stop the new fentanyl analogues, which sometimes started killing people before the DEA had even heard of them.

Thus was inspired the Federal Analogue Act, signed into law by President Ronald Reagan in 1986. The legislation specifically went after fentanyls and what would become known as designer drugs and NPS. It made anything deemed "substantially similar" to schedule I or II psychoactive drugs — in either effect or structure — automatically illegal the moment it came into being.

However, banning something "substantially similar" proved challenging. Just because chemicals have similar structures doesn't mean they will affect the human body the same way; in fact, quite often the effects can be dramatically different. Further, the law aimed at psychoactive substances, but what constitutes psychoactive can be debated. A strong cup of coffee can have a powerful impact, as can large amounts of chocolate and sugar.*

* The United Kingdom went even further with an analogue act thirty years later, in 2016, when it

75

The US Federal Analogue Act is still used to prosecute makers of analogue drugs, though these prosecutions can be difficult because the government must prove the defendant knew the substance was similar to a controlled chemical. Furthermore, little evidence exists that the Federal Analogue Act has had a strong deterrent effect. In fact, since its enactment the number of new analogue drugs being consumed by Americans has skyrocketed. Most NPS are made in China, and since China lacks an analogue

---

enacted the Psychoactive Substances Act, which sought to ban anything that could get a person high, with medicine, alcohol, cigarettes, and caffeine specifically exempted. The purpose of the bill was to combat "legal highs," such as synthetic cannabinoids and ecstasy knockoffs, which had been sold lawfully in head shops — but the bill had unseen ramifications. The Church of England and the Catholic Church were worried that using incense in services could lead to prosecution, and the bill's implementation was delayed over concerns that the difficulty of defining *psychoactive* might make the law problematic to enforce. Ultimately it was implemented and did successfully remove "legal highs" from store shelves, but the long-term ramifications aren't yet fully understood.

act of its own, generally, drugs there must be banned one at a time, as they are discovered. (There are three United Nations international drug treaties — from 1961, 1971, and 1988, to which China, Russia, the United States, and most other world powers are signatories — and they also operate the same way, without an analogue act.) Thus, brand-new drugs that are automatically covered by US laws start off perfectly legal for manufacture and export in China, although the country recently announced a ban of all fentanyl analogues.

The United States seems just as susceptible to new drugs as countries like Sweden, which lacks an analogue act. While Sweden has been devastated by dangerous analogues such as cyclopropylfentanyl, acrylfentanyl, and acetylfentanyl, the United States has been hit particularly hard by carfentanil, the veterinary tranquilizer that can be one hundred times more potent than fentanyl and five thousand times more potent than heroin. Carfentanil was responsible for killing more than eleven hundred Ohio residents between July 2016 and June 2017 alone.

At this point in the cat-and-mouse game between legislators and rogue chemists, warns Julijan "Sidney" Picej (an expert on new drugs who is from Ljubljana, Slovenia), the rogue chemists are so desperate for new products that they'll try anything. "Good combinations are long gone. Their approach to finding a new flagship product is, 'Anything goes, as long as it's not fatal if you use it the first three times,' " he said. "It's difficult for users and researchers to get any info, since the molecule was literally synthesized for the first time three weeks ago."

In the mid-1980s, it wasn't clear whether these types of "synthetic heroin" would become a plague or simply fade away. A University of California at Davis pharmacology professor named Gary Henderson studied the chemical impurities in China White and concluded that a single chemist was responsible for all of it. "Most likely he made a few grams of the drug — millions of doses — and then shut up his shop," he told journalist Jack Shafer in 1985.

Henderson became the scientist doctors turned to when their overdose patients had strange blood samples, and the DEA consulted when it turned up inscrutable chemicals. He had already been researching fentanyl for years; his lab focused on how it was used to dope racehorses, whose urine turned up traces of it. He worked to develop a technique to identify fentanyl and began to understand the nature of the drug, including its potential for chemical manipulation. "Perhaps hundreds," he said, when asked how many fentanyl analogues would be possible. "Maybe thousands."

Henderson was way ahead of his time when it came to predicting the horrors not just of fentanyl but of NPS generally. "It seems we are still watching reruns of *The French Connection* while there is someone out there using a computer to search the chemical literature looking for new drugs to synthesize," he told the US Senate's Budget Committee in July 1985, a statement that was remarkably prescient. He coined the phrase *designer drugs,* defining them as "substances where the psychoactive properties of a drug are retained, but the molecular structure has been altered to avoid prosecution." Often synthesized from common chemicals, they were skillfully marketed under attractive, exotic names, he added. His 1988 paper "Designer Drugs: Past History and Future Prospects" is nothing less than prophecy, speculating accurately not just on the future of NPS chemistry but on the implications for law enforcement. "In the view of this author," he wrote, "it is likely that the future drugs of abuse will be synthetics rather than plant products. A single gram of any very potent drug could be synthesized at one location, transported to distribution sites worldwide, and then formulated (cut) into many thousand, perhaps a million, doses. . . . Preventing the distribution of such small amounts of the pure drug will be exceedingly difficult. . . . In fact, any success we may have in curtailing the distribution of natural products such as opium, coca, and marijuana and preventing the diversion of pharmaceuticals will only stimulate the development of potent synthetic substitutes."

THREE

The 1989 police action comedy *Tango & Cash,* starring Sylvester Stallone and Kurt Russell as narcotics detectives with outsize opinions of themselves, may not have gotten great reviews, but it did inspire the name of a new fentanyl product, which began killing people in the northeastern United States in early 1991. The deceased included residents of New York City, Newark and Paterson in New Jersey, and Hartford, Connecticut. Almost all of the drug called Tango and Cash seemed to originate from an open-air drug market in the Bronx, near 138th Street and Brook Avenue, described in the *Hartford Courant* as, "a kind of regional wholesaler to dealers from cities around the Northeast." Over the weekend beginning February 2, 1991, Tango and Cash caused a dozen deaths and more than one hundred overdoses.

The *New York Times* quoted a thirty-nine-year-old heroin user named Richie, who was pursuing the drug despite its toxic effects. "When an addict hears that someone O.D.'d, the first question they ask is: 'Where'd they get it?' Because they want to find some of it for themselves."

The deaths continued. During 1991 and 1992, 126 people in the Northeast died from this new fentanyl product, which was also sometimes called China White. More than twenty of the deceased came from Philadelphia. "Some of the Philadelphia junkies died so swiftly that syringes were still embedded in their arms," reported the *Baltimore Sun.* Alpha-methylfentanyl, even though it had been scheduled in 1981, was discovered in some of the Tango and Cash batches. (News reports from this era weren't always clear about whether the drugs involved were fentanyl or a fentanyl analogue like alpha-methylfentanyl, so the term *fentanyl* is used below to reference both.)

For almost two years, police remained stymied in their search for the drug's source. But then in December 1992, they received a valuable clue from a Boston drug dealer named Christopher Moscatiello. In the midst of a fentanyl sale, he mentioned to a customer that his Wichita, Kansas, supplier had nearly died from a fentanyl overdose.

Moscatiello didn't realize it at the time, but the customer was actually a DEA agent.

DEA began pursuing the tip, despite the fact that Kansas seemed an odd place for a fentanyl laboratory, since the Midwest wasn't yet associated with deaths from the substance. But it turned out the supplier in question had Eastern ties. He was a Pittsburgh businessman named Joseph Martier. In August 1992 paramedics responding to a 911 call found Martier passed out in a storage building near Wichita, having overdosed on fentanyl. In February, 1993, the DEA arrested Martier and raided his facility, alleging that his was the country's only lab making fentanyl. This drug, the agency noted, was "the serial killer of the drug world."

Also taken into custody was Martier's partner, a drug cook named George Marquardt. No ordinary illicit chemist, Marquardt was an oddly philosophical, hyperintelligent chemistry prodigy. A retired DEA agent later called him "the very best illicit chemist in the history of American drugmaking."

As a child Marquardt had been fascinated by "an anti-drug film in which a mouse on LSD chased a cat." Before he was old enough to drive, he was making heroin with a friend, and after doing research for the University of Wisconsin (from which he pilfered lab equipment) he pretended to be a member of the Atomic Energy Commission, falsely adding the claim to his CV in an attempt to trick a Milwaukee college into accepting him as a physics lecturer. The ruse succeeded.

Marquardt single-handedly fashioned his own mass spectrometer, a complicated scientific instrument used to identify chemicals, and became a drug mercenary for hire, eschewing the academic world because it didn't pay enough. But he was genuinely fascinated with the magic of chemistry and had a selfless streak as well. At one point, he said, he synthesized clandestine AZT for people with AIDS. Marquardt made his name, however, with hard drugs, venturing further and further into a dangerous underworld, emboldened by a belief — similar to one held by Walter White of the series *Breaking Bad* — that drug kingpins wouldn't kill him because he made a superior product. He first learned about fentanyl in 1978, while doing jail time after being busted at his Oklahoma meth lab. Upon his release he began producing it, but not before doing his homework. "I read the forensic science literature religiously," he said. "I read publications like *Police Science Abstracts.* Surveyed all the appearances of fentanyl everywhere that I could find out from the literature. And gave careful thought to what these people had done wrong." He reported spending more than a week at a time cooking up batches, and he sought to make different varieties of fentanyl so his products would appear to come from different labs and thus confuse the authorities.

The DEA, however, believed it could trace the 126 Northeastern deaths back to Marquardt and Martier's lab, and Marquardt was charged with distributing and manufacturing fentanyl. He immediately confessed to his crimes. "I just don't bother with the lies," he said. "When the game's over, it's just over. If you can't deal with the consequences of these things, you should have carried a lunch bucket." In the end, Marquardt's products were thought to have killed more people than initially suspected — perhaps two hundred or even three hundred. He served twenty-two years in prison and was released in 2015.

Marquardt now swears he is done with fentanyl, but he has little remorse. "I don't feel like I'm supplying a product to an innocent or naïve population," he said. "I attach no blame to them. They are what they are. I am what I am. We're both criminals."

The moral discussion of accountability becomes more complicated when one considers legitimate university scientists who, like Marquardt, were also making fentanyls. They sought to patent new chemicals that would benefit the study of medicine and, ultimately, people suffering from pain. For this reason, most people would give them the benefit of the doubt, despite the fact that they were often motivated by financial gain as well — and that such scientists sometimes unwittingly paved the way for rogue chemists to exploit their work.

A fentanyl analogue called 3-methylfentanyl, patented by a University of Mississippi professor of medicinal chemistry named Thomas Riley, provides a case in point. Riley developed it from Paul Janssen's original fentanyl, and hoped that 3-methylfentanyl might perhaps maintain fentanyl's potent analgesic (or pain-reducing) qualities, without sharing its dangerous attributes, and catch on as a medical product. In 1973, he and two other collaborators published a paper about their studies of 3-methylfentanyl on rats, but the results were not what Riley hoped. It was never commercially marketed, and he never made any money off it.

With addicted users, however, 3-methylfentanyl was a huge hit. In the late 1980s it killed eighteen people in western Pennsylvania. Predating Tango and Cash, this was the first major case of fentanyl-related deaths since the California overdoses earlier in the decade.

More than a decade later, 3-methylfentanyl was at the center of an armed hostage crisis in Moscow. On October 23, 2002, a huge crowd had gathered in a converted ball-bearing factory for the performance of Nord-Ost (Northeast), a musical celebrating Russian heritage that was the most expensive production of its kind in the country's history. The show came to an abrupt halt when dozens of Chechen rebels seized control of the facility, taking about eight hundred attendees hostage and threatening to kill them if the Chechen war with Russia wasn't immediately ended. The standoff lasted for several days, and on October 26 Russian security police pumped a gray aerosol gas into the building, intending to knock out the hijackers before forcing their way in. The guerillas were killed, but so were about 120 of the hostages, who were already weakened by days without food or water. Some died en route to the hospital.

Though authorities initially declined to say what chemical agent had been used, the Russian health minister and a Russian newspaper later identified it as 3-methylfentanyl. Subsequent analysis of survivors' clothing indicates it was possibly a chemical cocktail containing numerous drugs, including carfentanil.

Russia claimed that the gas used was nonlethal and intended to simply put both the rebels and the civilians to sleep. Though some praised the Russian effort for saving the majority of the hostages, many international observers criticized it as a type of chemical warfare that not only violated international treaties but also was based on foolhardy science.

"There is no way known to medical science that can put a large number of people to sleep without killing a sizable percentage of them," said Harvard biology professor Matt Meselson. "In medicine you are dealing with one patient. You can see when he is asleep and, assuming your hand isn't shaking too badly on the valve, you probably won't kill him. But the military objective is different. You have to put 100 percent of the people to sleep — not 50 percent, not 70 percent — and you have to put them to sleep fast. There isn't any way to do that effectively and safely." Analysts continue to worry that fentanyls could be used in large-scale attacks, particularly by terrorists, considering that a tiny amount can do such damage. In January, 2019, Massachusetts senator Ed Markey wrote letters to the State and Defense Departments, warning of the possibility of such an attack on Americans. "To my knowledge, no such strategy exists at present for addressing the threat fentanyl poses," he wrote.

In 1988, an international treaty scheduled 3-methylfentanyl — effectively outlawing it in much of the world — but by the early 2000s it had begun catching on as a street drug in Eastern European countries such as Estonia. The small former Soviet satellite, known for its brisk economic growth, already had a large heroin problem, but the heroin supply from Afghanistan was squeezed after the Taliban banned opium poppy farming in 2000. Fentanyl and 3-methylfentanyl began to take off, likely entering the country from Russia, which it borders. Over the next decade a thousand or more Estonians died from fentanyl and 3-methylfentanyl overdose, a startling number for a country of only 1.3 million.

Though the heroin supply has reemerged, the destruction from fentanyl and 3-methylfentanyl continues in Estonia. "The dealers realize it's easier to traffic and package fentanyl than heroin . . . and so they strictly control the market in favor of fentanyl. Even though drug users themselves say they would prefer heroin, it's simply not allowed [by dealers] in Estonian markets," observed Aljona Kurbatova, head of the Infectious Diseases and Drug Abuse Prevention Department at Estonia's National Institute for Health Development.

A 2016 study showed Estonia to have the highest increase in drug-overdose deaths in the world, and the entrenchment of fentanyl and 3-methylfentanyl there serves as a portentous warning for number two: the United States. Despite hopes that the crisis has peaked, experts believe fentanyl and its analogues could be just picking up speed. Fentanyl is also threatening to become an epidemic in other countries. Australia has already seen five hundred fentanyl deaths from 2010 through 2015 (the most recent year for which figures were available), and the number is believed to be surging. The UN Office on Drugs and Crime (UNODC) reported that the most common method of illicit fentanyl use in Australia seems to be extracting the drug from pharmaceutical products such as transdermal patches and that this is also the case in Germany. While Europe's problem with fentanyl is smaller than North America's, a sharp uptick in deaths indicates the crisis may also be spreading to the United Kingdom, which according to one survey buys more fentanyl from the Dark Web than any other European country.

Even aside from fentanyl, fentanyl analogues have triggered a crisis in some countries. In 2016, Sweden suffered forty-three deaths associated with acrylfentanyl, an analogue discussed in scientific literature during the 1980s but unknown in Sweden until it started killing people. In 2017 another analogue, cyclopropylfentanyl, caused more than seventy deaths there. Now, because of the fentanyl analogues, fentanyls as a class have displaced heroin as the number-one killer drug in the country. The analogues there are purchased almost entirely over the Internet, from China.

Other European and Eastern European countries are also starting to see fentanyls from China, but that's a fairly recent development. Until recent years, European fentanyl was procured locally — stolen from pharmacies, for example, or harvested from

91

patches in hospital waste — or received from Russia and its Eastern bloc neighbors.

Russia itself imports vast quantities of ecstasy and synthetic cannabinoids from China, and the country has widespread public-health problems with drugs including heroin and "bath salts." Russia also harbors a huge psychonaut community, whose members create new drugs and discuss them on Internet message boards. It's difficult to gauge whether Russia suffers from widespread fentanyl addiction, because its data reporting is very poor. The country has undoubtedly been producing the synthetic drug for a long time, however, both legally and illegally. Before the dissolution of the USSR, it was producing fentanyl for its army. "It was included as a painkiller in the emergency kits for Soviet Union soldiers," said Roumen Sedefov of the European Monitoring Centre For Drugs and Drug Addiction. "After the Soviet Union collapse, we think there may have been huge stockpiles of fentanyl, in Lithuania and other countries, and a lot of it was diverted into Europe and sold on the illicit market. This may have fueled, partly, the epidemic here in Europe." William Leonard Pickard, a famed LSD chemist now serving a life sentence for conspiring to manufacture and distribute LSD, studied the Russian fentanyl epidemic in the 1990s while a student at Harvard's Kennedy School of Government. He uncovered Mafia-run laboratories in Azerbaijan, where chemists who were winners of the Russian chemistry olympiad synthesized fentanyls including 3-methylfentanyl. They were imprisoned, but he feared that other out-of-work chemists formerly employed by the Soviet Union could spread fentanyl far beyond the country's borders.

In 2018, a former colonel in the Russian army named Sergei Skripal was poisoned in Salisbury, England, along with his daughter. The poison was reportedly fentanyl. Skripal had been convicted in Russia of spying for Britain years earlier but was sent to the United Kingdom as part of a "spy swap," an exchange for sleeper agents in the United States. Both he and his daughter survived. Russian foreign minister Sergey Lavrov denied Russian involvement.

The fentanyl analogue 3-methylfentanyl has never been used as a medical drug. There is no legitimate need for anyone to have it, with the exception of official forensic labs in places like Estonia, where tiny quantities are needed to verify the types of street fentanyl that are killing people. Still, numerous Chinese labs make it for illicit use.

Though 3-methylfentanyl has likely killed thousands of people, its inventor, Thomas Riley, who died in 2005, appears to have been unaware of the fallout. His widow, Phyllis Riley, doesn't believe he knew the drug was used illicitly. One of his former colleagues, retired University of Mississippi pharmacology professor Marvin Wilson, was Riley's coauthor, along with Danny B. Hale, of a 1973 paper about 3-methylfentanyl published in the *Journal of Pharmaceutical Science.* Wilson acknowledged that drug peddlers could have learned about 3-methylfentanyl from their paper. "Chemists of the [DEA] believe that any competent chemist could make the substance after reading Dr. Riley's description in the chemical literature," read a 1980 *New York Times* article on the subject. Wilson recalled they weren't much concerned with its abuse potential. "Because it was so potent, a lot of us at the time thought that it probably won't get into the abuse channels, because it would be so potentially dangerous, and small changes in the dose could have dramatic effects on the body. We weren't thinking of it as a new heroin."

The conflict between legitimate medical

science and illicit drug chemistry has come to the forefront as NPS have spread. Not just fentanyls, but deadly hallucinogens, synthetic cannabinoids, fake ecstasy, and other stimulants have all gotten their starts in scientific labs. Academics say nothing can stop legitimate scientific creations from crossing over into the realm of abuse — without stifling science. Nonetheless, the trend has caused some outraged family members of overdose victims to demand that the university-sanctioned creators of these drugs be held accountable.

"We as scientists just haven't been able to differentiate the receptors that lead to abuse from those that are associated with the analgesic," Wilson laments. "And that's a conundrum. Scientists come up with knowledge, and people choose to use that knowledge in different ways. Some beneficial, and some not so beneficial. But to not continue the scientific endeavor, certainly is not a good option for mankind either."

Marvin Wilson and his colleagues were not alone in underestimating the potential popularity of fentanyl. Experts ranging from health-care professionals to top scientists knew how powerful and addictive fentanyl was, and yet very few of them expected it to seize hold in the general population. The underestimation of fentanyl's potential extended to the DEA, even as recently as 2015. That year the agency's *National Drug Threat Assessment Summary,* which focuses on drug abuse trends, read: "Fentanyl will remain a threat while the current clandestine production continues; however, it is unlikely to assume a significant portion of the opioid market. Fentanyl's short-lasting high, coupled with its high mortality rate, renders it unappealing to many opioid users who prefer the longer-lasting high that heroin offers and who wish to avoid the increased danger from fentanyl."

One year later, fentanyl had shot past heroin and was killing more Americans annually than any other drug in American history. And the fentanyl analogues, which are being developed and marketed at an increasingly rapid clip, threaten to make the problem worse. Seventeen analogues were reported to the UN Office on Drugs and Crime between 2012 and 2016, some of which were developed from information found in scientific papers published thirty or forty years ago. These fentanyls — including ocfentanil, furanylfentanyl, acetylfentanyl, and butyrfentanyl — had never been made into marketable drugs. They could have existed only on paper, but at a time when old research is more accessible than ever before, these chemicals have roared to life.

We are now living in pharmacology professor Gary Henderson's dystopian future, which he described in his 1988 paper "Designer Drugs: Past History and Future Prospects." Just as Henderson predicted, the production of illicit fentanyl has become an international business. Like most NPS, the majority of illicit fentanyl is made in Chinese drug laboratories. It's then sold over the Dark Web to individual dealers or shipped to Mexican drug cartels, who press it into counterfeit pills, cut it into heroin, coke, or meth, or package it up as powder and bring it into the United States.

What Henderson didn't predict is that many fentanyl users don't even realize they are taking it. Thinking they are buying another drug, they instead receive a product cut with fentanyl. They don't know they have put a potentially lethal drug into their system until it's too late. Today, in many places, little heroin can be found that hasn't been cut with fentanyl. "There are very few people that just make pure heroin nowadays, because of the quality of 'El Diabolito,' " a Sinaloa trafficker told *Fusion,* referencing fentanyl.

That dealers would kill off their own clients may seem counterintuitive.

"It brings more business," said Detective Ricardo Franklin, of the St. Louis County Police Department's Bureau of Drug Enforcement. "Sure, it kills more people, but from a user standpoint, they're not thinking about the death. When they hear someone OD'd, they think it must be an amazing high. A friend who will tell a friend who will tell a friend, and in the end it's promotion."

"If addicts find something that killed somebody, they flock to it," said Jack Sanders, a former fentanyl dealer from St. Louis. "They want the strongest product possible. Most people, they want to be drooling. The dealers don't look at it as if we're losing customers. They look at it as if we're gaining more customers."

Today, Janssen Pharmaceutical of Johnson & Johnson makes only one fentanyl product — the fentanyl patch. Marketed as Duragesic, it helps relieve chronic pain, including in cancer patients. Patented in the United States in 1986, Duragesic was approved by the FDA for advanced pain treatment in 1990, with medical fentanyl no longer required to be diluted with droperidol. By 2004 it was a certified blockbuster, clearing $2 billion in worldwide sales. But like Purdue Pharma, the makers of OxyContin, Janssen Pharmaceutical engaged in deceptive marketing, suggesting Duragesic had less abuse potential than other opioids. In 2000 the FDA said that this and other claims Janssen made about the patch were "false or misleading," and four years later the FDA instructed the company to "immediately cease" such claims, including the claim that the patch was less abused than other opioids.

Sales dipped after Duragesic's patent expired in 2006, and Janssen stopped marketing it two years later, according to a company spokesperson, but the patch continues to be trafficked in medical theaters, and different companies sell other fentanyl medical products, including a lollipop. The patch in particular continues to be trafficked on the black market. Not long ago on the Dark Web emporium Wall St. Market, for example, Duragesic patches were being offered for one hundred dollars each, from a vendor called BigPoppa7777.

Even as it devastates communities in North America and around the world, fentanyl remains a critical pharmaceutical product. Overall, fentanyl was prescribed by doctors 6.5 million times in 2015, according to the DEA, a number that dropped to about 6 million in 2016, and about 5 million in 2017. Still producing many medicines, the Janssen division within Johnson & Johnson continues to prosper, today boasting more than forty thousand employees in labs and offices around the world.

Paul Janssen didn't live long enough to see the mass destruction fentanyl has wrought. Upon his death in 2003, at age seventy-seven, he was widely celebrated as a lifesaving innovator. Obituary tributes noted Janssen's passion for the country of China. Janssen was the first Western company to set up a pharmaceutical factory there, and in 1993 Paul Janssen became the first non-Chinese person to receive a pharmaceutical honorary doctorate in China. Janssen's factory was in Shaanxi province, near the excavation site of the famous army of terracotta soldiers, sometimes called the Xi'an Warriors, buried more than two thousand years ago with China's first emperor, Qin Shi Huang, to protect him in the afterlife. When the statues were threatened by mold, Janssen analyzed the damage and provided antifungal sprays developed by his company to save them, even setting up an on-site lab.

The soldiers remain one of the most popular tourist attractions in China.

The opioid epidemic sweeping through the United States, Canada, and Estonia undoubtedly would have horrified Paul Janssen, as would the fact that Chinese laboratories today produce most of the world's illicit fentanyl. According to Andrew Wheatley, spokesperson for the Janssen Pharmaceutical Companies of Johnson & Johnson, Duragesic patches sold in the United States are manufactured in the United States, and those sold outside the United States are manufactured in Belgium, and none of the controlled-substance active pharmaceutical ingredients in either Janssen or Johnson & Johnson products are manufactured in China.

Janssen and other pharmaceutical companies like Purdue are now facing lawsuits from states and other entities around the United States for their contributions to the opioid epidemic, but Paul Janssen continues to be remembered as an unparalleled medical drug innovator. Since 2005, Johnson & Johnson has been giving out a biomedical research award named for him. But the proliferation of illicit fentanyl may alter his legacy. His focus throughout his professional life — up until the day he died, while

101

attending a scientific conference in Rome — was the science and business of creating chemicals to help ease suffering. To his core, Janssen believed in medical science's ability to benefit humanity. When fentanyl was first synthesized in 1959, nobody could have predicted that it would eventually create so much suffering. Nobody could have known it would become as common as cheap liquor in America's inner cities and much more deadly, or that anyone with an Internet connection could have it sent to his or her door.

FOUR

One consequence of the Federal Analogue Act of 1986 was its effect on science and medicine. Some believed the law derailed development of potentially beneficial treatments and medical drugs by making it difficult for researchers to study new chemicals on human subjects. "The placement of medical research approval within law enforcement, the DEA, is unthinkably stupid and inappropriate, and cannot be tolerated," wrote Sasha Shulgin in 1993. "We, as the research community . . . have quietly acceded to a non-scientific authority that can oversee and, to an increasing degree, influence the direction of our inquiry."

Shulgin was easy to dismiss, by some. He wasn't a medical doctor but rather a psychedelics chemist, who manipulated the structures of chemicals to try to create new drugs. He had a record of pushing the bounds of legality in his studies, and the passage of the Federal Analogue Act meant that most of his new creations would likely be *a priori* illegal. But those who understood Shulgin's research knew that he wasn't just looking for new ways to get people high. He was on a lifelong journey of exploring the relationship between drugs and the human mind. He knew that some new psychoactive substances could have terrible effects, but he also believed many could be lifesaving medicines.

Astronauts take voyages into outer space; psychonauts, by contrast, take voyages into their own psyches, testing new, just-created recreational chemicals that might make them incredibly high — or might make them lose their minds. Many brag about their exploits. Some have done themselves irreparable harm.

Alexander Shulgin, better known as Sasha, who lived to eighty-eight, stood above them all. He took thousands of psychedelic trips, on hundreds of drugs that were never before consumed by humans. Many he invented himself. He spread their gospel to the masses, publishing his recipes in books that became underground best sellers. More than anyone else, he helped create the world of novel psychoactive substances (NPS) we live in today. Some believe Shulgin deserved a Nobel Prize. Others wanted him locked away.

Shulgin first began thinking deeply about drugs as a young man while serving in the Navy during World War II. Aboard a destroyer escort in the Atlantic, he faced terrifying spurts of conflict followed by long periods adrift. To pass the time he read through a giant chemistry textbook, memorizing its contents. In 1944, off the coast of England, his thumb got infected. When his ship arrived in Liverpool, Shulgin was prepared for surgery at a military hospital and given a glass of orange juice he believed contained a powerful sedative. He promptly passed out and slept through the procedure. Only later did he learn there had been no sedative at all. The incident inspired a profound belief that, more than anything, one's mind determines what happens when one takes a drug.

This lesson stayed with Shulgin when he was a biochemistry PhD candidate at UC Berkeley in 1955. He tried mescaline for the first time and experienced seeing the world around him as if he were a child. The psychedelic, originally derived from cactus plants and still at that time legal, evoked awesome sense memories. Again he wondered: Was this the drug, or was this his mind?

"This awesome recall had been brought about by a fraction of a gram of a white solid," he wrote, "but . . . in no way whatsoever could it be argued that these memories had been contained within the white solid. Everything I had recognized came from the depths of my memory and my psyche."

Shulgin soon realized his calling: to explore psychedelic drugs from a scientific perspective, which he began doing during his employment, in the late 1950s and 1960s, at Dow Chemical, the industrial giant that manufactured the crippling herbicide Agent Orange, which was sprayed in the Vietnam war. While under the company's employ, Shulgin synthesized a biodegradable insecticide branded "Snail Slug 'n Bug Killer" ("This one really works," read the packaging), which was enormously profitable. After that, he was given carte blanche and began experimenting with psychoactive drug structures. He tweaked chemicals like mescaline — which, after being consumed for thousands of years in its natural form by Native peoples in the Western Hemisphere, had been the first psychedelic synthesized in a lab, in 1918.

Shulgin believed drugs were the most efficient way to tap the powers of the world's greatest resource — the human brain. He hoped, by studying how psychedelics affected people, to benefit science, medicine, psychiatry, the arts, and even religion. "He argued to his superiors that this could be therapeutically important, at doses at which there was no risk of psychotic effects," said Shulgin's Dow colleague Solomon Snyder.

Once he had created a new compound, Shulgin tested it on himself, starting at very low dosages, and occasionally would get a reaction he had never experienced before. This wasn't standard scientific protocol; human clinical trials would have been untenable and unethical, and no animal could usefully describe a psychedelic's effects. Shulgin's drug testing often began on his morning hike from his Bay Area home in Lafayette, California, along a canal to Dow's Walnut Creek facility a few miles away. Dow went along with his ideas and even patented some of his creations. One was a psychedelic known as DOM, which Shulgin found to be even more intense than LSD.

"The body tremor feels like poisoning, there is no escaping the feeling of being disabilitated, but at least there is no nausea," he wrote, after sampling a particularly strong dose. "The music was exceptional, the erotic was exceptional, the fantasy was exceptional. . . . This may be a bit much for me." Shulgin never distributed the drug, but according to his protégé Paul Daley, he coached the famous psychedelic chemist Nick Sand on how to make it in the mid-1960s. Hoping to fund the production of his famous Orange Sunshine brand of LSD, Sand sold quantities of DOM to the Hell's Angels. At some point along the way, DOM was renamed STP — Serenity, Tranquility, and Peace — and the Hell's Angels began disseminating tablets of it.

Provoked by California's banning of LSD, thousands of people gathered not long afterward, on January 14, 1967, in San Francisco's Golden Gate Park for an event called the Human Be-In, its name inspired by civil rights sit-ins. The event would set the tone for that year's upcoming Summer of Love. The Grateful Dead and Jefferson Airplane performed, while the psychedelic thought leader Timothy Leary advised the crowd to "Turn on, tune in, drop out." Unfortunately, many who took STP landed in the emergency room, for the tablets the Hell's Angels distributed were of a much higher dosage than Shulgin recommended.

Spooked by Shulgin's forays into a realm

increasingly associated with lawless youth culture, Dow Chemical asked him to cease using its name on his publications. He took the hint, left the company entirely, and began working exclusively out of a lab next to his house, on a twenty-acre plot near Berkeley called the Farm. Here, he would continue to hone his research and build his reputation, eventually becoming known as the "Godfather of Ecstasy."

Ecstasy is not a narcotic that sets users floating on a cloud, like the opioids; it's not a traditional amphetamine that seems to instill one with superpowers, like meth; and it's not a psychedelic that lets users see the world as if for the first time, like LSD. Instead, it's something of a combination of the three, fusing the cerebral and the sensual to instill a sense of profound happiness. It has become one of earth's most popular illicit substances in recent decades, emerging from the electronic dance music scene and gradually infiltrating the mainstream while transcending geography and culture. Sasha Shulgin didn't invent the drug known as ecstasy, MDMA — which is also sometimes called Molly — but he earned the title "Godfather of Ecstasy" for popularizing it.

MDMA was created by the German pharmaceutical company Merck when it was trying to develop a blood-clotting drug. Another local company was also doing work in this area, so Merck patented MDMA late in 1912. Merck had no idea of its psychoactive effects. Very little was done with MDMA in the ensuing decades, until the US Army began using it and similar drugs for studies on animals in 1953. What inspired the program or what the army was looking for is not clear — possibly a truth serum, possibly a "happy bomb" (a chemical weapon that incapacitated but didn't kill an enemy). In 1960 MDMA's synthesis was described in a scientific paper written by a pair of Polish scientists, and Sasha Shulgin first synthesized MDMA in 1965 while working at Dow. Shulgin's approach was to take the structure of a known drug and use it as scaffolding — a skeleton structure to which he would add or subtract other chemical elements or groups, to see if anything interesting was formed. MMDA, which is more psychedelic than MDMA, may have led Shulgin to first synthesize that structurally similar drug in 1965. Shulgin did not, however, immediately realize ecstasy's effects, possibly because he took too small a dose.

The formula leaked out, and MDMA

began to be used recreationally; in 1972 police discovered it on the streets of Chicago. Shulgin was alerted to its effects by a University of California, San Francisco, graduate student. Shulgin then resynthesized the material, began documenting his experiences, and was astonished. "I feel absolutely clean inside, and there is nothing but pure euphoria. I have never felt so great, or believed this to be possible," he wrote. "The cleanliness, clarity, and marvelous feeling of solid inner strength continued throughout the rest of the day, and evening, and through the next day. I am overcome by the profundity of the experience, and how much more powerful it was than previous experiences, for no apparent reason, other than a continually improving state of being."

Shulgin didn't extol MDMA for it to be a party drug, but as a tool for psychotherapy. He believed it had the strong potential to benefit people's psyches. In 1978 he coauthored, with Purdue University professor David Nichols, the first scientific paper describing MDMA's effects. "Qualitatively, the drug appears to evoke an easily controlled altered state of consciousness with emotional and sensual overtones," they wrote. Nichols, another towering figure in the realm of psychedelics studies, went on to coin the term *entactogen* (meaning, roughly, "to produce a touching within") to distinguish MDMA from stimulants and psychedelics.

MDMA works by subduing a part of the brain, the amygdala, which controls our response to fear, and thus the drug can have a therapeutic effect, helping users work through painful experiences. Shulgin introduced MDMA to key figures in the psychotherapeutic community, including his friend Leo Zeff, a retired psychologist, who was initially skeptical but tried it and was immediately sold. Zeff promptly un-retired and introduced MDMA to "countless other therapists, teaching them how to use it in their therapy."

The love drug couldn't be contained. In the 1980s MDMA became a dance-club favorite from New York and San Francisco to Ibiza, initially going by names like Empathy and Adam, the latter implying a Garden of Eden–type innocence. The name ecstasy took hold in the early 1980s. The new "yuppie psychedelic" appealed because, unlike LSD, it wasn't "supposed to teach you anything or take you anywhere," according to a 1984 *San Francisco Sunday Examiner and Chronicle* column. "It was designed to simply stimulate the pleasure centers of the cerebral cortex. Its partisans compare Adam to Aldous Huxley's Soma, the blissful, all-obliterating drug of *Brave New World*."

Ecstasy was available at such hot spots as Dallas's Starck Club, where patrons could buy the drug at the bar. A receipt at the end of the night might read: "2 gin and tonics, 1 ecstasy tablet."

The DEA banned ecstasy on July 1, 1985, reasoning that a University of Chicago study of a similar chemical, MDA, showed it to cause brain damage in rats. Even the study's authors seemed to acknowledge this was a leap of logic: "It would be premature to extrapolate the present findings to humans," it read. Shulgin was entirely unimpressed. This new law, he argued, would impede psychotherapy. Indeed, it is hard to make the case that the ban saved lives, especially considering that today's ecstasy is chock-full of impurities. "If you look at the period where MDMA was sold legally in night-clubs, where you could buy it with your credit card at the bar, there were no fatalities," said DanceSafe founder Emanuel Sferios. "Zero fatalities!"

Ironically, Sasha Shulgin for years maintained a unique relationship with the DEA, which was more tolerant of his work than might be expected. The DEA even granted him a rare license to handle schedule I drugs, which he maintained for more than two decades. The agency enlisted his help in gaining an understanding of recreational chemicals, consulted his 1988 book *Controlled Substances: Chemical and Legal Guide to Federal Drug Laws,* and gave him awards for his service.

The relationship with the agency broke, however, after the publication, in 1991, of Shulgin's psychedelic instruction manual for amateur chemists, *PiHKAL: A Chemical Love Story,* cowritten with his wife, Ann Shulgin. With its title acronym, for *Phenethylamines I Have Known and Loved,* no publisher would take it on, so he and Ann published it themselves, along with a 1997 follow-up, *TiHKAL — Tryptamines I Have Known And Loved.* Phenethylamines and tryptamines are the two main families of psychedelics. Together the two books contain formulas for more than 230 drugs, including many substances Shulgin didn't invent, like LSD; some psychedelics Shulgin did discover, like 2C-B, which would become popular; and others, like GANESHA (2,5-dimethoxy-3,4-dimethylamphetamine) and 4-HO-MET (4-Hydroxy-N-methyl-N-ethyltryptamine), that remain obscure. "It is our opinion that those books are pretty much cookbooks on how to make illegal drugs," Richard Meyer, spokesman for the DEA's San Francisco field division, told the *New York Times Magazine.* "Agents tell me that in clandestine labs that they have raided, they have found copies of those books."

On October 27, 1994, a phalanx of DEA official vehicles raided Shulgin's property — a hillside expanse dotted with psychedelic cacti — combing the grounds in search of violations of Shulgin's DEA license. They found some small infractions, packages from senders who hoped he would test their ecstasy to see whether it was actually ecstasy, and while he hadn't tested the materials, he hadn't disposed of them either, which was the problem. Ultimately, Shulgin was fined $25,000 and lost his DEA license.

Authorities around the world also began regarding Shulgin as a menace. Britain took the unprecedented step of blanket banning every compound that appeared in *PiHKAL.* This, of course, has not stopped Shulgin's work from having seismic influence. Just as he had hoped, his formulas were distributed widely, and with the rise of the Internet in the 1990s, a new community of tech-savvy psychonauts sampled his ouevre as if from a menu. Shulgin's influence is felt in every corner of the psychedelic Internet, from Bluelight, an informational message board focused on illegal chemicals and harm reduction, to Erowid, a comprehensive encyclopedia of recreational substances, new and old, and their effects.

How many overdoses and deaths Shulgin's drugs have caused is hard to know. According to Erowid, three people died from a phenethylamine named 2C-T-7, and two others from a tryptamine called 5-MeO-DIPT. There are surely others, but the number of fatalities is likely small, even though Shulgin brought well over one hundred new drugs into the world. Generally, with some notable exceptions, psychedelics don't tend to be especially toxic, and they cause death at a tiny fraction of the rate of opioids, cocaine, meth, and benzodiazepines, which include Xanax and Valium.

Shulgin's playbooks inspired chemists around the world to go into business, and many have used his scaffolding technique to invent numerous drugs much more dangerous than Shulgin ever made. Chinese laboratories selling his chemicals have profited in untold millions, and the same channels that help spread his psychedelics — including Internet message boards and Dark Web emporiums — are also used by people advocating and selling much darker drugs. Meanwhile, armed criminal gangs have also gotten in on the action. The mescaline derivative 2C-B, Shulgin's favorite of all the chemicals he invented, in recent years has come to be heavily trafficked by drug organizations in Colombia and is a favored club drug in places like Medellín. Known as *cocaína rosada* (pink cocaine) for its color, or simply *tusi* (the Spanglish pronunciation of "2C"), it's snorted like cocaine and, due to its psychedelic qualities, has displaced cocaine in popularity among some sets.

Shulgin anticipated that lab-made drugs like fentanyl could displace plant-based substances like heroin, and he lived long enough to see the adulteration of MDMA. "He was saddened seeing it escape from the relative control of the psychoanalytic community into the rave scene," Paul Daley said. "In particular, he didn't like being called the Godfather of Ecstasy. What was being sold as ecstasy on the street was often not. The folks who could really benefit from the MDMA experience all of the sudden had access only to impure materials, of unknown quality and dosage."

The heavily cut "ecstasy" tablets now common on the rave scene stand in contrast to pure MDMA's acceptance in the medical community in recent years. One of the pure drug's leading advocates is Ann Shulgin, who said MDMA's banning effectively shut down significant medical research on the drug for years. "If MDMA hadn't been scheduled, it would have probably almost wiped out PTSD," she said. "It is the most perfect drug for PTSD. Instead, they have millions of veterans all over the world suffering."

Approximately one of every thirteen Americans suffers from post traumatic stress disorder, and veterans are twice as likely to be afflicted, according to the US Department of Veterans Affairs. However, in August 2017 the FDA granted MDMA a "breakthrough therapy" designation, helping to accelerate a third and final phase of medical trials to test its efficacy in treating victims of PTSD. If the trials are successful and approval is granted, certified psychotherapists will be allowed to treat patients with 125 milligram ecstasy pills in their offices, effectively legalizing MDMA for medical use, perhaps as early as 2021.

"They take the MDMA and have this expansiveness," said therapist Julane Andries, who treated PTSD patients during phase two of the trials. "They're not feeling fear. They're not feeling shame. They're not feeling anger. They can look at themselves and have compassion." As reported by the Multidisciplinary Association for Psychedelic Studies, which has been spearheading this movement, one year after the phase two trials, 68 percent of the patients no longer met the criteria for PTSD.

But while ecstasy gained credibility among therapists, in the 2000s it became increasingly difficult to find — in its pure form — on the street.

FIVE

The easiest way to make MDMA, Sasha Shulgin wrote in *PiHKAL,* is to use a precursor called safrole. A naturally occurring chemical compound found in nutmeg and other spices, safrole was once used as an ingredient in root beer before it was banned as a food additive by the FDA. Animal-testing studies showed it could lead to cancer.

Safrole oil smells like licorice, and is obtained by harvesting sassafras trees, which are found in various parts of the world including eastern Asia and North America. In the United States the trees don't produce enough oil to make harvesting them profitable, but in countries like Myanmar, Vietnam, China, and Cambodia, the rise of ecstasy in the 1990s set off a scramble to turn native trees into a cash crop. Cambodia was particularly susceptible to exploitation by the ecstasy trade. The impoverished

Southeast Asian nation of sixteen million people shares long, porous borders with Thailand, Vietnam, and Laos, across which traffickers on bicycle, motorcycle, or even on foot dart through forests to evade detection. With few patrols and a history of corrupt officials turning their backs to drug crime, Cambodia maintains a reputation as a smuggling haven. It also possesses an abundance of a rare type of sassafras tree prized for its capacity to generate rich, highly potent safrole oil. Known as *mreah prew phnom,* it's found in large quantities in a protected, mountainous area of the country called the Phnom Samkos Wildlife Sanctuary.

The 1988 United Nations drug treaty produced an agreement to expand the drug war from crackdowns on illicit drugs to crackdowns on the compounds used to make them, including safrole oil.

Traditionally in Southeast Asia, safrole oil has been used in small quantities to make medicines, including those used to salve skin irritations. But increasing demand for MDMA toward the end of the twentieth century created a multimillion-dollar trade in Cambodia, served by increasingly large and sophisticated operations. The oil was distilled inside factories that were protected by armed guards, and proprietors worked in tandem with poachers of pythons, pangolins, tigers, and other jungle animals. The distillers and poachers would eat the animals or sell them on black markets.

The harvest required entire *mreah prew phnom* trees to be cut down and their roots chopped off and boiled in giant pots for nearly a week. The product, safrole oil, sold for $200 a gallon, each gallon enough to make thousands of ecstasy tablets. Apparently, many sassafras farmers were left in the dark as to its purpose. "Some erroneously suspected that it was used for *yama,* or methamphetamine," wrote Myanmar-focused publication the *Irrawaddy* in 2009. "One thought it was used to make an atomic bomb."

The environmental damage became catastrophic, not just for the destroyed trees but also because leaking oil killed off fish, frogs, and other animals. "The illicit distilling of sassafras oil in these mountains is slowly but surely killing the forests and wildlife," said David Bradfield, who served as adviser to the Wildlife Sanctuaries project of Fauna and Flora International in 2008. "The production of sassafras oil is a huge operation, which affects not only the area where the distilleries are actually located, but ripples outward, leaving devastation and destruction in its wake." He added that the livelihoods of as many as fifteen thousand indigenous people — hunters-gatherers in the wildlife sanctuaries — were in jeopardy.

Cambodian production ramped up, spiking after neighboring Vietnam banned production of safrole oil in 1999 and then again after China enforced stricter controls in 2004. Three years later, facing the real possibility that the *mreah prew phnom* tree might be felled into extinction, Cambodia banned the production of the oil.

Simultaneously, Southeast Asian nations accelerated efforts to crack down on the safrole oil trade. In October 2007 three shipping containers — containing some fifty tons of the Cambodia-produced safrole oil — were seized at a port in southern Thailand. The containers — two bound for China, one for the United States — possessed an estimated cumulative value of $150 million.

International agents intent on wiping out the trade sent an even louder message a year later. In June 2008, Cambodian and Australian federal police descended upon the Pursat province in western Cambodia, where they destroyed fifty safrole oil laboratories and arrested scores of people. Hoping to deter anyone else from continuing the practice, the officers — clad in gas masks and hazmat suits — publicly burned more than twelve hundred seized drums of the oil, blanketing the sky with giant clouds of black smoke. Enough safrole to make more than 200 million ecstasy pills — billions of dollars worth — went up in flames.

Meanwhile, law enforcement agencies were pulling off ecstasy busts of historic proportions. In 2005, officials seized about a ton of the pills in Melbourne, Australia. In 2007, a drug baron named Rob Karam (who was out on bail and awaiting trial in the 2005 ecstasy seizure) traveled to Hong Kong to negotiate a massive ecstasy sale with the Calabrian Mafia, of southern Italy. The deal could have been worth billions. But the man Karam met with was working undercover for the Australian Federal Police. His information helped the government intercept about four tons of ecstasy pills shipped inside tomato cans.

The international effort to disrupt the ecstasy trade was surprisingly successful. Though big drug seizures don't always make a significant dent in supply, and eliminating one precursor chemical (another name for a critical drug ingredient) sometimes causes chemists to switch to another, this one-two punch was extremely effective. After peaking in the early years of the 2000s, MDMA became increasingly difficult to find.

In the United Kingdom, where EDM (electronic dance music) culture was popular, the drought was most immediately evident. "There wasn't any MDMA to be had, which is unusual in a market with 500,000 participants every week," said journalist and drugs expert Mike Power.

The site Pill Reports, where users post the results after testing their drugs, showed that much of the so-called ecstasy that began appearing on the UK scene was adulterated. This fact did not stop dance-floor denizens from swallowing pills anyway, but those who were paying attention quickly realized that something was amiss. The lack of safrole oil had forced the hands of ecstasy suppliers. "A number of international syndicates took a vote on whether or not to raise the wholesale prices on pills or look for cheaper substitutions," an anonymous source with inside information is quoted as saying in Power's book *Drugs Unlimited*. "Apparently the vote came down on the side of substitutions and it was after this that we started seeing more and more pills with what we could consider adulterants."

The MDMA drought affected dance-music culture across the world. In Europe it helped usher in a new class of exotic drugs known as "legal highs." In the United States, adulterated ecstasy contributed to a spike in rave deaths. And at the bottom of the planet, in New Zealand, it ushered in a more insidious substance: meth. The problem got so bad that a quirky man who talked with God decided to do something about it.

Born in 1971, Matt Bowden was a precocious kid. Growing up in New Zealand, he loved music and attended university early, at age sixteen. He studied computer science but soon dropped out. "I got bored," he said. "I didn't think I needed a degree to get along in life." He played in a metal band and taught guitar for a living. In his twenties he was drawn in by the electronic music scene and its illicit substances.

By the late 1990s he was a club kid on the nightlife scene. During the summer of 1998 — the New Zealand "summer of love," he called it — he was living in Auckland and the city was awash in MDMA. The dance-music scene was exploding, and everyone seemed to be hugging one another. The festivities continued on for a few years, until about 2003, when international eradication efforts slowed New Zealand's ecstasy supply to a trickle.

The drug landscape in small, far-flung New Zealand has long been different than that of most countries. Composed of two main islands and hundreds of smaller ones in the southwestern Pacific Ocean, New Zealand is the most isolated well-populated country in the world, a full thousand miles from Australia. Because of this isolation, certain drugs simply don't proliferate there. "We are surrounded by water and have strong border controls that have always made it challenging for drugs like cocaine and heroin to get into New Zealand," said Ian Hastings, a retired senior drug-squad detective. "In some ways that is a blessing, but in many other ways it's not." Without ecstasy, and without cocaine — which in some countries had filled the void in ecstasy's absence — homemade crystal meth instead began taking root in New Zealand. In 2003 the percentage of the population using it rose to 2.7 percent, the highest in its history.

Many of Bowden's friends and family members became addicted to meth, as did he. During this time he noticed a stark change in the local culture. "Everyone in the nightclubs started roughing each other up," he said. "People were paranoid." Fights routinely broke out, whereas before club-goers had been warm and friendly. A friend of Bowden's entered a fit of psychosis while under the influence of meth, stabbing himself with a samurai sword and dying from the wounds. Another friend was killed when a meth lab exploded. These deaths greatly troubled Bowden, so he brainstormed ways he could help. He had some experience in the drug business, having apprenticed with a pharmacologist, and he had worked for a time developing stimulants with legal ingredients, known as "herbal highs." Now Bowden wanted to develop a successor to ecstasy and a safer alternative to meth, one that would satisfy the urges of the all-night-raging crowd.

Internet message boards discussing drugs had become popular, and Bowden began reading about one compound called benzylpiperazine (BZP). Over the years it had been developed both as a treatment for parasites and as an antidepressant, though it didn't quite fit the bill for either. It had speed-like qualities, and in the United States first came onto the DEA's radar in 1996, when it was being used in California. Though it hadn't really caught on, there were concerns about its potential for abuse. As Bowden dug deeper into its clinical trial history, however, he concluded that it was relatively safe. "What attracted me was the history of research with amphetamine addicts," he said, adding that they reacted favorably to switching over to the less-dangerous BZP. Like meth it got users' blood pumping. Unlike meth, however, it didn't seem to lead to addiction. "After you had too much, you felt you had too much," Bowden explained. "You weren't tempted to keep taking more."

Because it had never been banned in New Zealand, BZP was legal. Bowden set out to bring BZP to his fellow ravers and then to the entire country.

Bowden is not a typical drug lord. Though he became incredibly rich from selling chemicals that are now illegal, he said his ultimate goal was to save kids from overdoses and addiction. His attempt to overhaul New Zealand's drug laws was bold and unorthodox, not unlike the man himself. He doesn't crave obscurity like most kingpins. Rather, he seeks out high-profile opportunities to make his case, and for a time could be seen on New Zealand television wearing flamboyant suits, science-fiction-inspired garb from his steampunk fashion line, and platinum blond, feathered hair. His passions over the years have run from learning complicated chemical processes and delving into the minutiae of legislative bills to performing rock operas as his David Bowie–inspired alter ego, Starboy.

He also claims to talk to God.

"Growing up, I had a strong Christian period," he explains, over a Skype video call, speaking quickly and in a thick Kiwi accent. "I guess I had a vocation, or calling. I had a relationship with the Creator that was based on a belief that God is alive and can talk to us and cares about our lives. If we care to talk to the Creator — and ask, 'What's the path I'm supposed to be on? What am I supposed to be doing?' — he'll answer and lead us and guide us."

Bowden decided to dial this hotline to heaven during a loveless period in the early 1990s. "I asked, 'Hey, when are you going to bring the right girl for me to marry?' " God responded, Bowden claims, explaining that he would know his great love because she would deliver him a cocktail. This did not happen overnight, however. Bowden had to wait for seven long years. In the meantime, his life began unraveling as he became addicted to meth. One night, feeling particularly sorry for himself, he went into a strip club and found himself making eye contact with the woman on stage.

"This light shined down upon this man as he was walking into the room," the dancer said. "He was looking at me with this big Cheshire grin and this bright green shirt and this blond ruffled hair." Before long she made her way to the bar and then, just as was prophesied, brought him a drink. And that's how Matt Bowden met his wife, Kristi, a cover model for the Australian versions of *Penthouse* and *Hustler,* who is known in the industry as Kristi Kennedy. This was July 4, 2000, and they would go on to marry and have two children.

Around that same time, Bowden launched another life-changing endeavor: he began spreading the gospel of BZP. A member of a class of drugs called piperazines, BZP is more like an amphetamine than ecstasy. Employing chemists in labs in India to synthesize the drug, he began by giving away samples to friends in the club scene. They seemed to like it. He claims it helped some people — including him and Kristi, who had been hooked as well — kick their meth addictions. His initial experiment successful, Bowden set to mass-producing BZP.

131

He settled on manufacturers based in China. "From looking at the Internet, I saw where the pharmaceutical industry goes when they need to produce molecules," he said. "So we went to the same sorts of factories." He began distributing BZP in head shops around the country. It started to catch on, until hundreds of thousands of New Zealanders were taking it. Beginning in 2004, New Zealand's meth usage rate began to drop.

BZP also gained popularity in Europe, sold under names like Legal X and Cosmic Kelly; Bowden wasn't selling it there, but his party elixirs appear to have inspired others. "Piperazines were the first new drug to adulterate MDMA that we saw," said Rainer Schmid, of Vienna General Hospital in Austria, who runs one of the most sophisticated chemical analytics laboratories in all of Europe. "This was a direct result of Bowden."

BZP seemed to be a great solution to the decline of MDMA. For the most part, it was safe. And though the United States had scheduled it, the drug was still legal in Europe and New Zealand, where it was sold everywhere from gas stations to local malls. A pack of six tablets might cost forty dollars. Some twenty-six million BZP pills had been sold in New Zealand by 2008, making it the country's second-most-popular recreational drug — trailing only marijuana. The fighting, overdoses, and violence that had defined New Zealand's crystal meth culture declined.

But soon a new change occurred: copycat chemists soon began releasing BZP products with escalating dosages and without proper labeling. Worried that government regulators would come down on them, Bowden confronted other New Zealand dealers. "You all stole my intellectual property," he told them. "You've all broken my copyright." Yet instead of getting angry or threatening to sue, he asked them to join forces. "Let's get around a table and work together to develop some safety standards," he said. Together he and the majority of the country's BZP manufacturers formed a group called the Social Tonics Association of New Zealand (STANZ), which developed a "code of practice" regarding the production and distribution of its drugs, seeking input from the police and government. The idea was to make BZP as safe as possible. The association attempted to set rules for maximum dosages and age limits, but the best way, it reckoned, was for the government to regulate it.

At this point Bowden's career began to shift. He focused less on growing his party-pill empire and more on spreading the gospel of safer drug consumption. Drug dealers never run public awareness campaigns, but Bowden attempted to convince the people and politicians of New Zealand that a regulated drug industry would be a tremendous public-health benefit. Since some people are always going to take drugs, he argued, offering something that wouldn't kill them would be a public service.

"I'm not actually promoting drug use," Bowden said. "I'm promoting safer policy."

STANZ commissioned a study to help it understand the health consequences of BZP use. The group hoped it would sway the government to its side, and the results were encouraging. "We weren't seeing a lot of adverse events," Bowden said. Though BZP caused a number of hospitalizations, STANZ found "no record of any death, long-lasting injury or illness attributed solely to BZP."

The New Zealand government was willing to hear Bowden out. In 2004 the Ministry of Health commissioned further studies of BZP, taking seriously the task of understanding the drug — so seriously, in fact, that an addiction specialist and advisory committee member named Dr. Doug Sellman went to a head shop, called Cosmic Corner — which carried brands with names like Kamikaze and Rapture — and took BZP himself. "They gave me this little packet. I went home on a Friday night and took it and sat in front of the television, waiting," he said. Not much happened, except he stayed up until the middle of the night and had a bad hangover the next day. "You don't have to worry, really, about this drug," he told the committee, and its report recommended BZP not be banned.

In 2005, at the recommendation of the Ministry of Health, the New Zealand government passed a law requiring BZP buyers to be eighteen and regulating the drug's dosage and manufacture — just as STANZ had hoped. But a year later, after reviewing a series of new studies and consulting the public — Bowden said the media had begun painting BZP in a negative light — the Ministry of Health determined that BZP posed a "moderate risk" and thus should be reclassified. In 2008, the New Zealand government banned BZP.

The battle, however, was just beginning.

SIX

New Zealand's government was not alone in feeling squeamish about the new crop of drugs that had replaced MDMA. In the United Kingdom, a synthetic cathinone — the lab-made version of the stimulant found in khat leaves — called 4-methylmeth-cathinone, became a sensation in the late 2000s. Known as mephedrone, it was first synthesized by a French chemist in 1929 and revived in 2003 by an Israeli psycho-naut chemist going by the name Kinetic, who, on a hunch, decided to make it from scratch. Using techniques reminiscent of those employed by Sasha Shulgin, he sampled this new drug himself, and then — while he was still high — took to the Internet to share his synthesis process and describe his trip. "50mg didn't do too much. I thought I'd wasted my time until I snorted another 100mg about 30 minutes later, and then it hit me," he wrote on a discussion board called the Hive. "Each time I could feel the rushes of energy coming across me, and after that, a fantastic sense of well-being that I haven't got from any drug before except my beloved ecstasy."

Kinetic, who is now known as Dr. Zee, soon began receiving kudos from other commenters. "That's a wonderful piece of pioneering research, congratulations man!" wrote one, posting an image of a man popping champagne. Before long amateur chemists were brewing up batches themselves and gushing that mephedrone hit the sweet spot between amphetamines and ecstasy. It began spreading to the general population. Though the American analogue act scuttled mephedrone, it was permissible to take in the United Kingdom, where it became the first blockbuster NPS. Sold by vendors from Israel and Eastern Europe operating on the surface web, it was the first recreational chemical most English people had ever bought over the Internet, and was soon also for sale in stores, ushering in the "legal highs" era. An increasingly agitated press called it "meow meow" — based on an abbreviation of its chemical name, M-CAT — but that only drove its popularity, which began to rival that of traditional intoxicants. The results of one survey put it as the fourth-most-popular drug in the United Kingdom, after marijuana, ecstasy, and cocaine. "I prefer mephedrone to MDMA," said a twenty-seven-year-old fashion industry worker named Dave Timms in 2009. "It makes me laugh when I see people try it for the first time. Many are skeptical that something that's legal can actually work. But it does."

Chinese chemists began producing mephedrone in huge quantities, most famously Zhang Lei, who operated out of Shanghai and called himself Eric Chang. Running a company named China Enriching Chemistry, he manufactured and sold mephedrone, meth ingredients (also known as precursor chemicals), "bath salts," and other drugs on the surface web. Chang was remarkably flagrant, even after 2010, when mephedrone was scheduled in the United Kingdom and many other countries. His chemicals were sold all over the world, and his trafficking network reportedly involved corrupt airline stewards. According to US officials Chang earned $30 million from American customers alone. "He was a very busy guy, living in a fancy apartment — complaining his wife never saw him because he was so busy," reported Mike Power. Interpol pursued Chang, and the United

States charged him under the Foreign Narcotics Kingpin Designation Act. He was finally captured by Chinese police in 2013 as part of an operation that spanned continents. Soon afterward, Russian television released a harrowing video taken in a hotel outside Moscow, where a mammoth SWAT team stormed a hotel where Chang's wares were distributed, described as a "transshipment base." Brushing aside frightened, barely clothed hotel guests, the SWAT team seized vast quantities of powders and made scores of arrests.

In December 2015, the Shanghai First Intermediate People's Court sentenced him to fourteen years in prison and a fine of 500,000 yuan ($74,000) for the crimes of "narcotics manufacturing" and "teaching criminal methods to others." The relatively mild punishment was owing to the fact that the NPS Chang was producing tended to be unscheduled in his home country.

The story of mephedrone bore all the hallmarks of the NPS revolution, part of a pattern that has played out again and again. Originally synthesized in a legitimate lab — but then resuscitated for recreational purposes — it filled the void of a popular banned drug, MDMA. It gained fame in specialized corners of the Internet before being manufactured in China and breaking to a wider audience, all the while leaving regulators and police scrambling to try to control it. In particular, mephedrone helped inspire the United Kingdom's 2016 blanket ban of psychoactive substances.

Mephedrone is an example of a synthetic cathinone, a stimulant made to resemble the natural psychoactive chemical occurring in the khat plant, a shrub whose leaves are chewed by many in the Middle East. "Khat is alcohol for Muslims," a Yemeni told *Time*. Synthetic cathinones were for a time in the late 2000s and early 2010s sold legally in US and UK shops, often marketed as "bath salts"; these are not actually crystals for the bath but rather a nebulous substance that can contain many different chemicals intended for recreational consumption.

Other synthetic cathinones began to take off as well in the early 2010s, including Flakka, a drug that, as demonstrated in YouTube videos, has caused some people to lose control of themselves and run naked through the streets. Flakka's chemical name is α-PVP (alpha-pyrrolidinovalerophenone), and it had a particularly lethal run in the Fort Lauderdale, Florida, area, killing more than sixty people in less than a year and a half, just before the middle of the decade. In 2015 a Broward County narcotics officer said it had become more popular there than cocaine.

By that year Flakka had been explicitly banned in both the United States and China. Yet, with no analogue act to stop them, Chinese chemists immediately began modifying the molecule just slightly, so it was still legal. Soon, a new version of Flakka was being sold on the Internet, called α-PHP. Then, when that was banned in China, it was replaced by something called α-PHPP. Chinese manufacturers next sold something called 4-Cl-PVP — although in August 2018, China scheduled that chemical, and so manufacturers quickly moved on to something else.

"They just added a random chlorine group at the fourth position on the benzene ring," explained new-drugs expert Sidney Picej, regarding 4-Cl-PVP. The problem is that when something "random" is added to the chemical structure, it often makes the drug's high worse and the drug itself more dangerous. "It makes it bulkier," added Picej, "which affects its ability to effectively cross the blood-brain barrier or activate a certain receptor. [These new] stimulants make your heart go crazy, with a slight dysphoric buzz.' "

Methylone, another synthetic cathinone, was developed by Sasha Shulgin and a colleague for use as a possible antidepressant. To many, methylone was a satisfying replacement for MDMA. Matt Bowden even began selling it, until it was clear his government planned to ban that one as well.

Methylone and mephedrone were the best-known synthetic cathinones to be cut into ecstasy pills and have been tied to a number of overdose deaths over the years. Official statistics are hard to come by, but the number is most certainly small, relative to the number of deaths attributed to a much more toxic MDMA-substitute drug called PMA (paramethoxyamphetamine). PMA and a related compound, PMMA, were linked in the early 2010s to more than one hundred deaths in the United Kingdom alone, according to the *Guardian,* as well as dozens more in Canada and other countries throughout the world. "It has similar effects to MDMA, but it takes about two hours to come up. It leads users, after an hour, to be like, 'Hey, I'm not feeling anything,' so they take another dose," explained Amy Raves, a California-based harm-reduction activist.

"Nobody takes PMA or PMMA on purpose. Nobody ever has," said Emanuel Sferios, the founder of DanceSafe, adding that people think they're taking MDMA. "These drugs are only being manufactured because they're cheap and easy to produce and replace for MDMA, and they give the user a stimulant effect."

International attempts to knock out ecstasy had opened the door to a wide array of curious new chemicals; some were dangerous, and some benign, and considering that most of them hadn't had significant clinical trials (if any), the health consequences of their use were being tested in real time.

Governments around the world — from Japan to France, Australia to Canada — reacted predictably, seeking to criminalize each new drug as it emerged. In Matt Bowden's home country, however, against the odds, public officials tried to confront the problem in a different way.

After New Zealand made BZP illegal in 2008, Matthew Bowden was frustrated. His pills had ushered in a drop in overdoses and violence in the local party culture but apparently to no avail. "There'd been no deaths, no lasting injuries, no real serious hospitalizations for people using the product as directed, but they decided to make it illegal," he said. He worried the nightlife denizens would turn back to crystal meth. To console himself, Bowden took some time off. He grew his hair out and, under the auspices of his glam rock alter ego, Starboy — wearing KISS-style face paint and steampunk accessories — started working on a new album. In 2010, however, a new drug called to him: fake marijuana.

Bowden was well aware of synthetic cannabinoids' dubious safety reputation. Still, that didn't deter him when, he said, he was approached about manufacturing new fake pot compounds. He figured he could do things differently. And so, as before when he was looking for a meth substitute, he focused on making a safer product, working with pharmacologists to try to find a less harmful synthetic cannabinoid. "We were creating hundreds of new [cannabinoid] molecules, working out which ones were going to be less toxic," he said. The best ones they synthesized and patented.

He renewed his public-relations efforts, hiring a well-connected law firm, led by former New Zealand prime minister Sir Geoffrey Palmer, to help him persuade the government that the country needed a recreational-drugs industry that was required to do product testing, meet safety standards, and clearly label its offerings — not one that operated in the shadows.

Remarkably, politicians started listening. Before long, they even crafted a bill.

"Quite simply they will now have to do what any manufacturer of any product that is consumed or ingested already has to do — make sure it is safe," argued Parliament member Peter Dunne, speaking in favor of the Psychoactive Substances Act of 2013, which would effectively legalize not just BZP but a host of other party drugs and synthetic cannabinoids as well, including the ones made by Bowden. This would be a completely unprecedented piece of legislation, moving New Zealand in the opposite direction from the rest of the Western world — which was making new drugs illegal as fast as it could.

New Zealand focused on these substances, instead of legalizing traditional ones like MDMA or marijuana, because the country's hands were tied by the United Nations international drug-control treaties, which outlawed the most common recreational drugs and to which it is a signatory. An issue with the Psychoactive Substances Act was that none of these new drugs (including Bowden's) had gone through clinical trials, and holding such trials would be extremely time-consuming. To address this, the law would permit new drugs that had previously been sold without incident to be grandfathered in.

It was an extremely complicated bill, one presented under the auspices of regulation, rather than legalization. Quite possibly not everyone in the New Zealand Parliament fully understood what he or she was voting on. When the results came in, on July 17, 2013, they were staggering: 119 to 1, in favor.

Legalization advocates rejoiced, as did Bowden. They were optimistic that this new law could show the world how to avoid an NPS crisis, by putting safety and control above prosecutions and imprisonment. Sales were restricted to those over eighteen years of age. Pills couldn't be sold in gas stations or grocery stores. And packages displayed warnings not to drive after consuming their contents. This was a mind-boggling policy shift. People around the world suddenly began paying attention to this small island country, best known to many for its sheep.

"New Zealand's Designer Drug Law Draws Global Interest," read a CBS News headline, noting that some British parliamentarians hoped to bring a similar policy to the United Kingdom. New Zealand's government — which Bowden praised as "small and maneuverable" — was suddenly in the vanguard of progressive drug law. And it had Bowden to thank for it.

Though Bowden had been having his new products manufactured in China, he began to believe that his partners there weren't keeping his new creations secret. And so he began building a lab of his own, in Auckland, which opened in 2013. It featured state-of-the-art equipment and, eventually, five employees. By his accounting, their work was a success. "Our products were not producing addictive behaviors or overdoses," he said.

For Bowden, the dream he had pursued for more than a decade was finally coming true. Working out of his lab, he and his team manufactured large quantities of his party-pill meth and ecstasy replacements, as well as synthetic-cannabinoid alternatives to strains like Spice and K2, which were causing so much damage. He hadn't made much money off his drugs previously, Bowden said, focusing instead on his goal to make safer products. But eventually he decided it was time to cash in. After legalization, when the synthetic-cannabinoid profits really started to accumulate, he bought property

— including a palatial house for his family in the lush countryside. In that moment, he seemed to have everything he could ever want; a loving wife selected by a divine matchmaker, a beautiful family, and a successful business doing something he felt proud of, grounded in utopian ideals and endorsed by the government.

But within a year Matt Bowden's revolution went up in smoke. Public opinion quickly shifted against the now-legal drugs.

A combination of factors turned the tide. For one, not many stores applied to sell the drugs, perhaps because shop owners didn't want to go through the cumbersome approval process. As a result, the few stores that did receive licenses sometimes had lines around the block, creating loitering masses who got high and created disturbances. "Imagine if you only had one liquor store in town. You would have a queue of people," Bowden said. "So that's what we had. There would be these big queues of people, smoking and getting a little wasted in the streets." The media began picking up on this problem, as well as the preponderance of emergency-room visits, and the fact that some were becoming addicted to the cannabinoids.

A controversy also began to erupt around

the issue of animal testing, a critical component of drug development. Protests sprang up, which Bowden said led to the spread of misinformation: "Some were saying, 'The party-pill guys want to kill our dogs!' " Bowden affirmed that he never, in fact, tested on dogs. He also claimed that when he began attempting to develop a safer alternative to alcohol, the beer, wine, and spirits lobbyists began campaigning against him.

And so, in 2014, an election year, New Zealand reversed course, revising the legalization bill to make the party pills and synthetic-cannabinoid strains illegal. Some of the same lawmakers who had voted in favor of the legalization bill a year earlier now claimed not to have realized what they were endorsing. The drugs that had been grandfathered in were now un-grandfathered. Under the revised bill they could still win authorization for legal sale, but the revised bill also curtailed animal testing, which threw a wrench in the process. Effectively, it all but blocked the possibility of new drugs receiving approval.

"The immediate effect was that the industry was handed on a silver plate to the black market," Bowden said. "All the manufacture standards, all the dosage control, it went out the window."

After New Zealand's legalization repeal, Matt Bowden still planned to try to bring his drugs, including BZP, up to code, but the collapse of the industry he had so heavily invested in left him financially obliterated. Owing unpaid back taxes and other obligations that amounted to some NZ$3.6 million (US$2.4 million), he was forced, in May 2015, to liquidate his company. "I did make some mistakes," he admitted. "I was sloppy with accounting back when we were a small company starting out."

Unable to secure new loans, Bowden was locked out of his lab and lost his estate and other possessions, even the steampunk fashion line he had worked on with Kristi. According to a 2015 news report, the "fixed assets" of Bowden's company, including "lab equipment, music equipment and the costume and prop hire branch of the business" were sold off for NZ$230,000 — money that went to creditors. Broke and owing millions, Bowden faced the possibility of jail time over the unpaid back taxes, a criminal offense. And so he, his wife, and their two young children fled the country in 2015 and landed in Chang Mai, Thailand.

In July 2017, ten Auckland deaths were

attributed to synthetic cannabinoids. The fatalities caused a national uproar. The country's National Drug Intelligence Bureau soon released a report, placing blame on the Mongrel Mob — New Zealand's biggest gang, known for extensive facial tattoos — for controlling much of the drug's distribution. "It is believed they have started manufacturing their own product in order to increase and retain control of the supply chain," wrote New Zealand news website *Stuff*. The worst fears of Bowden and others, who had hoped to bring synthetic cannabinoids into the light, were being realized. The strains associated with the Auckland fatalities were not the same ones that had been previously sold legally in New Zealand — they were much, much stronger. "Dose escalation is going crazy," Bowden said.

By the end of 2018, more than fifty New Zealand fatalities had been tied to synthetic cannabinoids. The deaths prompted international news coverage. Most of the stories made only passing, if any, mention of New Zealand's political experiment. Little analysis was undertaken to determine whether legalization — with workable safety testing and clear labeling — might have saved some of these lives. "The law was ruined over the animal testing BS," Bowden said, noting that, because the law was changed, human beings were instead serving as the unwitting test subjects.

The scourge of deadly synthetic cannabinoids was by no means limited to New Zealand. Media reports of mass overdoses and "zombie" outbreaks began appearing across the United States — the same country where, in medical labs, many of the most potent strains were invented.

SEVEN

Mike is a forklift operator from downstate Illinois, whose name has been changed to protect his privacy. In the early 2010s, while living in Decatur, Mike was able to work reliably, though he was required to undergo regular drug testing. For that reason he tried to limit his use of drugs he knew the company would check for, such as marijuana. He was glad, then, to hear about an alternative. Fake marijuana was not only cheap and available legally in stores, it also didn't show up on drug screenings. The drug was so new — and there were so many different strains — that tests hadn't been formulated for it yet. If one was on the job, on parole, or even just had untrusting parents who administered tests, it was perfect. "That's why most people start smoking it," Mike said. "Because it's untraceable."

Whenever he got the urge — which was increasingly often — he would head down to the corner market and buy a gram bag for fifteen bucks. Sometimes he would get lucky, and a ten-gram bag would be on sale for only twenty-five dollars.

Some people knew it as Spice, but Mike called it K2. These were just two of the many brand names slapped on the multicolored, glossy packets containing the drug, including King Kong, Scooby Snacks, and Laugh Out Loud. One was called Power Diesel, a nod to the marijuana strain known as Sour Diesel. Sometimes it was labeled "potpourri" or "incense." Also deceptive were the notes on all packages warning that their ingredients were "not for human consumption."

In superficial ways the fake blends — more precisely called synthetic cannabinoids — were like regular marijuana. Mike would smoke them out of a glass pipe or even roll them up in a joint. But that's where the similarities ended. "It would get you extremely high," Mike said. "The taste, the effect, the high — everything's different." It wasn't a mellow, relaxing high; it made his heart race. Sometimes it was enjoyable, but sometimes it made him throw up or pass out. Unlike marijuana, K2 is not a plant. Rather, it's a chemical compound that is usually dissolved in a solvent (often acetone)

154

and then sprayed onto dried plant leaves so it resembles marijuana. Furthermore, though K2 was then sold in sealed, professional-looking packages, there was no quality control. Some packets were mild, with little effect at all. Others were extremely potent.

There was a lot of overlap, Mike said, with the heroin community. People in a state of heroin withdrawal would smoke some K2 because it might make them pass out — temporarily freeing them from the physical agony of opiate withdrawal. Eventually, though, came the sickness. K2 withdrawal, he said, is "even worse" than fentanyl withdrawal, which he also experienced. "You puke constantly, every day. Your skin turns green. People was thinking I was dying."

Mike went cold turkey, and it took him more than three full weeks to get well. It was a misery he wouldn't wish on anyone. "Pure sickness," he said.

Mike had never heard of John William Huffman, an organic-chemistry professor in the Deep South nearing retirement around the time Mike was getting hooked on fake marijuana. But Huffman helped set in motion the explosion of synthetic cannabinoids in the first place.

Born in 1932, Huffman grew up in the northern part of Illinois, in Evanston. He had a chemistry set full of compounds that would soon be removed from such products, including the ingredients for making gunpowder. His father was a doctor, and Huffman was expected to be one too, but as a premed student at Northwestern University he took a shine to organic chemistry, and his path changed. He got his PhD at Harvard in 1957 and, after a stint at Georgia Tech, became an organic-chemistry professor at Clemson University in South Carolina. In the late 1980s he received a grant from the National Institute on Drug Abuse (NIDA) for the synthesis of the psychoactive component of the khat plant, cathinone.

When this grant ended, Huffman sought additional funding from NIDA for the synthesis of THC carboxylic acid, which is produced in the body after one consumes marijuana. In 1990, a graduate student alerted him to some interesting compounds developed by the pharmaceutical company Sterling-Winthrop, which was hoping to create new nonsteroidal anti-inflammatory drugs, along the lines of aspirin or ibuprofen. And, indeed, Sterling Winthrop's compounds had good analgesic, or pain-reducing, effects. But there was also something strange about them. They bound to a cannabinoid receptor. This was curious, because the compounds had a totally different structure than THC, the main psychoactive component of marijuana.

Sterling-Winthrop wasn't interested in these compounds — the company wanted a pain reliever, not a wild-card drug associated with recreational chemicals — but Huffman was interested in why they interacted with the same receptor as THC. NIDA saw the potential research benefits in this pursuit (new medicines could potentially emerge) and agreed to fund Huffman's project, giving his lab more than $2 million for research. Between the early 1990s and 2011, when Huffman retired, his Clemson lab made more than four hundred new synthetic-cannabinoid compounds, studying how they interacted with the cannabinoid receptors that are found in the central nervous system and the immune system. The goal was to understand the receptors better, to potentially help develop everything from pain-relief medicine to cancer treatments. "These receptors don't exist so that people can smoke marijuana and get high," Huffman said. "They play a role in regulating appetite, nausea, mood, pain and inflammation."

"These compounds that Huffman made were pharmacological tools — tools we can use to understand what's happening in the brain," said Marilyn Huestis, senior investigator at NIDA. "He created an entire line of chemicals . . . that enlightened us so much." Huffman said one of his compounds has shown potential, in mice, to battle skin cancer and brain tumors. Other scientists have also made progress; in 2018, for example, Pennsylvania State University College of Medicine researchers found 10 synthetic cannabinoids that stopped colorectal cancer cells from growing.

Huffman was far from the only scientist making synthetic-cannabinoid compounds. After cannabinoid receptors were first identified in 1988 by St. Louis University Medical School pharmacology professor Allyn Howlett and her graduate student William Devane, scientists rushed to try to develop new medicines, and much of this research was introduced into the public domain. But when these drugs were plucked from the scientific literature, manufactured, and sold as products like K2 and Spice, the work of Huffman, more than anyone else, was implicated, in large part because his compounds carried his initials: JWH.

His most famous creation, made in 1993, was called JWH-018 — the eighteenth compound he developed in his series. Four years later it was described in a publication, and soon made the leap from the academic world into the recreational one.

Head shops and bodegas in Europe and North America in the late 2000s and early 2010s often offered synthetic cannabinoids for sale — not under the counter or in a back room but right on the shelves, with bar codes.

At first glance, they might have appeared to be herbal smoking blends, the kind head shops have always sold, which tend to be made of benign chemicals that don't really produce a high. Since their chemical structures didn't resemble THC, they weren't subject to the Federal Analogue Act of 1986, which stipulates that, to be illegal, drugs have to be not only "substantially similar" to already banned drugs but also intended for human consumption — hence the "not intended for human consumption" warning on the cannabinoids' packaging.

Nobody selling the packages had any idea what was in them. They could have contained JWH-018 or CP 47,497 (a synthetic cannabinoid originally developed by Pfizer) or any number of the hundreds of different varieties. Even today, synthetic cannabinoids remain the fastest growing class of drugs. The United Nations Office on Drugs and Crime identified more than two hundred different varieties by 2015, and since then the numbers have continued accelerating. Some are twice as potent as marijuana; some are one hundred times as potent or more. And since there is little formal testing, almost nobody knows how safe each blend is, not even the scientists who invented them, including Huffman.

THC "is not terribly potent," Huffman said. But synthetic cannabinoids have no THC. The chemicals in synthetic cannabinoids and THC both bind to cannabinoid receptors but in different ways. THC is only a "partial agonist" of these receptors — meaning it doesn't fully activate them. The synthetic cannabinoids, on the other hand, tend to be "full agonists," making them supercharged and unpredictable. While marijuana works almost immediately, some synthetic versions take a while to kick in, instigating users to smoke more and then overdose.

"THC will lower your blood pressure," Huffman said. "But these synthetic cannabinoids will increase your blood pressure, to the point where some of the young people who have taken it have had strokes." In the early 2010s poison-control centers were flooded with calls, and stories of overdoses began to emerge, including, in January, 2012, one apparently suffered by actress Demi Moore. She was taken to a Los Angeles hospital after smoking what friends described, in a 911 call, as "not marijuana, it's similar to incense." They added that her body temperature rose dramatically, and she went into convulsions and nearly lost consciousness.

Moore made a full recovery, and a spate of local and federal laws took aim at the JWH drugs and others. In 2012, President Obama signed the Synthetic Drug Abuse Prevention Act, which outlawed twenty-six varieties of synthetic cannabinoids and cathinones. Owing to the speed of innovation in the drugs culture, however, the law "was obsolete before the ink of his signature dried," in the words of *Wired*. "Drug formulations not covered by the law's language, and almost certainly synthesized in direct response to legal pressure, are already on sale."

In the ensuing years synthetic cannabinoids started disappearing from bodegas and head shops and were instead sold in traditional street deals. Along the way they became even more popular. In 2015 the DEA said that, among high school seniors, synthetic cannabinoids were the second-most-popular drug after marijuana. "I think if we talk to a lot of kids five, ten years from now and ask, 'How did your drug use start?' they might say K2," said Courtney Pero, a narcotics sergeant in Plano, Texas. Now, synthetic cannabinoids are turning up in oils sold for vaporizers and e-cigarettes. One popular vaping liquid, CBD oil, is purported to have health benefits; it can be derived from both marijuana and hemp plants, but it's not psychoactive. A November 2018 study by Virginia Commonwealth University researchers, however, showed that legally sold, hemp-derived CBD products from a company called Diamond CBD contained a synthetic cannabinoid called 5F-ADB, despite claims on its website that its oils are "100% natural." Kevin Hagen, CEO of Diamond CBD's publicly traded, Fort Lauderdale–based parent company, said the company did its own independent testing and did not find any synthetic cannabinoids, adding that their formulas had changed since the study was undertaken.

The American and European demand for

synthetic cannabinoids set into motion a huge manufacturing industry, which sprouted up in China and, to a lesser extent, in India. The industry created millionaires who could hardly keep up with demand, and whom American law enforcement began targeting. One alleged kingpin was a Chinese national named Haijun Tian, who after arriving on a flight from China to Los Angeles International Airport on March 4, 2015, was arrested by agents from the DEA and the IRS's Office of Criminal Investigation.

Trumpeting the news in a press release, the DEA called Tian "the highest-level synthetic designer drug trafficker apprehended to date in the United States." Federal prosecutors charged him with importing a synthetic cannabinoid called AB-FUBINACA, and said his Chinese factory was making two tons of fake marijuana per month. They asked that he receive a seventeen-year sentence, but a judge gave him only thirty months. Ironically, Tian benefited because his manufacturing plant had exploded in 2013, in the midst of the American investigation against him. At this time the United States hadn't yet banned AB-FUBINACA — which was patented by Pfizer in 2009 as a potential analgesic —

and there was no evidence he synthesized it after the explosion, though he did admit to importing it.

The United States has had a difficult time prosecuting sellers of synthetic cannabinoids. Laws prohibiting the drugs began sprouting up early in the 2010s — not just federal laws but a patchwork of city and state laws — from New York City to Illinois and Texas. There are hundreds of different varieties of synthetic cannabinoids, and they don't all have similar structures, making prosecution under the analogue act difficult. Further, many different players are involved in the process, from the synthesis to the packaging to the distribution. "It's not like there's one K2 distributor," said Christopher Rosenbaum, University of Massachusetts assistant professor of toxicology. "Everybody is making their own stuff, calling it K2 and selling it, which is the most unnerving aspect."

"It's being shipped in raw form to [vendors] in Europe and North America, and there you have the second step of the manufacturing process, mixing, dissolving, and spraying the material on herbal matter," said Martin Raithelhuber, an illicit-synthetic-drug expert with the United Nations Office on Drugs and Crime. "Then they package and label it in a way that appeals to people in that country. And even then, maybe it's shipped to another distributor who would offer it on an online platform."

The raw compounds are easily available from Chinese or Indian manufacturers for as little as $1,000 a kilogram, and then vendors mix up the batches using techniques such as soaking dried plant leaves in kiddie pools full of the chemicals or combining them inside spinning cement mixers.

The profit margins are astronomical, but these crude techniques mean that some batches are much more potent than others and cause immediate overdoses. In March, 2016, in the Florida town of Clearwater, reports emerged of drugged-out citizens stumbling around or slumped over in parks. Police responded to dozens of calls involving people who had consumed what they called Spice. "The spike that we're seeing and my personnel are dealing with on the road are unprecedented," Clearwater policeman Eric Gandy told news station WFLA. "Looked like one of our zombie movies. . . . I had fifteen people walking around in various states of incapacitation."

New York became a crisis zone as well, and over three days in July 2016 the city

165

experienced a rash of 130 suspected K2 overdoses. Many victims were believed to have purchased their drugs at a deli located near the border of the Bedford-Stuyvesant and Bushwick neighborhoods, an area of Brooklyn that some began referring to as "zombieland" because of all the synthetic-cannabinoid users staggering around or passed out. In September, an NYPD raid turned up more than thirty thousand packages of the drug at a storage facility rented by an employee of the deli. A subsequent *New England Journal of Medicine* report examined the drug that many of the victims had consumed. It was packaged under the over-the-top name "AK-47 24 Karat Gold," and contained the synthetic cannabinoid known as AB-FUBINACA. This analogue, the report noted, was fifty times stronger than JWH-018.

During one August 2018 week more than one hundred people overdosed on synthetic cannabinoids in and around a New Haven, Connecticut, park. Some threw up or convulsed, while others collapsed. "Even while we were trying to return [emergency workers] to service, they were passing victims on the ground," said fire chief John Alston. Compared to fentanyl, deaths are not as common with synthetic cannabinoids, and no deaths were reported in these incidents, though Washington, DC, saw at least a handful of synthetic-cannabinoid deaths in 2018, along with more than three thousand overdoses. The homeless are particularly at risk, because of K2's inexpensive price, said a DC outreach worker. In late 2018 the Centers for Disease Control and Prevention issued a warning that some synthetic cannabinoids are tainted with the chemical brodifacoum, which is used in rat poison.

As all this was happening, from Demi Moore's overdose to the "zombie" outbreaks in Florida and New York, John William Huffman was easing into retirement. He had worked in relative obscurity almost his entire career, until, in 2008, he learned that JWH-018 had been identified in a Spice packet that was being sold in Germany. It was the first recreational synthetic-cannabinoid strain to be pinpointed in that country and the first time Huffman heard about people smoking his creations. Initially, he was bemused. "Gee it took these people a long time to put one and two together," he said.

For the first time in his career, the media sought Huffman out. Most reporters kept the focus on his science, but in 2010 a BBC radio host named John Humphrys aggressively questioned him. "Are you ashamed that you made it, now it has been banned?"

"Not at all," answered Huffman.

He nonetheless admitted he had opened a "Pandora's box" and lamented the destruction his creations and the other fake marijuana strains have caused. Even he didn't understand synthetic cannabinoids' effects on the body. Huffman remained unclear whether people die because they take too much, or if the drugs could be unsafe at any dosage.

Legalization of marijuana is the solution, he believes, so long as it's sold only to adults and highly taxed. The research is still inconclusive whether or not full marijuana legalization would substantially reduce synthetic-cannabinoid consumption — though a 2011 study of twenty-five hundred users of both synthetic cannabinoids and marijuana found that 93 percent preferred traditional marijuana. An August 2016 report from the New York City Department of Health speculated that marijuana legalization could be a preferable alternative from a public-health perspective.

Huffman said that while much is still unknown about synthetic cannabinoids, they are, inherently, an extremely risky substitute for marijuana. "Synthetic cannabinoids do not belong to the same structural group as THC," he said. "They are really dangerous compounds."

People started using synthetic cannabinoids because they were cheap, potent, and didn't show up on drug tests. But another dangerous new drug that gained traction around the same time — a psychedelic — was simply filling a hole in the marketplace.

EIGHT

When someone refers to "acid," they usually mean LSD, lysergic acid diethylamide, a psychedelic first popularized in the 1960s. For all the controversy associated with that drug, it has never caused someone to fatally overdose, but that's not the case with newer, knockoff novel psychoactive substances (NPS) also sometimes referred to as "acid." These new types of "acid" have little in common, chemically, with LSD. But not long after LSD became scarce in the early 2000s, these new synthetics began to appear — with devastating consequences.

The story of LSD and the knockoff NPS begins with a six-foot-five-inch-tall man who carried a metal briefcase. He was hard to miss. When he entered the Kansas strip club, strippers and patrons alike noticed the tall man in tattered clothes who wore a beard with no mustache, Amish-style.

Krystle Cole noticed him too. From a

modest family, Cole grew up outside of Topeka, Kansas — "a spiritual black hole" full of "white trash," she called it in her self-published memoir, *Lysergic*. She detested her classmates so strongly that she dropped out of high school at age fifteen and attended community college. To support herself she worked as a carhop at a Sonic Drive-in and then, later, a stripper. Patrons loved her tall, blond look, but she threw some of them off with her stage show. "I'd dress in black leather and lead myself around the stage with a dog collar and leash," she wrote. She was desperately lonely. When the Amish-looking man paid her attention, it seemed that her prayers for companionship were answered.

Gordon "Todd" Skinner was twice Cole's age. Despite his strange facial hair, he wasn't Amish, and Cole was not sure what he did for a living. But the two hit it off. They spoke for hours at the club that day, and she later accepted his invitation to go back to his place. Cole reeled when she saw Skinner's home — a decommissioned, Atlas E missile base. Why would a person want to live in a missile base? she wondered. How did a person *get* a missile base? From the government? Who was this strange man?

Soon afterward, he gave her MDMA. It

171

was her first time using the drug. "I felt like we were better friends already than I usually ever was with any of the people in Kansas," she wrote, adding that the drug experience made her soul feel "reborn."

Skinner acted cagey when she asked what he did for a living, and he frequently left the state on business. But that didn't stop Cole from being drawn into his playground of mind-altering substances. He entertained Cole and other guests — including beautiful young women and older men — by serving up batches of drugs, many of them obscure. They spent days and nights romping on mind-altering trips in the silo and indulged in expensive luxuries like his cutting-edge music system, which they blasted at full volume. The particularly intrepid psychedelic cowboys in the group hooked themselves up to IVs so they could control their dosages. "The parties could get really wild," Cole told Vice.

With Skinner assuring her that money was not an issue, she quit her job as a stripper, and he began supporting her financially. Skinner was involved with other women, but he bought Cole fancy clothes, took her on trips around the country, and let her drive his Porsche. They went deep together on his substances. "We experienced God, if you want to call it that," she said.

The neighbors in Wamego, Kansas, had long been suspicious of the goings-on at the missile silo. Built into the landscape on property totaling more than twenty-five acres, the silo — one of many built by the government to withstand nuclear attack, for millions of dollars each, in the early 1960s — was horizontal and underground, some fifteen thousand square feet of tunnels, cylindrical passageways, and vast, high-ceilinged rooms. "It was like a fortress, surrounded by chain-link fence and barbed wire," Cole wrote. Sites like this are all over Kansas, many of them deemed obsolete and decommissioned only a few years after being built, and since purchased by eccentrics. Aboveground, Clydesdale horses and llamas had the run of the property. Skinner told Cole that the facility was home base for a metal-spring factory, which seemed plausible, considering Skinner's mother did in fact own a multimillion-dollar enterprise called Gardner Spring in Tulsa, Oklahoma, where Skinner had been raised.

People in the community found it strange that the building was closely monitored by video cameras, and that off-duty police officers guarded the premises. "Over time, there was lots of money being spent and not much happening, and the officers got suspicious," Wamego police chief Ken Seager said. "Our feeling was it was a money-laundering operation, so the Wamego detective contacted the DEA and recommended getting the IRS involved." But nothing came of it. And the DEA took no action in the late 1990s when Wamego police uncovered LSD in town that they believed was perhaps tied to the silo. "We couldn't prove there was anything going on, but we suspected it," Seager said.

Eventually, Skinner came clean to Cole. "I have to tell you who I really am," he said, explaining that he was the "head of security" for the most famous group of LSD dealers in history — the Brotherhood of Eternal Love.

Founded in the mid-1960s, the brotherhood hailed from Orange County, California. Its early members included crew-cut-wearing roughnecks who had seen the light. Their goal was to use LSD to get street toughs turned on to God and transcendental meditation.

The youths teamed up with chemist Nick Sand, an affiliate of Sasha Shulgin, who made more than three million doses of LSD that he called Orange Sunshine. Selling for as little as ten cents per dose — and often given away for free — Orange Sunshine would be consumed by a who's who of infamous hippie-era counterculture figures, including Charles Manson, the Hell's Angels, and Timothy Leary, who became the brotherhood's close confidant. An author and Harvard psychologist who was fired in 1963 after his psychedelics studies got out of hand, Leary championed LSD for therapeutic purposes. He helped both popularize and demonize LSD in the public consciousness, and many pharmacologists believed his actions set back potential medical research on the drug for decades. After Leary was arrested for marijuana possession and imprisoned in San Luis Obispo, California, in 1970, the brotherhood conspired with the radical group Weather Underground to bust him out. Traversing a telephone pole and a barbed wire fence, Leary escaped the prison's confines and was driven to Canada. There he received a fake passport and was transported to Algiers, where he was taken in by the Black Panthers. He was finally arrested in Afghanistan in 1973.

Skinner's precise relationship to the Brotherhood of Eternal Love is hard to determine, but by 2000, he had a lab at the silo that was enormous in scope. DEA officials would later estimate it had enough chemical components to make at least thirty-six million doses of LSD. Krystle Cole had no way of knowing it, but she had stumbled onto one of the largest LSD operations in history.

Not long after they met, Skinner and Cole flew to Oakland. There, he introduced her to a man he described as his business partner, William Leonard Pickard, who was in his fifties, and his much-younger fiancée, a Russian émigré named Natasha.

Like Skinner, Pickard was a tall, imposing figure, and Cole was immediately mesmerized by "his wavy, shoulder-length, silver hair," which "helped his face to radiate a grandfather's loving warmth."

She wouldn't learn it until later, but Pickard was also an LSD chemist and believed to be a member of the Brotherhood of Eternal Love. Pickard was a student and friend of Sasha Shulgin, and his story was full of twists and turns. He had once trained as a monk and had been imprisoned for making LSD. He had earned a master's degree from the Kennedy School of Government at Harvard (Shulgin wrote him a letter of recommendation), where he studied fentanyl abuse in Boston and Moscow, anticipating the current fentanyl epidemic in a presentation to the Harvard Faculty Club in 1996, one of the few to do so. He also served as deputy director of UCLA's Drug Policy Analysis Program.

Pickard and Skinner first encountered each other, Skinner said, in 1997 at a San Francisco conference on ethnobotany. They met again at another conference a year later and got to talking about their backgrounds and interests. Skinner said he could help Pickard raise money for drug research, Pickard claimed, including from Warren Buffet — whom Skinner claimed to know. Skinner portrayed himself as fabulously wealthy. "He was incredibly generous. I'd never seen anything like it," Pickard later testified. "I assumed his funding was legitimate."

Skinner soon invited Pickard out to Kansas to see the missile silo. Though Pickard denied it, according to reports he and Skinner became partners. Pickard's alleged role was to manufacture LSD, while Skinner was said to provide security and launder their money. By the turn of the millennium, their new operation was responsible for a tremendous portion of the world's LSD supply, according to the DEA.

Lysergic acid diethylamide was discovered, almost accidentally, in 1938 by a Swiss scientist named Albert Hofmann. In the employ of the Sandoz pharmaceutical company, Hofmann was experimenting with variations of an unpredictable, poorly understood fungus called ergot, which grows on rye and throughout history has caused mass outbreaks of gangrene and convulsions. But it also seemed to have great potential as a medicine, and from the fungus Hofmann created a series of synthetic compounds, some of which became successful drugs, including one called Methergine, that stems post-childbirth hemorrhaging, and remains in use today. The twenty-fifth in the series was called LSD-25, and nothing about it at first seemed particularly notable. When tested on animals it caused them to become "restless during the narcosis" (or drugged stupor), but otherwise was considered a bust, and so Hofmann set it aside.

Hofmann moved on to other projects, but five years later, in 1943, he was compelled to revisit LSD-25 by a "peculiar presentiment — the feeling that this substance could possess properties other than those established in the first investigations," he wrote. He remade it and then — in another cosmic twist of fate — dosed himself, perhaps by accidentally touching a bit of the mixture, and became dizzy and restless. "I perceived an uninterrupted stream of fantastic pictures, extraordinary shapes with intense, kaleidoscopic play of colors," he famously wrote of that first experience.

Unsure exactly what had happened, three days later at his Basel lab he deliberately drank 250 micrograms of the compound, dissolved in a glass of water. He believed this to be a tiny amount, though it consti-tuted what we now think of as about twice a normal LSD dose. Soon he was tripping, hard. Unable to continue taking notes — or even to coherently form sentences — he asked his lab assistant to help him home. Because cars were restricted during war-time, they took bikes through Basel, back to his home. A neighbor woman brought him some milk. Believing it could cure his "poisoning," he gulped down two liters of it — but even she appeared as a "malevolent, insidious witch," and he began to believe his body had been invaded by a demon. Hofmann called for his family doctor, who could find nothing abnormal — other than dilated pupils — and helped calm him down. Soon Hofmann settled into the experience and began perceiving everyday things as profound and transcendent. "It was particularly remarkable how every acoustic perception, such as the sound of a door handle or a passing automobile, became transformed into optical perceptions," he wrote.

Hofmann would have a complicated relationship with his invention, which he referred to as his "problem child." Still, he believed LSD could be of strong benefit to medical science, and many concurred, with some academics speculating it could help cure mental illness. Stanislav Grof, an influential Czech psychiatrist who has conducted thousands of psychedelic sessions with patients, compared LSD's potential benefits for psychiatry and psychology to "the value the microscope has for biology and medicine or the telescope has for astronomy." The CIA, however, thought it might be better suited for mind control, running covert, wide-ranging experiments with the drug beginning in the early 1950s as part of a project called MKUltra, secretly dosing people and following them around to see how they reacted. (A San Francisco–based subset of the program called Midnight Climax enlisted prostitutes to entice unknowing johns into taking drinks containing LSD; CIA operatives would then secretly watch them having sex.)

Separately, in the 1960s, the US Army tested LSD and other drugs on volunteers, hoping to develop techniques to incapacitate enemies. Much later in life, the volunteers' medical and psychiatric histories were studied. "There were no aftereffects that could be discerned," said Sasha Shulgin's protégé Paul Daley. "The only thing statistically significant in the LSD volunteers was that they lived longer."

During the 1950s a psychiatrist named Humphrey Fortescue Osmond legally treated alcoholics with LSD and coined the term *psychedelic* in letters with fellow mind-expander Aldous Huxley. Hofmann's company, Sandoz Pharmaceuticals, distributed an estimated quarter-million doses of the drug, which was widely used in psychiatry research in the 1950s and 1960s. But as LSD made the leap from the medical realm to the recreational, it developed a bad reputation in the mainstream, and Sandoz began curtailing its production. In its place, illicit chemists began manufacturing LSD, and the drug was at the center of the counterculture movement.

Getting banned in the United States in 1967 did little to dent LSD's popularity, and since then the drug has risen and fallen in the public's consciousness, with varying degrees of acceptance. Though its potential medical use was never entirely established, LSD maintains a reputation as a wonder drug of sorts, one that elicits profound reactions in people while maintaining a remarkable safety record. In fact, some users have taken hundreds or even thousands of doses and lived to tell the tale, though they became extremely sick in the process.

In 1972, the Brotherhood of Eternal Love was caught in a massive sting operation, which disrupted — but did not end — the group's operations. In the following decades most other LSD manufacturers, and the Brotherhood, managed to stay under the radar of law enforcement. There were relatively few LSD labs to find, and those were hard to track; they didn't emit strong odors and weren't prone to exploding, like meth labs, so police struggled to locate them. LSD is notoriously difficult to make, in part because the precursor agent needed for its synthesis, ergotamine tartrate, is hard to obtain. In Skinner and Pickard's time, US chemists often received it clandestinely from Eastern Europe.

In 2000, with the meth crisis ramping up, LSD was low on the DEA's list of priorities. In fact, by the time Krystle Cole arrived at Skinner's lab in 2000, the DEA hadn't busted an acid lab since 1991.

Shortly after introducing her to Pickard in Oakland, Skinner announced to Cole that they needed to go to Las Vegas. They hopped into his Porsche Boxster — his "West Coast car" — and Skinner revved the engine and took off. "At one point, I looked over at the speedometer and it read 136 mph," Cole remembered. The car fishtailed, and they smashed into a light pole. They weren't wearing seat belts, and Cole injured her neck, but Skinner immediately hopped out of the car, "digging his clothes and what looked like wads of hundred-dollar bills out of the smashed trunk while I lay down on the ground."

Cole was taken to the hospital, where she was diagnosed with whiplash and a concussion, but that didn't stop them from flying to Vegas the next morning. There they met Pickard and Natasha. Cole relaxed in their luxury suite at the Mirage casino with Natasha, while Skinner, according to Pickard, engaged in " 'smurfing,' or money laundering, buying $200,000 worth of chips, gambling a bit and then redeeming the chips for the casino's cash."

Skinner's busted-up Porsche, meanwhile, would come back to haunt him. The bills for the car joined a long list of alleged debts he had incurred — hundreds of thousands of dollars worth. Some of the jilted contractors and vendors sued, including the store from which he had purchased his expensive stereo, claiming he owed $120,000. Skinner also failed to produce the funds for Pickard's drug research. "I was taken for an enormous ride," Pickard told *Rolling Stone.* "I'd been lied to. Once I realized it was all a charade, I felt very used and started backing away."

Skinner had problems of his own with Pickard. He believed Pickard took issue with a man who had outed another man who was supplying their operation with ergotamine tartrate. "Skinner said Pickard had tried unsuccessfully for three years to convince him to kidnap or drug the person and then take the victim to Guatemala," wrote the *Topeka Capital-Journal.* According to Cole, Skinner believed Pickard was responsible for having this man killed. (Pickard was never charged with or convicted of murder.)

Skinner's distrust of Pickard grew. He

began secretly plotting with the DEA and meeting with federal prosecutors. "I have what I believe is the world's largest LSD laboratory," he told them. Though initially dubious, the Department of Justice granted Skinner immunity for agreeing to turn over the lab and testify against Pickard. Skinner soon invited Pickard for a meeting, and — though Pickard remained angry at Skinner for not producing the money he had promised — they got together on October 23, 2000, at the Four Points Sheraton Hotel in San Rafael, California. Natasha, who was now Pickard's wife and pregnant, sat at the bar while the men met upstairs and spoke for about a half hour about their future LSD plans, agreeing to reunite in Kansas in the coming weeks. Listening in from an adjacent room, the DEA picked up every word.

On November 4, Pickard and a friend from California named Clyde Apperson arrived at the Wamego missile silo, driving a moving truck and a Buick. Skinner made an excuse and departed the premises, while Pickard and Apperson began loading up the chemistry glassware and ergotamine tartrate, which took about two days. The two men then got back into their vehicles and departed. Prosecutors believe they were headed to a new lab in Colorado, though

Pickard later claimed they were actually planning to destroy the materials.

The Kansas Highway Patrol made its move and stopped the mini-convoy. The officers apprehended Apperson, but Pickard fled on foot, "sprinting across snowy ground into the woods, two highway patrolmen half his age in hot pursuit, a chase that was eventually joined by DEA agents, helicopters with infrared scanners and tracking dogs," *Rolling Stone* reported. The next day Pickard was turned in by a local farmer, who said he was hiding out in his truck and his shed.

Back at the missile silo, a crew of men in hazmat suits turned up chemicals capable of producing between thirty-six million and sixty million doses of LSD, according to DEA spokeswoman Shirley Armstead. The final tally wasn't in yet, but investigators were predicting that the lab "could have been supplying a third of the LSD in the United States and maybe the world," she noted. The government agents patted themselves on the back. With this one bust, they had dealt a perhaps unrecoverable blow to America's LSD production, it seemed.

Skinner testified against his former partner Pickard. An acquaintance of Sasha Shulgin named Roger Ely also testified at the trial. Ely, who has worked as a chemist with the DEA since 1987, said Shulgin had introduced him to Pickard. Ely added that he and Pickard had discussed "the use of the Internet to get illicit drugs; the use of encrypted messages to elude law enforcement investigators; Russian drug trafficking; and synthetic illicit substances."

Pickard received two concurrent life sentences without parole. He remains incarcerated in federal prison, in Tucson, Arizona, relying on his monk's training to maintain inner peace, jogging loops around a quarter-mile asphalt track and writing a now-published, six-hundred-page, semiautobiographical book about LSD chemists called *The Rose of Paracelsus.* He maintains a cult following of fans, who cite him as an example of federal drug sentencing gone haywire.

Because of his cooperation, Skinner was free to go. He and Cole traveled around the country, living for short stretches in Seattle, Mendocino, Tucson, and Tulsa. They sold drugs, including MDMA, and lived "like psychedelic royalty," Cole said.

Along the way their relationship withered, and Skinner began to get abusive, Cole claimed, displaying "hints of a violent side to him that I'd never seen before." She said that he "dosed my house with some sort of mystery psychedelic that made me trip for three days." Cole said she wanted to stop selling drugs, and began seeing a man closer to her age, Brandon Andres Green. At this point, according to Cole, Skinner became unhinged and jealous. Green was beaten, tortured, and drugged at a Tulsa hotel. Skinner, Cole, and a man named William Ernest Hauck were charged with kidnapping. Hauck testified against Skinner, and Hauck and Cole both pled no contest to the charge of being an accessory after the fact. The details of who did what exactly are murky, but neither Skinner nor Cole came out looking good. In the end, Cole was ordered to pay $52,000 in restitution to Green and walked away free, though Green said she actually paid only a small fraction of her debt. She now owns an art gallery in a Wichita, Kansas, mall, which features her psychedelic paintings of animals and nature.

Convicted on kidnapping and assault charges, Skinner received a life sentence plus ninety years; there is speculation that Skinner was also unofficially being punished for his drug crimes.

It was a story with life-changing consequences for everyone involved, and also likely altered the national recreational-drug landscape. In the aftermath of the Kansas missile silo saga, LSD became increasingly difficult to find. According to the DEA, LSD-related arrests dropped from 154 in 2000 to 100 in 2001 to 22 in 2002. The agency claimed that this war-on-drugs success story was owing to the "90.86 pounds" of LSD they had seized.

"These defendants," read a DEA press release, "were proven, by overwhelming evidence, to be responsible for the illicit manufacture of the majority of the LSD sold in this nation. The proof of the significance of these prosecutions and convictions lies in the fact that LSD availability in the United States was reduced by 95% in the two years following their arrest."

Many take issue with the DEA's numbers and methodology. For starters, the amount of actual LSD they seized was dramatically overstated; what they actually found was about ninety-one pounds of materials containing trace amounts of LSD. The total weight of the drug was perhaps less than one pound. An analysis by *Slate* estimated that the lab had about ten million LSD hits — a lot, but less than claimed. Further, even by the DEA's own estimations, the LSD

189

supply had already begun to fall in the years before the bust, perhaps due to factors including the takedown of Nick Sand's LSD lab in Canada in 1996 and the growing popularity of MDMA. So it's far from clear that the Kansas sting alone was responsible for the drug's steep decline.

Ultimately, the closure of the lab may have been less impactful than the headlines it generated. "I don't think Pickard was necessarily producing 95 percent of the supply, but it seemed really clear that as soon as that bust happened, other LSD manufacturers shut down," said Mitchell Gomez, the executive director of DanceSafe, who is knowledgeable about the case and LSD manufacturing of this era. "As soon as they got busted, everybody just freaked out."

After the Kansas bust, LSD became very difficult to find. The psychedelic drug landscape began to shift, and a new drug began to gain traction. This chemical was often sold as acid or LSD, but it was completely different. Some enjoyed its trippy effects, but it was poorly understood and extremely difficult to dose properly. Unlike LSD, it could be fatal.

NINE

Located about five hundred miles due south of the Wamego missile silo, McKinney, Texas, is an affluent exurb of Dallas, named the best place to live in America by *Money* magazine in 2014. Its population more than doubled between 2000 and 2010 and now stands north of 150,000. Its landscape is cluttered with earthmovers clearing farmland for brand-new, cookie-cutter housing developments. It's not for everybody; new developments include Adriatica, a faux-Mediterranean community full of McMansions. But parents are drawn to McKinney for its good schools, safe environment, and booming economy, which is boosted by a plethora of nearby Fortune 500 companies.

In the early 2010s a dark time began in McKinney. Along with similarly prosperous nearby towns like Frisco and Plano, it was battered by a wave of mysterious new drugs, and overdoses plagued young people in the area. The overdoses shocked the community, especially because almost nobody knew what these new drugs were — not the families, not the paramedics, not the police, and often, not the kids themselves.

In 2013, Lee Stockton was a freshman at McKinney-Boyd High School. Housed in a gleaming brown and yellow brick building, the school appears from the outside to be the essence of new exurban wealth, with a video screen welcoming students and gorgeous athletic facilities surrounded by woods. But sports weren't Lee's passion so much as psychedelic drugs, with which he became fascinated. "Me and my friends got interested in the spiritual enlightenment that they promise, the whole culture behind it," he said.

Like many high school students, Lee dreamed of something bigger. "I feel like here in America we're so closed off mentally." One day he hoped to travel the world, visiting "shamanic tribes in the Amazon" and "Buddhist temples in the East." For the time being, however, Lee would have to make do with inner journeys. He wanted to try LSD, but it wasn't easy to find. A guy he knew sold him what he said was LSD, but when Lee tasted its metallic, bitter flavor — having done his Internet research

— he knew he had been duped. He spit it out, and the dealer later told him it was actually something called 25C-NBOMe, one of a group of chemicals with the unfortunate nickname "N-bombs." As with other NPS, when it began to be sold on the Internet, 25C-NBOMe was called a "research chemical" — a euphemistic name intended to confuse law enforcement — but really, it was simply a new way to get high. It started showing up on the websites of illicit drug manufacturers around 2010 and was still legal when Lee first took it; the DEA outlawed it on November 15, 2013.

Users of N-bombs found the effects similar to LSD, but N-bombs were much cheaper. Drug dealers, seeking bigger profits, began selling N-bombs as LSD, figuring the effects were close enough than no one would complain.

Lee's dealer told him about Silk Road, the Dark Web emporium where one could buy all manner of illicit drugs. Lee logged on and resumed his search for LSD. But while some vendors were selling it, they charged more than he was willing to pay. As he continued poking around, he kept coming back to 25C-NBOMe. He plunged into online research about the chemical, studying its effects, and concluded that it might give him the type of high he was searching for.

Lee placed his Dark Web order and the 25C arrived soon afterward in the mail. The liquid chemical had already been laid on sheets of blotter paper, which meant he could easily tear them into small squares known as "tabs" without having to do any measuring — no muss, no fuss. That was a good thing, considering each dose was a tiny 650 micrograms, which, like LSD, is all but impossible to measure by eyeballing. (For comparison, even a small dose of ecstasy is about one hundred times larger.)

Lee went to a local park and took the dose; the taste, again, was awful. The drug kicked in about fifteen minutes later. As Lee looked out over a small lake, visuals began sweeping in. The experience was more intense than he had expected, but it wasn't unpleasant. "You're clearheaded, completely lucid," he said, "it's just that everything around you is morphing around."

Lee Stockton is not his real name. In one moment the teen can seem wise beyond his years, in the next, way over his head. When it came to the N-bombs, Lee decided he wasn't just going to take them — he was going to try to make some money selling them. And so, not long after that first trip, at only sixteen years old, he began peddling tabs to young people he knew. Unlike the dealer who had tried to dupe him, he didn't claim the drug was LSD, just that it had similar effects. He had no idea if it would catch on. "Kids at other schools were like, 'Hell, no, dude. I know one kid who touched acid, and he was never the same,' " he said.

But at McKinney-Boyd the synthetic psychedelic was an almost immediate success. Selling for five bucks apiece (ten times what Lee paid), the tabs found willing customers in the most unlikely of places. "Kids you would never even expect, like kids on the football team, would drop on the weekends. It was so casual." Lee would order one hundred tabs on Silk Road and sell them until he ran out before ordering more. The money was decent, and there were other perks. "I liked the reputation it gave me," he said.

His product came from an American address, though he believed the drugs themselves were manufactured in China. He sometimes tried different sellers and also experimented with other types of N-bombs, like 25I-NBOMe and 25B-NBOMe. Other students were dealing them as well, and McKinney-Boyd was soon overrun. Kids would go on nature walks and trip out, or hit up electronic dance music concerts, heading down to Dallas on the weekends to see popular DJs. Lee estimates that well over one hundred McKinney-Boyd students were taking the N-bomb drugs at one point — perhaps even closer to two hundred. This was no small number in a school of three thousand, and a highly regarded one at that. "I don't know what it was, but there was something about McKinney-Boyd, they loved hallucinogens. It was like the 1960s for a while there," Lee said.

But McKinney-Boyd's throwback era wouldn't last long. During Lee's sophomore year the school erupted in scandal and near tragedy — owing to a series of drug overdoses, fueled, in part, by Lee's dealings.

Within a single day in early April, 2014, at least three local kids were sent to hospitals. (Since most of those affected were underage, the police did not release many details. Some close to the situation say the number of children affected was much higher.) Two of the three students were found naked, and one in particular was walking along a highway without his clothes. According to a knowledgeable source, this student believed his 25B-NBOMe to be LSD and took more than the recommended dose. He and a small group of friends were hanging out at a friend's home when he began overheating, which is what seems to have prompted him to remove his clothes and go out into the cold, rainy weather. He was walking along Highway 380 when he was stopped by police. "He just kind of freaked out and attacked the police officer," said the source.

Another student, a fourteen-year-old girl in middle school, had an equally intense reaction. According to a relative who was an eyewitness, she and a friend were having a sleepover and decided to experiment with the new drug. The friend chickened out, but the girl — a good student, active in sports — took the hit and reacted violently. "When I got there, she was in a powerful [state]," said the relative. "You ever seen a picture of a deer, how their eyes look, just solid black? She had doe eyes." Suddenly possessed by inhuman strength, the diminutive girl ripped down bathroom cabinets and towel racks. She smashed herself against the bathroom walls, as if trying to go through them. "That part of the house was trashed," said the relative.

The girl too was overheating, and so her mother wrestled her into the shower and turned on the cold water. This, the relative believes, may have saved her. When the paramedics arrived, all of their efforts were needed to get her onto the gurney. At the hospital she had to be strapped down.

She ended up making a full recovery. But at the hospital, none of the medical professionals had any idea what she had taken.

This is very common when it comes to NPS, say toxicology experts. With so many new "research chemicals" pouring into the country, all health-care providers can hope to do is treat the symptoms. "Getting too hung up on the exact chemical they've taken is walking down the wrong path," said Kristina Domanski, MD, a toxicologist in the North Texas Poison Center at Parkland Health and Hospital System in Dallas. "It's hard to stay on top of these, because in six months what we see might be totally different from what we see today," said Ashley Haynes, another toxicologist at Parkland.

The danger isn't just in the drugs themselves but in the fact that nobody knows how much they should be taking. "There's an old saying in toxicology — the dose makes the poison," said Shannon Rickner, also a toxicologist at Parkland. A hot spot for MDMA use when the drug broke big in the mid-1980s, Dallas has reemerged as a center of this new drug scourge. One substance-abuse counselor in the area said in 2016 that between 25 and 30 percent of the kids she was seeing were taking these new synthetics. Ecstasy was easier to understand: law enforcement officers and parents knew what they were looking for, they understood the drug's effects, and they knew how it was usually distributed, but these new drugs were unlike anything they had seen.

The McKinney students who overdosed in 2014 weren't young burnouts mindlessly popping poison into their mouths. Many were honor students who had read online accounts of others' psychedelic trips and wanted to experience the mind-expanding possibilities for themselves.

This was the profile of Montana Brown, from Frisco, Texas, the town just west of McKinney. He and his brothers thought they had done their homework.

Montana Brown was the life of the party. He and his brothers were called the "three musketeers" by their dad, and though he was the youngest, Montana was the ring-leader. He had dark brown hair and a big smile that often turned into a smirk when he cracked wise. He played football and had an insatiable appetite for life. He smoked e-cigarettes and constantly drank coffee. He also got in trouble. He was known to go searching for magic mushrooms among the cow patties in a field near his house in Frisco.

He was on probation for providing pain medication (which he received after a tubing accident) to a classmate, for which he served a brief stint in juvenile detention. But he had countless friends and the strong love of his family. When one of his family members told him they loved him, he liked to say, "Love you more." His dad explained: "He was very competitive with his love."

On December 13, 2013, when his older brother Rory was about to leave for college, Montana decided to throw a party with their middle brother, Jack. They made plans to celebrate at their home while their parents were out of town. They had been known to smoke some marijuana but wanted something special, so they asked around about some mushrooms. Montana's older brothers had done them before and wanted to take them with him; they couldn't find any, however. So they contacted a friend they worked with at Applebee's, named Stephen Wagner, who said he could hook them up with some LSD.

"Originally, we didn't want to do anything *that* crazy," Jack, the middle brother, said.

He was sixteen at the time. He's well built, with blue eyes and rectangular glasses. Many thought he and Montana were twins. "But we looked it up on the Internet and said, 'OK, this isn't that bad.' " It might be intense, but LSD was a drug that people had been taking for decades. They had little reason to fear it.

Stephen procured the acid for ten dollars a tab. After work that night, around eleven o'clock, Stephen and the three brothers popped the small paper squares in their mouths. Montana and Jack took two each, and Rory and Stephen took three. While they waited for the acid to kick in, Rory, Jack, and Stephen smoked pot in the garage. Montana abstained; because of his probation, he was worried a drug test might be in his future. When they emerged, everyone was buzzed, and it was starting to feel like the type of going-away soiree they had envisioned. "We came back inside, and the high seemed a lot more noticeable," Jack said.

But Montana soon became uneasy. In a text message with a friend, he questioned whether he had made the right decision taking the drug. "Dude im feelin pretty apprehensive lol," he wrote. "I dont even possess the vocabulary to express the sensations that are flowing outta me right now," he texted soon afterward. "Im trippin balls right now bra."

The acid hit the three brothers much harder than they had expected. Sounds entered their ears differently; colors appeared brighter. "Later, it became a lot of visuals, but at first you just kept thinking the same thing over and over," said Jack.

Montana experienced the symptoms particularly acutely. It's not clear what exactly he was thinking about, but, as with the others, the same thoughts raced through his head, again and again. He began to lose control. Jack and Rory were hanging out on the stairs leading down to the living room, when Montana, at the bottom of the stairs, suggested they join him. "Let's get some music down here," he said, gesticulating oddly with his hands. "Let's get some music down here," he said again, repeating the strange gesticulations. "Let's get some music down here."

Unbeknownst to Montana, the drug they had taken wasn't LSD, it was 25I-NBOMe. His brothers didn't know what to make of him. He was repeating himself — "Let's get some music down here" — overtaken by a phenomenon known as "thought loops," the endless repetition of a single idea in the brain that is sometimes experienced by N-bomb users.

Eventually he stopped talking and sat down on the stairs. Then he fell into convulsions. Rory and Jack called a friend who had been through EMT training. The friend arrived only minutes later, discovering a chaotic scene where nobody seemed to know what was happening. It was too late. According to the coroner, Montana died at 2:10 a.m. He was fifteen years old.

Montana's dad and stepmother raced to get flights back to town. Stephen, Jack, and Rory were hospitalized, and their memories from the night are hazy, but they recovered. A full autopsy wasn't performed, and scientists themselves know very little about how NBOMe drugs interact with the body. But Montana's father, Eric, speculated that he was the only one of the four to die because his veins had already been constricted by his indulgences in coffee and e-cigarettes. "So it was the perfect storm when this substance was put into his body," he said, "such a narrowing of his veins that no blood could get to his heart, his lungs, his brain."

Rory blamed himself for Montana's death. He was the eldest brother and felt he should have protected Montana. Eric Brown began worrying that he would lose another son, this time to suicide. By his own admission, Rory was in a very dark place. But a few days after his brother's death, Rory was lying in bed when he saw a vision that changed his perspective. "I saw a light on my wall, and there he was," Rory said. "He said, 'It wasn't your fault. It was part of a plan.' And he hugged me."

Eric's marriage didn't survive the fallout of his son's death. To cope, he has poured himself into spreading awareness about the type of substance Montana took. He has run group meetings with parents, staged interventions for teens going down the wrong path, and helped establish new Texas legislation that gives the state more power to act quickly to criminalize new synthetic drugs that come onto the market. It's known as the Montana Brown and Jesse High Act, also referencing an eighteen-year-old Amarillo boy who died in 2013 after smoking synthetic cannabinoids.

Eric regularly updates his son's memorial Facebook page and pores over the web traffic analytics. It's been seen by millions of people, and he regularly talks to those who have questions about N-bombs and don't believe they can trust the Internet. After a seventeen-year-old Plano student named

Evan Johnson overdosed and died from N-bombs in December 2014, his mother was disheartened to see, near the top of her computer's Google search history, a Reddit discussion full of misinformation about the drug. "25x-Nbome series is a derivative of the 2c-Family of drugs and people have been shoving those drugs up their nose since the 60s. I don't think you have much to worry about as long as you used 25x in moderation," wrote a top poster, incorrectly. Though some information about the drug on the Internet today is more accurate, much remains scattershot and confusing, as is the case with most NPS.

Eric Brown has learned a lot about these new drugs by reading everything he can, but he's exasperated with the way NPS are dealt with in this country. As he describes it, almost nobody — from first responders to law enforcement to legislators — is properly educated on the subject.

Stephen Wagner, the Applebee's employee who helped procure the drug that killed Montana Brown, received six months in jail, as did Wagner's accomplice, Stephanie King. The man who sold Wagner the drug, Kai Wen Tan, received five years. (Tan did not reveal his source.)

This may be partial justice for his son's death, but Eric Brown maintains anger at the man who helped bring these drugs to life, David Nichols, a former medicinal-chemistry professor at Purdue and a collaborator with Sasha Shulgin. Though Nichols didn't invent N-bombs, his research and writing on them seems to have served as a blueprint for illicit-drug chemists, who began selling them for recreational use.

Nichols, now retired, defends his work. He spent his career trying to develop molecular tools that would lead to the improvement of humankind, he said. His supporters defend his scientific integrity and say his efforts may one day be responsible for breakthroughs in medical science — to help those with drug addictions, depression, or PTSD, for example. For now, however, he is a venerated scientist who, in the eyes of some, has blood on his hands.

Nichols has retired from Purdue University, where from 1974 to 2012 he studied how psychedelics work on the brain, with a focus on dopamine and serotonin receptors, becoming the best-known academic in his small field. Because psychedelics produce such unusual, profound reactions in people — from elation and spiritual discovery to misery — they can help in understanding the brain's neural pathways, and Nichols used them as a tool in this way.

Nichols takes great pains to distance himself from the drug counterculture. He is like the straightedge version of his old friend and colleague Sasha Shulgin, considered the other titan in the field of psychedelics research. Shulgin was more interested in the potential for enlightenment in the drugs he studied, rather than the science of their chemical pathways, and pushed the legal envelope much further than Nichols, who did his work entirely lawfully and by the book. (His son, Charles Nichols, an associate professor of pharmacology at the Louisiana State University School of Medicine in New Orleans, also studies psychedelics.)

Shulgin and David Nichols were united, however, in their fascination with the incredible power of mind-altering drugs. "For some people a single encounter with a psychedelic like LSD can permanently change the way they see the world, for better for worse," Nichols said. "How can a molecule do that? How is your brain structured that this small molecule can go in there, spend a few hours, and you come back out and you're never the same person?"

David Nichols grew up in a town called Park Hills, Kentucky, just across the river from Cincinnati. In World War II, Nichols' father served as a radio operator in a tank. "He saw lots of damage and lots of dead bodies," Nichols said, and his wife later suggested he probably had PTSD.

Nichols studied chemistry at the University of Cincinnati and in 1969 began his research on psychedelics as a medicinal-chemistry PhD student at the University of Iowa. He came to believe psychedelics perhaps could have helped his father, who died in 2005. "Substances like psilocybin and LSD could probably be used for PTSD, because they change your frame of reference, your perspective on things," he said, comparing some peoples' profound psychedelic experiences to "rebooting the computer."

For much of Nichols's career, however, psychedelics studies using human subjects were untenable. A year after Nichols began graduate school, in 1970, Congress passed the Comprehensive Drug Abuse and Control Act, which caused funding for previously common human trials to dry up.

Nichols was left with imperfect options, such as testing LSD on cats from the pound.

Finally, in 1990, University of New Mexico psychiatry professor Rick Strassman got the green light to test the super-potent psychedelic DMT on a human sample group; Nichols synthesized the research-grade DMT. He also made MDMA for drug trials involving sexual assault survivors, veterans, and police officers, with many subjects seeing dramatic results. DMT and MDMA are schedule I drugs, meaning the US government believes they have "no currently accepted medical use." Though they can still be studied, the DEA makes scientists jump through hoops to get approval. To satisfy the DEA's safety requirements, Nichols kept his controlled substances inside a steel, fireproof file cabinet behind a padlocked, thick oak door.

In 1993 Nichols cofounded the Hefter Research Institute, which runs studies on how psychedelics can treat smoking, cocaine, and alcohol addiction, and reduce depression and anxiety in people with cancer. It was funded in part by Bob Wallace, an eccentric software developer who was Microsoft's ninth employee. Hefter's tests often use psilocybin, the synthetic version of the drug in magic mushrooms, which is easier on the heart than MDMA and shorter acting than LSD, so studies can be completed in one day.

The antidepressants on the market often don't work much better than a placebo, said Nichols. "Nothing really works very well. Antidepressants give some symptom reduction in around 50 percent of patients. And that doesn't mean they 'cure' depression. It just means that the intensity of the depression symptoms is reduced to a certain extent," he said. "But I really think [psychedelics] will work in resetting people's brains in some way, so they become healthy again."

Nichols has never been a household name, but as his career progressed the drugs community became increasingly interested in him. Whereas the chemical studies he published were once tucked away in hard copy in libraries, in the Internet age they became easily accessible, as scientific journals began sharing their contents online.

The series of events that led to Montana Brown's death began on Friday, April 4, 2003. That day Nichols, still at Purdue, received an e-mail alerting him to the existence of some curious new compounds. They were formulated by a German graduate student named Ralf Heim, a PhD candidate in the department of biology, chemistry, and pharmacy at the Free University of Berlin.

Advancing the work of a German pharmaceutical and medical-chemistry professor named Sigurd Elz, Heim made the compounds by slightly tweaking the structures of a group of phenethylamine drugs popularized by Sasha Shulgin. These were themselves derivatives of mescaline and included 2C-B, Shulgin's favorite. Testing these new compounds on arteries dissected from rats' tails, Heim wanted to see how they interacted with a serotonin receptor known as 5-HT2A. This receptor is of great interest to scientists, as it exerts control on mood, memory, and other brain functions; understanding how it works could benefit fields from psychiatry to neuroscience.

Looking at the structures, Nichols did not expect that the compounds would be particularly active. But, in fact, the opposite proved to be true. In Heim's experiments they turned out to be incredibly potent.

To try to comprehend this phenomenon, Nichols and his students synthesized the compounds, including 25I-NBOMe (a derivative of Shulgin's drug 2C-I) and 25B-NBOMe (a derivative of Shulgin's 2C-B), in their own laboratory. They were the first to christen them with the NBOMe names, so-called because they each contain an N-methoxybenzyl group. "We made a bunch of them, to try to understand what was going on by looking at receptors that had mutations and so forth," Nichols said. His team, as usual, didn't test them on humans but rather used live rats. "My technician gave rats a dose that would have been typical for almost any psychedelic we had been studying. And the rats got unbelievable terrible diarrhea, because the dose was way too high. It was significantly more potent than LSD."

Nichols and three students from his Purdue lab first published their findings about the NBOMe compounds in 2006, in a journal called *Molecular Pharmacology,* noting that the new compounds produced "affinity increases up to 300-fold" for the 5-HT2A receptor. This led to greater understanding of the receptor, and they continued studying the compounds.

How exactly these drugs made the leap from the academic world to the commercial is unclear. Nichols suspects that rogue chemists learned of them — and lifted his synthesis techniques — directly from his *Molecular Pharmacology* study, which gives detailed chemical notes about his experiments and remains easily accessible on the Internet to this day. By 2010 the NBOMe drugs were being produced by Chinese labs and sold online. 25I-NBOMe, 25B-NBOMe, and 25C-NBOMe were the most popular, but other variations were sold as well.

In 2010 Nichols learned the story of a forty-nine-year-old Scottish man named David Llewellyn, who was profiled in a *Wall Street Journal* article. Llewellyn was an amateur drugmaker who ran a construction business, but after the latter went south due to the housing-market crash of 2008, he built a small NPS empire, manufacturing imitations of ecstasy, cocaine, and others. Selling pills and powders with names like Euforia and XT, he tapped into the burgeoning European "legal highs" market. "Everything we sell is legal," he claimed, "I don't want to go to jail for 14 years."

In reality, Llewellyn's chemicals skirted the edge of legality; most European governments sought to outlaw these substances but were flummoxed by the huge numbers of new drugs coming into their countries. Whenever one was banned, Llewelyn simply created another one. For example, when the popular NPS mephedrone was made illegal in 2010, Llewellyn abandoned it in favor of a new drug called Nopaine, which he and a colleague invented by slightly altering the chemical formula of Ritalin. Llewellyn was forced to constantly innovate in order to stay successful. In his search for new recreational chemicals the governments didn't know about, he had the idea to begin scouring scientific journals. He realized that one scientist in particular had a knack for developing drugs with legitimate scientific uses that he could easily reappropriate. With David Nichols's unintentional aid, Llewellyn's business boomed. He hired eight employees and opened labs in Scotland and the Netherlands to manufacture the drugs he sold over the Internet.

"[Nichols's] papers give a full description of the drugs he's using, including their chemical makeup," the *Wall Street Journal* article read. "This provides Llewellyn and others with a roadmap for making the drugs."

Though there weren't any reports that Llewellyn's drugs caused deaths, when contacted for the article, Nichols was disturbed, noting that the chemicals he worked on had never been subjected to human clinical trials, and he had no idea whether they were safe. "When people use this stuff chronically, on a weekly basis — suppose it produces liver cancer?" he asked.

David Llewellyn wasn't the only one appropriating Nichols's chemicals. They began to be produced in Chinese labs and sold as "research chemicals" all over the world by drug dealers, Dark Web dealers, and sometimes legally in shops. As Nichols's drugs caught on with recreational users, three of them were tied to deaths: N-bombs, MBDB (an MDMA analogue), and a stimulant called 4-MTA (or MTA), which is known as "flatliners" — because it literally knocks people out. MTA became popular in Europe in the late 1990s and was linked to a handful of deaths in the Netherlands and England. "My laboratory had shown that rats perceived the effects of MTA as being like those of ecstasy," Nichols wrote in "Legal Highs: The Dark Side of Medicinal Chemistry," a 2011 *Nature* editorial. "It seemed that that was the sole motivation for its illicit production and distribution to humans. I was stunned by this revelation, and it left me with a hollow and depressed feeling for some time."

As of 2018 at least twenty-eight deaths have been ascribed to N-bombs, but the actual total is undoubtedly higher, as the drug is often misidentified as LSD or 2C-I in news reports, and many times more people have been hospitalized in critical condition.

Some people are more likely to die from N-bombs than others, even when they've taken the same dosage. Nichols believes it's possible that certain individuals don't metabolize the compound properly. An N-bomb drug "creates problems by thickening the blood and thinning the blood vessels," said Dr. David Caldicott of the Australian National University medical school, who has seen N-bomb patients, "and this is the main catalyst behind a range of other issues including ventricular fibrillation leading to heart attack, renal failure, and even stroke."

Nonetheless, the drug is still widely available on the Dark Web and remains popular among those looking for cheap acid, as well as people who prefer it in its own right.

When asked what he would tell the father of Montana Brown, Nichols said: "It was never our intention to develop drugs for people to take. We were using them as molecular tools to understand how the brain works. And unfortunately, unscrupulous people took that information that we published and put it out on the street as drugs. Of course, his son made the choice to use

216

those. He knew that they weren't approved drugs. His son has to bear some responsibility, and he paid the dear price for it. I couldn't control what people did because what we published was in the open literature."

"Whatever helps him sleep at night," Eric Brown responded.

Arthur Caplan, University of Pennsylvania's chairman of medical ethics, told ABC News that journals should consider restricting access to complete drug formulas with a potential for abuse to help "make it tougher for the bad guys." Nichols, however, believes there is no feasible way to make sure these formulas are available only to reputable scientists and not illicit drug manufacturers. "The hallmark of experimental science is reproducibility. That is, when you publish something you also must provide all of the details of your experiments so that, in theory, someone else could reproduce your work," he said. "In order for anyone to either validate or invalidate your conclusion, they must have your exact experimental methods."

Nichols did say he was interested in a molecule — which he declined to name — that he decided not to publish about, for fear of enabling "mischief" among those interested in a new recreational drug. "I think it would have effects very much like ecstasy, and it would be very cheap to make, so the market would be flooded with it."

He calls out Virginia Commonwealth University professor Richard A. Glennon by name for what he calls "reckless" publishing about the drugs paramethoxyamphetamine and paramethoxymethamphetamine, ecstasy substitutes sold by drug dealers known as PMA and PMMA, respectively, which have killed well over one hundred recreational users. "He published [numerous] papers on PMMA where he said, 'It's like MDMA. It's the prototype for MDMA,' " said Nichols. "How many underground chemists could read that and say, 'Oh, PMMA. Let's make this stuff. It sounds like it's just like MDMA'?"

"They were already being abused, and people knew relatively little about them. So we studied them," responded Glennon. "It's hard to come up with treatment modalities for overdoses if you don't know what these things are doing."

"I did not develop these agents," Glennon added. "And, I published warnings about using them."

As with Sasha Shulgin, Nichols's legacy is still being debated. It's possible that his work will be of great benefit to science and humanity. It's also possible that his drugs will cause more deaths. In conversation he emphasizes the potential benefits, even imagining a future where psychedelics aid not just those suffering from trauma or addiction but also regular folks in their everyday lives. (Bob Jesse, an instrumental figure in the field of psychedelic research, calls this "the betterment of well people.") "Someday, probably long after I'm dead, you'll be having a midlife crisis and your doctor will refer you down the street to a psychiatrist or shaman, and recommend that you have a psychedelic session," Nichols said. "You'll have this session and you'll get a perspective on your life, where you're going, where you've been. They'll help you get your bearings."

The complexities surrounding synthetics are front and center again. It's not lost on David Nichols that N-bomb compounds may not have done such damage if LSD were still available.

"We don't have really solid data on this, but it seems to me from talking to people in the field that most people who have tried N-bombs did it under the impression that it was LSD," said Mitchell Gomez, the executive director of DanceSafe. "I think if people can have access to LSD, the vast majority of them are not ever going to consider using a drug like 25I-NBOMe."

"As one of my graduate students said," Nichols noted, referencing his former student Andy Hoffman, "make one drug illegal, and a more dangerous one will take its place."

This is cold comfort to Montana Brown's father, Eric. "I don't get the benefit, or the gain, of this research," he said. "Send it to the appropriate parties. Don't make it public knowledge."

■ ■ ■ ■

PART II:
USERS AND DEALERS

■ ■ ■ ■

TEN

Late in the nineteenth century, four St. Louis men launched a company that made stoves. Ovens were extremely unreliable then, as likely to burn food as undercook it. But, led by a man named Charles Stockstrom — like his partners, he had arrived from Germany — the company produced stoves boasting game-changing thermostat control knobs, which let the cook accurately control the temperature. They called their enterprise the Quick Meal Stove Company.

Eventually known as Magic Chef, the company's fortunes quickly blossomed, and it could barely keep up with demand. In the early 1900s it commissioned a massive factory in an Italian neighborhood of St. Louis called the Hill. The stunning brick complex was ideally located off Kingshighway Boulevard, a major north–south thoroughfare, and could even accommodate a railway, with tracks curving along its northeastern edge allowing train cars to unload directly at its receiving entrance. The company chipped in for the war effort in the 1940s to build bombs and fighter plane armaments, and meanwhile the stove business kept churning. At its peak Magic Chef employed some two thousand workers. It was part of the great hum of industry that helped make St. Louis one of the ten biggest cities in the country at the time.

Stockstrom commissioned an opulent home for himself and his family, a French Renaissance Revival mansion in nearby Compton Hill. It had eight gas fireplaces and more than thirty rooms, including a library, a butler's pantry, and a bowling alley in the basement. The Magic Chef Mansion, as it's now known, remains a popular St. Louis tourist attraction.

The factory, however, is not open for tours. After Magic Chef merged with another company and then was bought out in the 1950s, it abandoned its factory on the Hill, and though the building has since been used by other companies, it hasn't been fully occupied since. During the late 2010s it was slated for demolition, but in its last years it was populated with drug users who wanted a secluded place to get high and pass out.

Jack Sanders started going there for that purpose around 2013. By then, parts of St. Louis already seemed like a ghost town. Because of the flight of industry and much of the white middle class, the city now housed slightly more than three hundred thousand residents, despite being built for almost three times that many. But the Magic Chef factory nonetheless stood out for its stunning fall from grace. From the street its white brick frame still looked sturdy, but its half million square feet of decrepitude included smashed glass, pools of water, dangling wires, and thirty-foot ceilings crumbling to the floor. Pigeons and rats picked at discarded refuse, while wildly colorful, carefully drawn graffiti shouted out street gangs.

Long ago condemned, and prone to fires, the building was sealed off, but Sanders and other users took advantage of a secret entrance, an aluminum door that had been ripped up a couple of feet, allowing just enough space for someone to shimmy under it. Inside were boiler rooms, abandoned lavatories, break areas, and other quiet corners to get high in, as well as dark subterranean recesses called "the tombs," where anyone unwise enough to enter might get shanked for their stash. Those who understood the rules of engagement, however, often found a welcoming, if paranoid, community, where those with a shared, pressing need came to escape everything else in the world.

Sanders, a personal trainer who grew up in a well-to-do St. Louis suburb — and whose name has been changed to protect his identity — spent many nights there after his life went way off course. By 2013 he was homeless and crashing at the old Magic Chef factory regularly. He dragged a mattress into an empty area or sometimes shared space with other users on an old train car, one of the same brown boxcars that had once brought raw materials that helped Magic Chef build and sell more ovens than anyone else in the world. Jack had been using heroin excessively for over a decade, but something had begun to change. Heroin had never been a particularly safe pastime, in St. Louis or anywhere else, but he and others in the city had managed to forge a precarious existence for themselves. In 2013, however, it began to seem as if no one was safe. When fentanyl arrived, Jack's friends began dropping like flies.

According to the Centers for Disease Control and Prevention, in 2013 the "third wave" of the opioid epidemic began. Because of fentanyl, it is the most deadly one yet. In 2012, St. Louis saw 92 opioid-related deaths, a number that rose to 123 in 2013 and up to 256 in 2017. Another record-setting year is projected for the region in 2018.

"There really is no pure heroin in St. Louis anymore," said Brandon Costerison of the National Council on Alcoholism and Drug Abuse.

"It really became a problem for us around 2014, that's when we really started noticing fentanyl-related deaths," said Detective Ricardo Franklin, of the St. Louis County Police Department's Bureau of Drug Enforcement. "You'll get someone who assumes they are buying heroin and have no idea fentanyl is in it. Their body might be used to two [doses] of heroin, but if fentanyl is now mixed in, they are more at risk of an overdose." Even for a notoriously dangerous city like St. Louis, in 2016 drug overdose deaths began outstripping murders.

Jack Sanders himself had helped fuel the local rise of fentanyl. It was a devastating new demon that no one — from street users to the DEA — saw coming.

"Fentanyl completely changed the game," said Jack, who like many St. Louisans pronounces it "fentan-OL;" many elsewhere say "fentan-IL." Jack keeps his beard trimmed and his muscles toned. He's a rare local who can adroitly navigate both parts of the sharply segregated metro area: the poorer, largely black area to the north, and the mostly white, wealthier area to the south. When he's in his largely white home-town in the St. Louis suburbs he seems to know everyone, talking up his glory days on the high school football team or debating the merits of various IPA beers, and he always knows how to address his audience, quick with pleasantries that feel genuine.

Jack has prison tattoos and disfigurations, including a scar across his forehead. He received it one night years back when he was desperate for heroin. He found himself on the wrong block, in the wrong part of town, and was pistol-whipped in the head. "I got caught slippin'," he said.

Sanders's story is dark and complicated. Growing up middle class, none of his siblings became addicted to drugs, and he had a stable, nuclear family. His father worked as an engineer, his mother as a cook. He had the support of family and a wide circle of friends. They got into mischief at concerts put on by Phish, the Vermont jam band beloved for its psychedelic guitarnoodling, which Jack and his friends followed on national tours during high school summers. Jack wore dreadlocks and drove his family's 1983 Dodge Caravan, outfitted with a pony keg and a bong. "We had like three other cars full of people," he said. "There was a posse of us, like a little gang. We all took care of each other."

The community was just as important as the music. Jack's friends began selling marijuana they had grown themselves, in shows' parking lots. It didn't feel risky; everyone was on drugs. Jack himself began experimenting: LSD, mushrooms, hashish, peyote, and even DMT. "My friends are jackasses," he recalled with a laugh. "They put DMT in a bowl and put weed on top of it so I couldn't see it. So I hit it, and I sunk into the couch. It was like taking twenty hits of acid. You turn white as a sheet."

Plenty of recreational drug enthusiasts never take the plunge from psychedelics into addictive and often destructive opiates. Jack isn't sure why he started taking heroin. "I think I had a hole in my heart, and I was trying to fill it," he said. He mentioned childhood abuse, but declined to go into specifics. "I had a lot of shit happen to me when I was young, so maybe I was trying to somehow suppress that. But, is that the reason why I did heroin? No. I liked to get high."

Heroin got him higher than any other drug he had previously tried. He discovered, however, that he could get even higher. Jack's country buddies from the distant outskirts of St. Louis first introduced him to fentanyl. By the early 2000s it was already being abused in pharmaceutical form, including by many low-income rural residents. "They had boxes and boxes of these fentanyl patches," he said. He'd put one on his chest, his legs, his shoulders, anywhere. Maybe two, three, or four to get an even bigger kick. "I'd be retarded."

Even after trying fentanyl, Jack preferred heroin. Many users do. One online commenter described heroin as more "soulful." "It's cleaner, the high," Sanders said. "Fentanyl makes you feel really dopey, drowsy. It will make you nod every time. It's more like anesthesia."

Heroin may have provided a better high, but it wasn't a better product. Fentanyl, it became clear, was the real moneymaker.

Just across the Mississippi River from St. Louis lies the largely white Illinois town of East Alton. It's also poor, but its poverty feels different. St. Louis is full of pretty, decaying red brick houses, but East Alton has more mobile home parks and graying one-story shacks crowned by non-operational satellite dishes. Dollar stores, title loan shops, and bars with slot machines line the commercial streets.

It's just one of many small municipalities that dot the east side of the Mississippi, which include tiny fiefdoms catering to industrial polluters and the increasingly depopulated hamlet of East St. Louis. Many St. Louisans don't cross into Illinois unless they're after vice: gambling at spots like the *Casino Queen* riverboat, or prostitution, which is run out of massage parlors and strip clubs. The area has also been overwhelmed by fentanyl, and the surrounding Madison County set its all-time annual record for drug overdose deaths in 2018. "Fentanyl has taken over as the drug that is killing people here," said county coroner Stephen Nonn. "When we go to a death scene and you still see the needle in the arm, we know it was fentanyl because it works that quick."

Bree and Mike are a couple from East Alton. Mike is the forklift operator who began using synthetic cannabinoids when he was being tested for marijuana. When I met them he wore red-tinted sunglasses and a small gauged earring in each ear. Bree had on blue nail polish, running shoes, and two tube tops, one orange and one pink.

They were sitting at a picnic table out in front of a retro-themed diner called Gwig's Family Restaurant, whose sign featured a clip-art photo of the perfect cheeseburger, below a wooden pallet attached to the building that read, "Proud to be an American." Bree and Mike walked here, since their car had broken down. Mike's dad had promised to get them a new one, so Mike would be able to work again. They said they would pay him back when they got their income tax return.

At that time, Bree was twenty-nine, Mike was thirty; both names are pseudonyms. Their last year had been a nightmare of drugs, poverty, betrayal, and rehabilitation attempts, all in the midst of trying to get their children to come out right. She had an eight-year-old boy and a nine-year-old girl, and on this day her tube tops showed off her bump. She was due in about six weeks with her first child with Mike, a girl. They already had a name picked out.

Though they both previously had problems with fentanyl, they pledged to quit once she realized she was pregnant. And they did, for two months. Then she relapsed.

"It was my first time ever relapsing straight to fentanyl," she said. "Couldn't get off it. Oh my gosh, nothing worked. It was the worst. And the baby, she moved so much for three days straight. She was going through it terrible with me. I was having muscle spasms in my arms, my legs. I would soak in the hot tub probably seven times a day, and still my legs would even ache in the hot tub. There was nothing that would help. You couldn't sleep at all, during the day or at night. It was horrible. I wish they would take it off the planet earth. It's the devil's drug, it really is."

"We pretty much lost everything to that drug," said Mike.

"We did," agreed Bree. "We hit rock bottom."

Bree and Mike both had experimented with plenty of drugs, and Bree initially knew a little bit about fentanyl, since her ex-mother-in-law was getting the patches prescribed. She never meant to try it, however. In fact, the first time, she didn't realize what she was taking. "I thought it was just regular heroin," she said. "Turned out it was fentanyl, and the high is amazing. It's like a Xanax and a pain pill mixed. It's an instant head and body buzz. It's unexplainable. It's almost like crack. I've never liked crack, but people say with crack you gotta keep doing it to keep that high. Well, that's how fentanyl and heroin is. You've got to keep doing it all day to keep your high."

Mike lighted up an Edgefield cigarette and gave her one. "With fentanyl," he said, "you *have* to have it —"

"— or you get deathly sick," Bree interrupted. "Say you do one in the morning, if you don't have one by that afternoon you're already sick. Within four to five hours."

Public-health studies show that most users don't want fentanyl; often, it's cut into the drug they actually want (heroin, meth, cocaine, or prescription pills). Other times they'll get fentanyl because nothing else is available, and they fear withdrawal. But according to the DEA's *2017 National Drug Threat Assessment,* the St. Louis area is a region where fentanyl has begun to displace heroin in much of the market: "This change is evidenced by fentanyl being sold as fentanyl and not disguised as heroin; a large opioid user base that actively seeks out fentanyl; an increase in fentanyl traffickers in the area; and a shift from overdose deaths caused by heroin/fentanyl combinations to overdose deaths caused by fentanyl alone."

Bree overdosed on fentanyl about two years ago, before she met Mike. Again, she wanted heroin, but her heroin dealer had been murdered, so she needed a new supplier. An East Alton friend referred her to a guy from St. Louis, so she drove across the river and met him in an alley, near North Kingshighway Boulevard. He seemed trustworthy enough; tall, lanky, and in his early thirties. The problem was that he didn't have heroin, he had only fentanyl. "I was just thinking it was a better high," Bree recalled. "I said, 'All right, let's get it.' "

She bought fifteen "beans" for seventy dollars; "beans" is slang for gelatin capsules full of powder, which is how fentanyl is mostly distributed in St. Louis, as opposed to baggies of powder or pressed pills, which are preferred in other regions. She then drove back across the river. But she didn't go home. Since she and her mother were having a fight, she was staying in nearby Granite City — where she and Mike are both from originally — at a hotel room her friend had rented. She settled in and got out her syringe. "I shot like two or three of the beans, and I was so high," she said. "I took a couple Xanaxes." But then she realized something distressing — her purse was missing. And so she and two friends who were also staying at the hotel hopped into her van and went out looking for it.

Bree was driving.

After a bit she pulled over, "to kind of regroup and think," parking in a QuikTrip gas station. She leaned her head on the steering wheel and promptly passed out. The fentanyl was much stronger than the heroin she usually took, and the combination with the Xanax pills was nearly lethal. This is a common way to overdose. Xanax is a member a class of drugs called benzodiazepines, which also includes Valium. Like opioids, benzodiazepines are sedatives, and the pair can be incredibly toxic in combination; rocker Tom Petty and rapper Lil Peep had both types of drug in their systems upon their deaths in the fall of 2017. Bestselling writer Michelle McNamara, author of *I'll Be Gone in the Dark: One Woman's Obsessive Search for the Golden State Killer,* also had benzodiazepines and opioids in her system upon her 2016 death — Xanax and fentanyl, both reportedly prescribed.

Bree's two friends, perhaps worried about police finding them with an overdose victim, hopped out of the car. Someone called 911. The first responders administered naloxone on Bree, the lifesaving miracle drug marketed as Narcan, which reverses opioid overdoses. Three doses were needed before she came to. "They shot the adrenaline

236

thing right there," she said, tapping her chest plate. "They broke my collarbone working on me." She woke up in Granite City's Gateway Regional Medical Center. When she was released she found her purse. A different friend had taken it. "She acted like somebody else stole it, but she had it the whole time at her house," Bree said. "It had $200 worth of Valium in there. That's why she stole it."

Even after this daunting experience, Bree wasn't finished with fentanyl, returning repeatedly to St. Louis. The vice economy across the Mississippi River runs both ways. While St. Louisans traverse it for naked flesh, east siders come into town for their heroin or fentanyl, which can be procured with remarkable ease. "As soon as you go over the McKinley Bridge, you stop at one of them gas stations," Bree said, adding that they tend to be prowled by dealers. "They'll come up to anybody who's parking, getting gas, even getting cigarettes. They'll drive up to you and ask if you mess around. They give it to you for free. They give you samples first. One time we were over there and got about twenty-four of them for free, from like ten different guys."

There's one condition, however. You must have a working cell phone and give them your number. Soon they'll be back in touch, ready to sell you your next batch. "They don't give you time to really do it," said Bree. "As soon as you pull off, they're like, 'How was it?'"

ELEVEN

high_as_fxck_GER is a drug dealer from Germany. Over the Dark Web, he sells magic mushrooms, DMT, and 25I-NBOMe, shipping out packages all over the globe. He clears about 500 euros per week from these sales, and once in a while a special order comes in worth many multiples of that.

He thinks his customers like N-bombs because they don't show up on drug tests, and he doesn't seem especially concerned about the health risks. "The deaths I heard about happened because people think it was lsd or cocaine and overdosed," he wrote me. "With safer use it is as safe as all other drugs."

In 2015, barely out of high school, he began selling hashish and marijuana on the street. His customers started asking about harder drugs, and so he started buying psychedelics off the Dark Web and selling

239

them in person. He was arrested by local police a couple of times, and his customers left, so he moved his business exclusively to the Dark Web. He doesn't use drugs himself, he said.

He worries about the police constantly, but enjoys the image and lifestyle of Dark Web dealing. With his earnings he was able to get a driver's license (which are very expensive in Germany) and a car.

His girlfriend knows about his profession, but she doesn't mind. "Maybe she love the bad boy style XD," he wrote, using the emoticon symbolizing uproarious laughter.

Much of the fentanyl sold in the United States comes into the country from Mexico, where China-synthesized chemicals are processed, cut with impurities, and packaged by Mexican cartels and sent up through border crossings. But that's not the case with different varieties (i.e., analogues) of fentanyl and other novel psychoactive substances (NPS). They are moved mainly through the Dark Web, a technology essential to the new drug economy. In an era when the National Security Agency has vast monitoring powers over American citizens, the Dark Web serves as a sort of a technological shield, allowing users and dealers to conduct transactions in relative confidence and anonymity.

high_as_fxck_GER was one of many Dark Web dealers I talked to, either by encrypted message, over e-mail, or in person. They discussed how their businesses operated, both on logistic and moral levels. They almost all trade in Bitcoin, the near-anonymous cyber currency. Logging onto the Dark Web is very easy to do, even on a smartphone, through the use of a browser called Tor, which disguises the user's IP address. The URLs of the Dark Web drug markets themselves — gobbledygook strings of numbers and letters — can be obtained from sites accessible on the surface web such as Deep Dot Web.

Many of these markets, and the vendors operating on them, run sophisticated and lucrative operations. A Brazilian vendor called Mr. Pills sells its wares on numerous markets, advertising itself as a "Worldwide Drug Service." Mr. Pills sends packages to customers anywhere, but doesn't offer refunds to people in the United States, Indonesia, Russia, Finland, or South Korea, likely because delivery is considered riskiest to those countries, owing to factors ranging from strength of law enforcement to severity of punishment.

Like many other drug vendors on the Dark Web, Mr. Pills seeks to set the minds of potential customers at ease, portraying its operations as professional and safe on its description page:

Who We Are? A clan of Brazilian traders with a mission to export the very best quality products for the most demanding customers in the world, with the maximum safety and ethical description. Why You Should Buy Here? Quality, in first place. We only commercialize products with over 9X% UP purity and without any additives or mixtures. We take very seriously the security. We have a long experience sending drugs. In those years, we adopted techniques anti-dog and imperceptibly x-ray guarantee, taking all safety and description in sending as possible.

Many emporiums are operated by skilled sales staff people who don't seem to have ethical qualms about what they are doing. An operator at a market called French Connection claimed the site is "good and honest," and he doesn't see any issues with selling fentanyl. "It is like morphine . . . if well diluted no more risk than other opiate."

A market called Majestic Garden specializes in psychedelics and has banned opioids and other drugs it believes are dangerous. Its community of users say they have a moral mission.

"We are not normal criminals," said one site regular who asked not to be named. "We are advocates of the prohibited psychedelic medicines and only do this illegally because since the late 1960's these medicines have been illegal. In all truth, humans have 1000s of years of history growing and learning from psychedelic medicines. We do not allow addictive drugs and are advocates of safe and responsible use of the psychedelic medicines offered. We are also advocates of the professional research of psychedelic medicines and eventual legalization."

In mid-2017 a Dark Web market called Hansa was suddenly shut down. Visitors saw this message:

The Dutch National Police have located Hansa Market and taken over control of this marketplace since June 20, 2017. We have modified the source code, which allowed us to capture passwords, PGP-encrypted order information, IP-addresses, Bitcoins and other relevant information that may help law enforcement agencies worldwide to identify users of this market-place.

Netherlands law enforcement had been working with the FBI as part of a sting called Operation Bayonet, which also seized AlphaBay a couple of weeks earlier. Alpha-Bay had grown to become the largest market on the Dark Web, selling drugs, stolen credit card numbers, and guns, and generating more than a billion dollars' worth of trans-actions. A phalanx of international agencies joined forces to take the market down, ar-resting a twenty-five-year-old Canadian, Alexandre Cazes, who was living in Thailand and was found dead in a Thai jail cell a week later. (Officials say he took his own life.)

As a result, paranoia swept Dark Web drug vendors, who nervously chatted in private and on message boards about the possibility of law enforcement officials lurking in the remaining markets. This perhaps partly explained why an American vendor I con-tacted wasn't initially anxious to talk. His clever web name was U4IA, and I first mes-saged him on a site called Wall St. Market, where I had seen one of his ads. "Novel Opioid. Limited quantity. 99.7% pure. $60g," it said.

I hoped to ease his mind by using an

encryption program called PGP, which encodes messages and makes them harder for law enforcement to read. *PGP* stands for "Pretty Good Privacy." I probably came on a bit strong, however, asking him how potent his opioids were and where he sourced them from.

"Your kind of making me leery with all your digging," he responded.

I apologized and explained that I was a journalist writing a book about new synthetic drugs — chemicals that imitate traditional drugs like heroin, marijuana, ecstasy, and LSD, except they are even more dangerous. If he were still willing to talk to me, I would really appreciate it.

To my surprise, he was. "I actually wouldn't mind a voice," he wrote. "I feel people like me are unfairly classified as degenerate scum. (Although many are.)"

Indeed, U4IA sells some incredibly powerful fentanyls, which he sources from Chinese labs. He agreed to speak over Wickr, a messaging app that is more secure than sending text messages. He bought a burner phone, specifically for the purpose of contacting me. Over the coming months, he told his story.

U4IA has been selling drugs on and off since age sixteen, mainly to pay for his own habits. Back then he was hooked on coke and meth, which made him do crazy things. One night he smoked crack and walked into a bar. "I saw some dude dancing on my ex and didn't say a word just walked over and cleaned his clock," he wrote. Another time he and some associates robbed a crack dealer in the crack dealer's own house. Eventually U4IA's crimes caught up with him, and he did more than a year for robbery.

The stimulants made him feel paranoid and antisocial. But then he discovered synthetic opioids. Out of curiosity, he tried one called U-47700 — originally created by Upjohn in the mid-1970s as a morphine alternative, it never received FDA approval — and everything changed. It was like an "antidepressant," he said. "I felt whole, confident, and happy, very little stress."

Soon he was fully addicted, adding to a stressful existence that also included a mortgage, child support for two kids, and about $10,000 in debt. His day job didn't cover everything. "I promised I wouldn't let my drug addiction cause my children to live in poverty," he said.

The Dark Web offered him a chance to move beyond selling marijuana and Molly to local kids. "There's more money, obviously, in a global market than a small-town market," he said.

U4IA hesitated at first when I asked to meet him in person. He didn't know that I wasn't a cop. But as our Wickr conversation entered its third month, I learned something new: he was a hip-hop fan. As the author of two books about rap music, it was a subject I could talk about. I sent him clippings about my latest, *Original Gangstas,* a biography of West Coast rappers like N.W.A and Tupac Shakur.

"Did Suge Knight kill Tupac?" he asked, referencing the owner of Tupac's record label.

"Nah," I said. "It was almost certainly the guy Tupac beat up that night, Orlando Anderson, or a member of his crew."

Somehow, this bit of insight won him over. He insisted I couldn't mention his location, or his real name, which sounded reasonable. He sent me the name of his town, which was driving distance from mine. And then, separately, he sent the location where we would meet. Our rendezvous was set for the next day, at 1:45 p.m., at a burger chain called Culver's.

The leaves on the trees ringing Culver's parking lot were just starting to turn when U4IA emerged from his truck in the parking lot: he had bulging muscles under his white T-shirt, camo pants, and piercing eyes. I was surprised to see he was carrying his baby daughter. She wore overalls, with big eyes and a smile.

We went inside, and he picked the most remote booth available, away from the largely elderly crowd. Sitting in a high chair, his daughter was in a great mood, giggling when he teased her with a french fry and pulled it away as she grabbed for it.

We spoke in hushed tones and soon got down to business. He told me that in the past he'd sold fentanyl, U-47700, and carfentanil, and had recently started selling methoxyacetylfentanyl, a fentanyl analogue also known as MAF. He had been selling this new product for only a few days but had already made a couple thousand dollars. Procuring it was remarkably easy. He hadn't even needed the Dark Web. All he had to do was search on a Chinese surface-web site called Weiku.com, which is based in Hangzhou and sells everything from household items to illicit chemicals. Immediately, a long list of vendors had popped up. He picked one, and they made a one-off deal: $500 for fifty grams of MAF, which was legal in China.

They spoke English in their communications, and the package arrived soon in the mail. Completely inconspicuous, it resembled a household cleaner, along the lines of Ajax. "It looked like you could pull it off a store shelf," he said. "You'd have to open it up to really see what was in there." (A Weiku representative told the *New York Times* that fentanyl wasn't permitted to be sold on the site, but that sellers got around this by slightly changing the search term.)

The product was extremely potent. To make a nasal spray solution — a popular method for ingesting some opioids — he needed only tiny crumbs of the drug, 0.001 grams per milliliter of water, he said, plucking a couple crumbs off his burger bun and placing them on the table to illustrate. When he sells it on the Dark Web, he charges sixty dollars for a five milliliter bottle. One spray, he said, is the equivalent of one OxyContin pill. It's an incredible markup; at that ratio, $500 worth of product could potentially make him $600,000, though he said he had made only about $2,000 so far.

His nasal sprayer was a small white bottle with a custom-made label reading: "Alpha Prescription Strength Nasal Cleanser and Decongestant." Below, in smaller letters, it said:

*Shake vigorously before each use and

keep out of reach of children.

It resembled a common drugstore product. For his addiction, he said, he uses his nasal spray every four hours or so. He needs a hit to be able get out of bed in the morning. Without it, he couldn't go to work to support his daughters, he said. He sees what he is doing as a public service for addicted users. "It's substantially cheaper for an opiate addict than supporting your habit other ways," he said. "By offering a cost-friendly solution, it keeps a user from committing crimes that hurt the innocent."

As he elaborates on his Dark Web page: "We should not have to spend 100s everyday just to get by and live a normal life because of an addiction that was put on a lot of us by the government or big pharma," referring to pharmaceutical companies that downplayed addiction risks while drawing billions in profit.

It is hard not to feel sympathy for his argument and for those with crippling, expensive addictions. However, U4IA's nasal sprays are high risk, argues the moderator of an online forum devoted to fentanyl, who asked that his name not be used. Properly preparing a fentanyl analogue nasal spray is extremely complicated, requiring compounds barely visible to the eye to be measured using a process called volumetric dosing, which requires them to be dissolved in liquid.

"People who are buying the spray assume that this person has the expertise to make a spray that won't kill them," the moderator wrote. "With pharmaceuticals, that expertise is well regulated, but . . . here there is no regulation, no quality control, and therefore if you buy this product you must absolutely trust this random stranger not to kill you. I don't know about you, but there is no way I would ever put that much trust in another individual."

"If it's not safe [I] will be the first one to hit the ground," said U4IA, when I relate the concerns of the moderator of the online fentanyl forum. "Because it is all tested not with equipment but with willing human subjects, [myself] included."

Many Dark Web dealers receive their Chinese NPS through a third-party intermediary, the same way Portland fentanyl kingpin Brandon Hubbard got his from Quebec prisoner Daniel Vivas Ceron, for example. Some, however, purchase their chemicals directly from connections in China, including one named Desifelay1000, a dealer whom I met on the now-defunct Dark Web site Pyramid.

Desifelay1000 comes from an Eastern European country he prefers not to mention and now lives in an eastern US city he prefers not to name. He loves Mary J. Blige, *Grey's Anatomy,* and playing soccer, and has a wry sense of humor. After being told that, owing to journalistic ethics, I couldn't pay him for an interview or buy his carfentanil, he responded, "I don't care about ethics. I'm a drug dealer."

He grew up fast, first trying China White when he was a teenager in New York. He began selling drugs on the street and went to jail for a stretch. Now in his late twenties, he started selling carfentanil and ketamine powder on a handful of Dark Web sites in 2016. Carfentanil, the veterinary tranquilizer that is one hundred times more potent than fentanyl, is measured in micrograms, and a nonlethal amount can barely be seen. He wouldn't go into the specifics of how he prepares the highly potent drug for sale, but said he chooses to sell carfentanil because a little goes a long way. "It is expensive and a single sale put much money in my hands," he said, adding that a gram starts at $800 and that his average order is about three grams.

He wakes up at 3:30 a.m. to facilitate sales

from Europe and countries farther east. He gets orders from all over the world and will sell to almost anyone, although not if they are from Indonesia, as he finds its drug punishments particularly draconian: drug traffickers there can be sentenced to death. The Dark Web is more lucrative than street dealing, and products sell faster, he noted, but he's constantly worried that one of his buyers will be a DEA agent in disguise.

He does a brisk business. "You know about Bitcoins? That is the best means of payment but I also do Paypal, Moneygram and Western Union," he said. He even accepts cash. Payment is required before delivery, and once he has the money in hand he can get the product to US customers within twenty-four to thirty hours, he brags.

He employs four people. "The most important characteristic for a successful worker is honesty, 'cause I can't exactly take my case to court," he said. "They're mostly people formerly in the same line of business. Three have records." While a criminal past might be disqualifying for many jobs, Desifelay1000 actually prefers it. Someone who is "compromised" — in violation of their parole, for example — is less likely to go to the cops.

Two of his employees are stationed far

afield, in Europe and Africa, where they do cash pickups in their specific regions. But most of his clients are from the United States. "Multiracial, every gender, mostly rich," he said, when asked to characterize his customers. "You will be surprised how many rich people use the product. I mean it ain't cheap."

He noted that one regular client, "a really rich man in Ohio," said he is suffering from AIDS, and that carfentanil brings him pain relief.

The practice of shipping dangerous drugs through the mail — which is used by Desife lay1000, U4IA, high_as_fxck_GER, and countless other DarkWeb dealers — is both brazen and common.

US Customs has made intercepting drug packages sent in the mail a top priority, recently increasing international mail facility staffing by 20 percent. In October 2018 the United States announced it was withdrawing from an international postal agreement allowing for inexpensive shipments from China, which the Trump administration said helped facilitate fentanyl sales.

With the help of sniffer dogs and advanced technology, including "lasers" that can scan unopened packages for specific drugs, more and more packages of NPS are being caught. And yet, considering more than 400 million international packages arrive in the United States every year, checking each one for drugs is logistically impossible. Customs intercepts only a tiny fraction.

Almost no one doubts that China is the starting point for most of these packages, a judgment underscored by the fact that when China schedules a drug, seizures in America plummet, a correlation that doesn't hold true when the United States or the United Nations schedules a drug.

Chinese officials, however, remain skeptical. "China doesn't deny that shipments to the U.S. happen, but there isn't the proof to show how much — whether it's 20 percent or 80 percent," Yu Haibin, director of precursor chemical control of China's Narcotics Control Commission, said in December 2017. He added that American officials had sent him information on only a half dozen fentanyl packages in the previous year.

A US Senate subcommittee report released in 2018 focused on six specific Chinese online sellers. They used shipping companies like FedEx and UPS to send $230,000 worth of fentanyls directly to American homes. When the markup was considered, the resale value of the drugs was in the hundreds of millions, the report stated.

The report found that it is extraordinarily easy to order and receive these chemicals from China, but determining who is sending them is difficult. The US Postal Service receives what is known as "advanced electronic data" — including the sender's name and address — from about half the packages sent from China to America. But many Chinese bundles are diverted through other countries before being sent on to the United States, a process known as "transshipment." These packages still go through customs, but because they do not come directly from China, sellers believe they are less likely to be scrutinized.

China has pledged to aid the United States in this matter. The country has a long way to go, according to anecdotal accounts. A Chinese synthetic-marijuana dealer named GN, who operates on a social media app popular in China called WeChat, said that sending drugs through the Chinese mail is easy, even when identification is necessary. "We have our people in the postal companies. They are pretty loose with the security."

Shanghai-based reporter Erika Kinetz

spoke not long ago to a new synthetic-drugs dealer who said he and his associates "lie to customs all the time." Getting packages through was a breeze, he told her. "They would have the paperwork filled out really badly. Or they'd use an English name instead of a Chinese name, so then that person becomes basically untraceable. Or they'd only put a family name. And it's like, 'Oh, Mr. Wang, great. How are we going to find him?' " One "fail-safe" delivery option, vendors told her, was EMS, a service of the state-owned China Post.

Desifelay1000 gets his carfentanil from China. He hooked up with his current supplier through referrals — consumers of the drug he knew from the United States — and traveled to China himself to seal the deal. There, he met his "conduit," a man paid a fee for making the introduction to a supplier. The conduit spoke a little English and served as his translator. Eventually he was taken to the supplier's lab. It was disguised, in an isolated area. Some Chinese labs produce both legitimate and illegal drugs, but this one made only illegal ones, he said, for markets in the United States, India, and Europe. The supplier claimed the carfentanil was top quality, and Desifelay1000 sampled a tiny quantity himself to be sure. He was satisfied, and they agreed to do business together.

He left the country with a positive feeling, and since then has found everyone he's worked with from China to be a good business partner. He trusts these partners more "than our own compatriots," he said. "The trust level with the Chinese is higher. I believe it is because they are poorer and generally really wanna sell, unlike Americans, most of whom are scammers."

A kilo of carfentanil from Chinese wholesalers can be bought for around $3,000, which breaks down to $3 per gram. Considering Desifelay1000 sells a gram for $800, his profit ratio is extremely high. But things became more complicated for him in March, 2017, when, under pressure from the United States, China scheduled carfentanil, along with three other fentanyl analogues. This spooked Desifelay1000's supplier. "Transportation within China is much more difficult now," he said. "They are quite worried about being caught." The takedown of behemoth Dark Web market AlphaBay in July 2017 affected him too, wiping out 25 percent of his sales, he estimated, and China's recent pledge to crack down on fentanyl analogues also worried some of his suppliers. But business remains profitable.

"I know I am harming some people," he admitted. "I am not proud of it. I really just do this for cash. I ain't stupid but I gotta make a living." He wouldn't say whether any of his clients had overdosed.

He hopes to transition to another career someday, something legitimate. Maybe he'll enlist in computer-training classes. For now, the job places huge stress upon him — the fear of prison, and the difficulties that come with living a double life. He tells most people he works in construction. There are very few who know his real story. "If I get caught then it is jail time," he said. "I trust no one."

TWELVE

Jack Sanders's efforts helped make St. Louis a fentanyl hot spot. Before anyone had heard of the drug, he saw it land in St. Louis.

Even as he descended into addiction, Jack maintained his football player's physique and his mental acumen, remaining alert and engaged through classes at a local community college, where he received a degree in personal training, traits that made him valuable to a friend named Marcus. He and Marcus had known each other for years, since Marcus was peddling heroin to high school kids. In the early 2000s Marcus was a high roller, one with contacts to a Mexican cartel and a sophisticated operation for ordering and receiving shipments of cocaine, marijuana, meth, and heroin. Jack heard Marcus communicating with his Mexican contacts over disposable burner phones. They used a complicated code, one that didn't even sound like English.

Jack needed to feed his heroin addiction. For Marcus he could serve as muscle, as protection. He knew how to operate a pistol and an automatic rifle and wasn't afraid to pull the trigger. And so Marcus began bringing Sanders along on his exchanges. His pay was all the heroin he could use.

Before leaving for a pickup, they would rent a car and put the drug payment money in the trunk. Jack sometimes drove and sometimes was "on the stick," carrying the firepower. They would pilot over the bridge into East St. Louis, Illinois, and stop at a mammoth travel plaza, such as the Pilot Flying J on State Route 203. With fast-food restaurants and public showers, the plaza is a favorite of long-haul drivers. There, Jack and Marcus would meet their counterparts, Mexicans or Mexican Americans who had come up Interstate 44 from Texas, through Oklahoma. East St. Louis was just a stop-over; the bulk of their orders were bound for Chicago.

The two crews simply exchanged keys and hopped in each other's car. Now the Mexicans had the cash, and the St. Louisans had bales of drugs in the trunk. This was the stressful part, the drive back across the river with enough contraband to put everyone

261

away for life, without parole. Marcus might be driving, Jack might be in the back seat with a machine gun, and they might have another partner along as well. They tried not to betray their nerves and were in agreement about one thing: they weren't stopping, even for police. "There was enough firepower in the car to put up a good fight," Sanders said. "So if it was a couple patrol cars, I told the fellas, 'We shoot the engines out, we shoot the tires out, we don't shoot the cops, unless we have to.'"

They would wait until they got back to open the exchange car's trunk and examine their haul. At first, the Mexicans' packages contained heroin, cocaine, meth, and marijuana. But sometime in the middle of the first decade of the 2000s — Jack doesn't remember the exact year — his crew started receiving a new product in their orders. These were smaller, vacuum-sealed bags that they had never seen before. The mysterious packages — which they hadn't ordered or paid for — were simply labeled "F."

Jack had experimented with fentanyl patches with his country friends, but he had never seen anything like this. It was not prescription-grade fentanyl but a white powder, so bright that it looked unnatural. Unlike their dark gray heroin, this fentanyl was the color of a napkin at a fancy restaurant. "White as snow and fluffy," recalled Jack.

The Mexicans communicated to Marcus and his crew what this new substance was all about. "Listen, you need this stuff," they said. Much cheaper than heroin, it would increase their profits, by making stepped-on heroin seem pure.

Marcus wasn't so sure. His business was booming, and he wasn't crazy about messing with a good thing. Jack, however, listened carefully when his crew was taught how to mix the fentanyl with heroin. The process wasn't exactly rocket science. It simply required a standard household item, a coffee-bean grinder. Not just any coffee grinder, though. A Mr. Coffee brand grinder was preferred, owing to its low-slung blades, which helped produce a more consistent grind. Of course, since fentanyl is so potent, this was far from a safe method — either for the person doing the mixing or for the person doing the consuming. Jack didn't know that at the time, however.

What he did know was that for each bit of this new powder added to the heroin, the more profitable the sale would be. They initially settled on a ratio of about one part fentanyl for every seven parts heroin. Just enough to give it some kick. They combined the powders, put them into the grinder, blended them together, and immediately had a much stronger, and cheaper, heroin product. At least in those first years, the customers seemed to like it, and it wasn't killing people. The Mexicans were really onto something, Jack had to admit.

"Somebody," he said, "had figured out that it was the perfect cut."

The drug's popularity grew. When illicit fentanyl began coming onto the market in serious quantities during the first half of the 2010s, some American drug dealers — those with web savvy, like Brandon Hubbard in Portland, Oregon — began buying it over the surface Internet or the Dark Web. Others, however, started receiving it from Mexican cartels, in huge quantities.

It was an outgrowth of the heroin trade. Whereas Afghanistan and Southeast Asia supply much of the world's heroin — and until the end of the twentieth century Colombia supplied the most to the United States — today, more than 90 percent of heroin in America comes from Mexico, according to DEA estimates.

The Mexican cartels have flooded major American cities like New York, Los Angeles, and Chicago with heroin, as well as other areas with established Mexican immigrant communities. But their traditional territories exclude great swaths of the American map, a situation that was exploited by individual, unaffiliated Mexican cells beginning in the 1990s. As detailed in Sam Quinones's book about the opiate epidemic, *Dreamland,* traffickers from the small Mexican county of Xalisco fanned out around the United States, largely in previously underserved markets like Nashville, Tennessee, and Boise, Idaho. Eschewing guns, violence, and ostentatious displays of wealth, dealers handed out business cards at methadone clinics, sat around waiting for a call, and then delivered products right to customers' doors, like pizza. "Guys from Xalisco had figured out that what white people — especially middle-class white kids — want most is service, convenience," Quinones wrote. "They didn't want to go to skid row or some seedy dope house to buy their drugs. Now they didn't need to. The guys from Xalisco would deliver it to them."

As the prescription-pill crisis began to emerge, both the Xalisco dealers and the cartels ramped up their heroin-trafficking efforts, reducing prices and providing an alternative to costly prescriptions. When people's OxyContin supplies ran out, they turned to heroin. Whereas US heroin deaths hovered around two thousand annually for decades, in the early 2010s the number shot up, reaching sixteen thousand by 2017 (the most recent year for which statistics were available).

Heroin made countless millions of dollars for Mexican distributors and continues to be extremely profitable, but it eventually became clear that it was an imperfect product from a business perspective, because it is expensive to produce. The opium poppy prefers a warm and mild climate, like that found in the Sierra Madre Occidental mountain range, which runs through the region of Mexico's dominant cartel, Sinaloa. Plants take about three months to bloom. Beyond the cost and time needed for cultivation, poppy fields' visibility makes them an easy target for law enforcement. Once the heroin is refined, traffickers face the added problem of transporting a bulky product across a heavily guarded border.

A Mexican cartel called Jalisco Nueva Generation was reportedly the first to sell fentanyl, and the biggest cartel, Sinaloa, followed quickly thereafter. Fentanyl's chemicals are cheap to buy from China, and fentanyl is much easier to bring northward, either by itself or mixed with drugs like heroin or meth, because quantities are smaller. Fentanyl is "the most profitable drug the Mexican cartels are trafficking," wrote former US State Department special agent Scott Stewart, an expert on the transnational criminal drug trade, for the global intelligence firm Stratfor. "Smuggling 1 kilogram of fentanyl into the United States is, from a dosage standpoint, essentially the same as smuggling in 50 kilograms of heroin."

"The cartels realize that fentanyl is much more profitable than heroin," said James Hunt, the leader of the DEA's New York division. "These guys are evil businessmen, but they are still businessmen. I don't know of any other product where you could invest $3,000 and make millions."

Sinaloa was for many years led by kingpin Joaquín Guzmán, known as El Chapo (Shorty). Beginning in the mid-1960s, when he was only nine, Guzmán said, he cultivated marijuana and poppy plants in the mountains of western Mexico's Sinaloa region, adding that he, like many others, turned to the drug trade out of poverty. "The only way to have money to buy food, to survive, is to grow poppy, marijuana," he told actor Sean Penn in a rare interview for *Rolling Stone* shortly before his early 2016 capture. Sinaloa and other cartels first rose to great fortune with cocaine in the 1980s, and Sinaloa also trafficked huge amounts of meth, marijuana, and heroin. El Chapo's influence surpassed even that of fabled Colombian drug lord Pablo Escobar, who was killed in 1993 by Colombian police, assisted by the American DEA. The United States represented El Chapo's largest market, but Canada was also targeted for what the cartel believed to be inferior law enforcement, and Sinaloa earned millions per day there on heroin and cocaine sales.

Sinaloa and the other cartels' illegal operations and turf wars have led to increasingly grisly killings and a rising death toll that has destabilized entire Mexican regions. More than thirty-three thousand people were murdered in Mexico in 2018, the most on record. Fueled by cash from American drug consumers, the cartels have corrupted government and police throughout the country, and El Chapo and others have become folk heroes in cities and the impoverished Mexican countryside, supplying medicine to the sick and Christmas presents to children.

Six months after escaping from a Mexican prison, El Chapo was recaptured in January, 2016, and a year later was extradited to the United States. At a Brooklyn federal courthouse, his trial began in November 2018. El Chapo was accused of trafficking more than four hundred thousand pounds of cocaine and making $14 billion in total drug sales, as well as murdering and torturing rivals and ordering *sicarios* (hitmen) to do the same. Prosecutors were armed with his own quotes from his *Rolling Stone* interview with Sean Penn to use against him.

"I supply more heroin, methamphetamine, cocaine and marijuana than anybody else in the world," he told Penn. Absent from his statement was fentanyl, though by the time of his trial Sinaloa was distributing more of it than any other cartel. The extent of the operation came into focus with a December 2018 raid in Mexico City, which uncovered a fentanyl operation inside a building of the Azcapotzalco municipal government, allegedly run by the Sinaloa cartel.

New York is the cartel's central US distribution point, meaning that El Chapo's legal defense may have been "funded in part with profits from fentanyl sales made just a few miles from his cell," noted the *Washington Post*. In February, 2019, he was found guilty on all of his 10 charges, each concerning drug trafficking.

The fentanyl sold by the Mexican cartels comes from Chinese manufacturers, which provide the cartels with both finished fentanyl and precursors — the chemical ingredients necessary to make fentanyl. "The Chinese role is that of a facilitator to Mexican and Latin American organized crime activities," said Robert J. Bunker, adjunct research professor at the US Army War College. Most commonly, the fentanyl and precursors arrive from China via shipping containers on boats that dock in Mexican ports. When it's finished, fentanyl is then usually brought into America on land in vehicles, through official border crossing.

The volumes arriving to Mexico from China can be enormous. In May 2015 Chinese customs agents seized one hundred pounds of fentanyl and more than fifty pounds of its analogue acetylfentanyl — enough to potentially kill millions of people — stashed in a Mexico-bound container. "Six customs officials became ill and one fell into a coma as a result of handling the fentanyls," reported the DEA, adding that great pains had been taken to obscure its specific origination point. "The fentanyls had been transferred through five different freight forwarders before arriving at customs."

"It's near impossible to stop these drugs, because they are so easy to smuggle in shipping containers," said University of Pittsburgh professor Phil Williams, an expert on international organized crime and terror.

Big ports are complex hubs of activity that resemble small cities. Searching every container would be impossible, and even when the containers are searched, the drugs are often well disguised or hidden. Port security protocol is sometimes circumvented altogether, as international criminal organizations, including drug cartels and Chinese organized crime groups called triads, use their own boats to bring the drugs from shore to shore. Still, "those that control Mexico's ports are in the best position to benefit from the fentanyl trade," wrote former US State Department special agent Scott Stewart.

Though Mexican ports have been taken over by the Mexican navy in recent years, the cartels maintain a strong influence there. Many drug shipments dispatch from Hong Kong, and Mexico's Sinaloa cartel has laundered vast amounts of drug money in the city's banks. But it was the shipment of a much-larger item through Hong Kong in 2016 — tanks — that underscored how hard it is to slow the NPS trade. Nine armored military vehicles were en route from Taiwan to Singapore, using a Hong Kong container terminal as a transit point, when China — which considers Singapore an ally and Taiwan a renegade province — discovered what was going on. China was outraged. "These shipments were going on for years and years," said Jean-François Tremblay, former Hong Kong-based senior correspondent for *Chemical & Engineering News.* "Nobody knew about it. And Hong Kong's part of China. And those were *tanks*!" If tanks go unnoticed in ports, much smaller drug shipments are almost impossible to stop.

The US Justice Department has designated the cartels Jalisco Nueva Generation and Sinaloa among the world's top five "transnational organized crime threats." Based in the southern Mexican state of Jalisco, which borders the Pacific Ocean, Jalisco Nueva Generation — not to be confused with the heroin traffickers out of Xalisco — is the second-most-powerful Mexican cartel. Traditionally best known for making meth, it has become a big player in fentanyl as well. "It's easier to sidestep into fentanyl, because they already had corruption networks set up at the ports and contacts set up with China," said Mexico City journalist Deborah Bonello.

Fentanyl isn't usually made from scratch by the cartels; they seem to lack access to skilled chemists capable of this synthesis. Instead, they receive the precursor chemicals from China, which they finish themselves in cartel labs, a relatively simple process. "Fentanyl can be produced anywhere a laboratory can be set up, such as a warehouse in an industrial park, a home in a residential area or a clandestine lab in the mountains," wrote Scott Stewart. The cartels then cut the fentanyl, a time-tested method used by traffickers to increase profits. Fentanyl is cut with many different powders; common cutting agents include caffeine, quinine, or antihistamines like Benadryl, the latter of which causes drowsiness and gives users the "nod," associated with high-quality heroin. (As with quinine, Benadryl can cause dangerous cardiac arrhythmia.) This cut fentanyl is then sent across the border, or cut into other drugs before being sent north.

Fentanyl augments the cartels' traditional

drug business, though there isn't much indication yet that they are greatly involved with NPS like fentanyl analogues or synthetic cannabinoids.

The cartels' foray into fentanyl mirrors their earlier move into meth. In the same way fentanyl's illicit rise was driven by doctors overprescribing opioids, meth's fortunes were also shaped by US drugstore politics.

As methamphetamine addiction rates accelerated in America in the 1990s, the drug was largely manufactured in clandestine domestic labs emitting toxic smells, often miles away from civilization. The chemists' preferred precursor to make meth was pseudoephedrine, the decongestant found in cold medicine. Buying up armfuls of Sudafed at Walmarts, CVS stores, and small-town drugstores, they harvested the pseudoephedrine. The Combat Methamphetamine Epidemic Act of 2005 stymied this practice, however, regulating the sale of these cold medicines and putting drugs like Sudafed behind the counter, requiring the purchaser to show ID.

As a result, meth production operations shifted largely to Mexican labs, run by cartels. Pseudoephedrine sales were regulated in Mexico as well, but China helped supply the cartels with both pseudoephedrine and another meth precursor known as P2P. In 2007 police found $205 million cash in the Mexico City home of a trafficker named Zhenli Ye Gon, who confessed to supplying the Sinaloa cartel with large amounts of meth precursors. During one six-week stretch five years later, Mexican police seized nine hundred tons of these precursor chemicals.

Meth remains an enormous business for the cartels, one that has been expanding in recent years. In August 2018, Mexican police seized fifty tons of meth from a Sinaloan mountain lab. Accordingly, a meth-overdose crisis has begun accelerating again in the United States.

The Mexican-Chinese alliance extends well beyond the drugs themselves. It includes everything from cartel-smuggled sea cucumbers — an overfished Chinese delicacy prized for its anti-inflammatory qualities and purported ability to boost the male libido — to complicated systems of money laundering. Some of these schemes involve cryptocurrency, some are designed to take advantage of NAFTA tax loopholes, and some involve illegal mining and clothing resale operations. For example, in one scheme, after cartel drugs are sold in the

United States, the resulting dollars are "washed" in the Los Angeles fashion district, used to buy inexpensive clothing made in China. The clothes are then taken to Mexico and because of NAFTA are not subject to tariffs that would have applied if they had come from China. The clothes are then resold in Mexican shops, and the cartels have washed their money, which is now in pesos and no longer tied to drug transactions.

"Hundreds of millions of dollars in goods transit the U.S. from China and go to Mexico through fraud to facilitate trade-based money laundering, undermine Mexico's tax base, and supply TCN [transnational criminal networks] with income," according to *Small Wars Journal.* "Further, China is in effect facilitating a multibillion-dollar income stream to the Mexican TCN and absorbing billions in illicit funds from U.S. customers of Mexican drugs, the precursors for which are supplied by China."

Money-laundering schemes are used in Canada as well, where the fentanyl epidemic is also at crisis levels. In 2018 the *Globe and Mail* uncovered one scheme involving fentanyl traffickers who granted loans to Chinese people who owned property in Canada. The borrowers sent loan payments to the lenders' accounts in China, which were then used to buy more fentanyl to ship back to Canada.

"For crime kingpins," wrote Canada's *Global News* in November 2018, fentanyl "has become a source of such astonishing wealth that it has disrupted the Vancouver-area real estate market."

THIRTEEN

Illicit fentanyl is sometimes made in the United States. It sometimes comes into the country on planes or boats. Most commonly, however, it enters in one of three ways: through the mail, from China; across the border, from Canada; or across the border, from Mexico.

Fentanyl and analogues arriving via postal carriers directly from China tend to be of the highest purity — 90 percent or higher. Most fentanyl analogues used in America, as well as most other NPS and fentanyl precursors, originate from mail shipments from China. Much of Canada's fentanyl arrives in the mail from China, and some of that is smuggled across the US border, which is more open than the US's border with Mexico.

While the majority of the pure, uncut fentanyl arriving to the United States comes from China in the mail, the majority of fentanyl by weight enters the U.S. from Mexico, either as pressed pills, in powder form, or mixed into other drugs. This fentanyl from Mexico is adulterated, and already contains a cutting agent like caffeine, quinine, or Benadryl. Its purity is thus much lower. According to the DEA, fentanyl seized at the US border with Mexico averages about 7 percent purity (which, of course, is still plenty strong enough to do major damage).

The cartels' fentanyl business is still in its nascent stage, said Mike Vigil, a retired DEA chief of international operations, who worked in Mexico. He believes that in the coming years an even larger percentage of US fentanyl will come from Mexico. "With any enterprise that is getting into another line of business, it doesn't happen overnight, but it's just a question of time before they dominate that market," he said. "They already have the existing distribution channels. I think more cartels will be involved, as well as criminal groups that aren't necessarily cartels but will see the money involved."

Having campaigned on a border wall to slow illegal immigration, as president, Donald Trump contended a wall would help abate the opioid crisis, but experts doubted that assertion, because the majority of fentanyl arriving from Mexico comes through the forty-eight official port of entry border crossings. These wholesale packages of fentanyl are most often concealed in vehicles — stashed in secret panels or in gas tanks, often alongside legitimate cargo like produce — and brought through official border crossings into California, Arizona, New Mexico, and Texas. Some is carried through secret, elaborately engineered underground passages, with sophisticated lighting and ventilation systems. El Chapo masterminded the first such tunnel, between Tijuana and San Diego, in 1989. The aboveground crossing between those two areas remains the favorite of his Sinaloa cartel and its rivals, judging by the quantities of drug seizures. In December 2017, a nineteen-year-old college student from Tijuana was caught trying to smuggle seventy-eight pounds of fentanyl in his car through the San Ysidro border crossing in San Diego. He was sentenced to seven years in prison. In August 2018, a thirty-nine-year-old US citizen living in Tijuana named Fernando Jesus Peraza was discovered with more than twenty thousand fentanyl pills at the San Ysidro crossing. He pled guilty.

As fentanyl use has increased, the drug is

being seized more often. While customs officials seized only about 1 kilogram of fentanyl in 2013, that number rose to 674 kilograms in 2017, the most recent year for which statistics were available. In August 2017, American officials found what looked like thirty thousand oxycodone pills in a vehicle outside Tempe, Arizona; they were actually fentanyl pills and reportedly a product of the Sinaloa cartel. Just a week later Mexican officials seized 140 pounds of fentanyl powder inside a truck rig in Sonora, just yards south of the border near Yuma, Arizona, along with another thirty thousand fentanyl pills. In January, 2019, 115 kg of fentanyl was seized by the US Customs and Border Protections from a truck at the Nogales, Arizona, border crossing, in what the agency described as the largest fentanyl bust in history.

Once the fentanyl arrives in the United States, it gets sent inland to mid-level regional distributors, to be broken down into smaller packages. "We're the main stopping point for the majority of Sinaloa cartel drugs that come across," said Doug Coleman, of the DEA, referencing Arizona. "They come to Phoenix or Tucson first, then a piece of them is shipped to meet local market, and the rest is shipped off to the rest of the United States." The drivers aren't usually official cartel members, but often Mexican American subcontractors who are in the United States legally. They take the drugs to other parts of the country using similar routes for cocaine and heroin, but fentanyl is much easier to transport, owing to its small size. "Law enforcement is set up to find volume," said journalist Deborah Bonello, an expert on Mexican drug cartels. "They're not going to tear up a vehicle to find a tiny quantity. I think that's something the cartels are hip to and they exploit."

St. Louis County drug enforcement detective Ricardo Franklin described elaborate schemes used by dealers to transport the drugs across country. "If state troopers are running interdiction, the dealers might have a car with a very large package and then another decoy car with a small package. The car with the smaller package will make a silly maneuver to get the officer's attention and get pulled over, so the car with the larger amount can carry on."

These shipments are driven to major cities like New York, Los Angeles, and Chicago, with stops along the way in satellites like St. Louis. There, they are subdivided further and farmed out to regional and mid-level traffickers, who tend to have gang affiliations. Some Sinaloa cartel members are moving into American neighborhoods, to broaden their business and exert more control over supply chains. In June 2017, Omar Zeus Rodriguez, a Sinaloa native believed to be tied to that region's cartel, was arrested by New Jersey State Police with five kilograms of fentanyl in his Range Rover; he lived on a quiet street in a New Jersey town called Willingboro, outside Philadelphia. "They're in sleepy towns," said Larry Williams, a New Jersey State Police detective, speaking of cartel members living in New Jersey. "They'd rather be in a Willingboro or another place where they can't be robbed or can't be found. They want to blend into their surroundings." Despite the cartels' reputation for bloody warfare in Mexico, they understand that violence doesn't play in the United States. "They're smart," said Jimmy Arroyo, a DEA special agent working to disrupt Mexican drug trafficking. "They know that if they kill people, they will attract attention."

In more rural communities that don't have traditional gang structures, the regional distributors might be more like extended families. "Places like West Virginia have these relatively new distribution gangs, where it's a family that operates it, and the members usually have opioid-use disorders," said Mario Moreno, former press secretary for the White House Office of National Drug Control Policy. "They maintain their habit while selling fentanyl on the streets."

After the fentanyl arrives to the mid-level regional distributors, it is divided up again for local dealers, who sell it directly to customers. This is where Jack Sanders came in.

Having been convinced fentanyl was a moneymaker, Marcus and Jack continued accepting more packages of the powder from the Mexicans, along with their usual shipments. These bundles were no longer free but still a good deal. Whereas a gram of heroin might have cost eighty dollars, they paid a maximum of only forty dollars for a gram of fentanyl. After combining the fentanyl and the heroin in the Mr. Coffee grinder and blending it, the crew would cut the blend even further, mixing in a healthy amount of the sleep-aid Dormin, which, like Benadryl, contains the antihistamine diphenhydramine.

After finishing the blend, Marcus, Jack, and their underlings would cap the mixture

— make it into capsules, or "beans." This was tedious work. "The guys hate doing it, because it takes so long," Jack said. "I would wear gloves. [Marcus] wore a doctor's mask and gloves. I was like, 'Dude, what's up with the doctor's mask?' But he was smart." Accidently ingesting even a tiny amount of the drug can cause grave health problems. They used one gram of fentanyl for every seven grams of heroin; by diluting the fentanyl in this way, Jack believed they were precisely controlling the product they were putting on the street.

But what he didn't realize was that the shipments they were receiving from Mexico had already been cut, perhaps also with diphenhydramine, though he didn't know the exact cutting agent. In fact, Marcus and Jack had no idea how much actual fentanyl was in each particular shipment they received. The only way they could have known the chemical makeup of their batches was if they had access to expensive mass-spectrometry equipment to test the chemical components.

The Mexican cartels preparing the fentanyl tend to use crude methods. "It's not like they're in a laboratory and measuring how much is in it, they just take the fentanyl and stir it with a spoon," said Doug Coleman of the DEA. "So you may take one hit with 1 milligram of fentanyl, and next you take a hit with 7 milligrams of fentanyl in it."

The same thing occurs today, across the country, even as the cartels become more scientifically sophisticated. Other than those who cut up the original product, nobody knows how much pure fentanyl is in the powders and pills being sold on the street. The cartel affiliates who drive the product across the border don't know, nor do the distributors who drive the packages for delivery around the country nor the local dealers selling them on the streets nor the users themselves.

This lack of dosage information, at root, is the primary cause for the fentanyl overdose crisis, the reason so many people are dying.

"It's like playing Russian roulette," said assistant US attorney James Delworth, who is based in St. Louis and heads the region's Organized Crime and Drug Enforcement Task Force. "There's no quality control in drug dealing. The way these products are cut with fentanyl is not in any way scientific. When users get it from a dealer who's gotten it from a distributor who's gotten it from another distributor, they're not going to have any idea what the strength is."

Around 2014, Jack Sanders was plying his wares in a North St. Louis neighborhood called Mark Twain. It's one of the most dangerous parts of the city and just a short drive from Mallinckrodt Pharmaceuticals, one of America's largest oxycodone manufacturers. At night, he squatted in an apartment building owned by a derelict landlord. It was a bare-bones existence. "There was water," he said. "There was no heat. You turn the stove on and open it for heat." His pit bull served as his burglar alarm. Though he stood out as a white guy from the suburbs, he could move about freely in the area, he said, because he had won the trust of local dealers by giving them free marijuana procured from a fellow Phish fan. "I could go into projects and walk in safely, walk out safely, without even having to have my gun on me, though I always would," Sanders said.

He sold his heroin and fentanyl just steps from where he slept, on North Kingshighway Boulevard, near where Bree got her fentanyl from a different dealer and about six miles north of the old Magic Chef factory. Jack's capped-up heroin and fentanyl beans were dispensed in ziplock bags with designs on them — hearts on the heroin bags and skulls on the fentanyl bags. All beans cost the same: five dollars each or a hundred dollars for twenty. (The heroin beans were actually a mixture of heroin and fentanyl.)

Customers would drive up, or arrive on foot, and place their orders with him. He'd take their cash and direct them to the "trap house" nearby, the place where the drugs were kept. "A trap house could be anything from an abandoned house to somebody's grandma's house," Sanders said. He wouldn't keep any drugs on him, but at the trap house, a teenager — maybe fifteen or sixteen — would give the customer the beans. The boys were chosen specifically for their young ages, "because he'd go to juvenile hall, not prison." For payment, Sanders said he gave them cash or bought them clothes or fancy sneakers.

The crew always feared violence, but Jack was guarded by "sentries" — armed watchmen posted nearby, keeping watch. "They'd basically get out a lawn chair and drink beer," Sanders said, adding that they would stash their big guns in a planter or a bush nearby, or even bury them under a bit of sand. Whenever they drew police attention, or someone got arrested, they would switch corners and trap houses.

How did he rationalize all this, the violence, the selling of poison, the exploitation of children? "I didn't feel anything. When you're addicted, you have no remorse. I didn't have a conscience," he said.

The cartels are often thought of as pyramidal in structure, with a powerful boss calling the shots. That style has begun to erode, particularly with El Chapo's arrest. The chain of command is not as powerful as it once was. "There's been this very severe fragmentation," said Deborah Bonello. "Power is now distributed more horizontally than vertically."

"The Sinaloa cartel has expanded to over forty countries, and it operates very much like McDonalds," said Mike Vigil, the retired DEA chief of international operations. "Subsidiaries in places like Belgium or France or Spain run their distribution networks, but they buy their product from the parent company, which is Sinaloa."

Jalisco Nueva Generation has suffered from internal division, and, owing to its especially brutal way of doing business and targeting of Mexican police officers, the Mexican government is particularly focused on the cartel, Vigil said. This gives Sinaloa greater leverage to operate, even with its leader out of commission. When El Chapo was extradited to the United States, a bloody inter-cartel war broke out that was won by Guzmán's family members and a senior leader named Ismael "El Mayo" Zambada. But despite the chaos, cartel business has continued unabated. "Sinaloa continues to be the most powerful cartel, even though El Chapo Guzmán has been taken out of the picture," said Mike Vigil.

In the United States, fentanyl has been hugely profitable for the cartels, and despite its staggering death count, it may have only scratched the surface. So far fentanyl has disproportionately affected the eastern part of the country, likely because, east of the Mississippi River, white powder heroin is more common and can be easily mixed in with white fentanyl powder. In the West, on the other hand, black tar heroin has long dominated, and it is more difficult to mix with fentanyl. St. Louis, located directly on the Mississippi, has seen both over the years, though white powder heroin is now more common. The predominance of black tar heroin out West is likely why, in San Francisco, users report that fentanyl is often clearly labeled as such, rather than being cut into heroin. There are indications, however, that dealers are beginning to find ways to mix black tar heroin and fentanyl, and that white heroin is moving West. These trends appear to be causing the fentanyl epidemic to surge in previously unaffected areas; the CDC notes that eight states west of the Mississippi are now showing "significant increases" in synthetic-opioid deaths, including Minnesota, Missouri, Texas, Colorado, Arizona, Washington, Oregon, and California.

And though many heroin users have by now encountered fentanyl, users of prescription pills still represent a largely untapped market. "Heroin has a much smaller using population than prescription pills," said Mario Moreno, former press secretary for the White House Office of National Drug Control Policy. "If the cartels can tap into the people who are misusing OxyContin and Vicodin and Percocet and can turn them into people who prefer fentanyl, they're going to make a lot of money."

Mike Vigil predicts that the Mexican cartels will eventually do away with heroin entirely. "They take a lot of risk of their opium poppy fields being eradicated," he said. "But with fentanyl, it's a huge profit-making drug with much less risk."

A February, 2019, investigative study on the Mexican fentanyl trade by *InSight Crime* concluded: "Mexico's government does not see fentanyl as an important issue yet and has not devoted significant resources towards finding the principal drivers of the trade inside its borders."

With sky-high US demand for illegal drugs coupled with a depressed Mexican economy, the cartels will continue to bloody their rivals and innocent parties throughout Mexico. They will continue to absorb young men into their ranks, who will opt for the status and money offered by the cartels rather than the low wages and lack of opportunity offered by the legal economy. "They have this saying here, *'Más vale vivir cinco años como rey que cincuenta como guey,'* " said Deborah Bonello. It's better to live five years as a king, than fifty as a loser.

■ ■ ■ ■

PART III:
THE SOURCE

■ ■ ■ ■

FOURTEEN

Much about the drug culture in China is surprising. While marijuana is the most popular recreational drug in both the United States and Europe, in China it barely registers. The 2017 version of China's annual report on drug control said that only thirty-five thousand people in the country use marijuana or cocaine — about one in forty thousand people. One should be skeptical about these official statistics, but anecdotal accounts confirm marijuana's relative scarcity there. The most commonly used drugs in China are heroin, methamphetamine, and ketamine, the lattermost a dissociative that dulls pain and causes users to feel removed from their environment.

Fentanyl and many other NPS popular in the West have not caught on in China, but exotic drug preparations abound. One might find illicit milk tea powders containing cathinone and seafood dishes spiked with ground-up poppy pods. Party drugs like ecstasy (which in Chinese translates as "head-shaking pills") are popular at karaoke bars where young people gather on the weekends. They are probably wise to do drugs away from home, because drug use is so taboo in China that abusers' own families sometimes turn them in to authorities. "Taking drugs" literally translates to "sucking poison," and consumption of psychoactive substances is highly stigmatized.

This stigma can be traced to the fallout from the country's two opium wars with England. China banned the opium trade in 1839, which put a stop to imports into the country of some twenty-eight hundred tons of opium per year by the British East India Company and set off the first war, which lasted until 1842. Not long before, China had been perhaps the world's wealthiest civilization, but its opium problem and the clash with British forces — seeking to protect their trade interests — imperiled the ruling Qing, China's last imperial dynasty, and Britain took control of Hong Kong as part of the Treaty of Nanking. ("The Opium War is seen in China as the original sin of Western imperialism," wrote John Pomfret, a former Beijing bureau chief for the *Washington Post*.) The Second Opium War

(1856–60) also ensnared France, and after it ended, opium returned to China with a vengeance. By the early twentieth century, about one in four of the country's men were said to be addicted.

Taking control in 1949, the Chinese Communist Party undertook dramatic steps to rid the country of the opium epidemic. Dealers were imprisoned or executed, and addicted users were sent to labor camps. In the early 1950s officials announced that China was now drug-free. "In a short period of three years, China wiped out the scourge of opium, which had scourged China for a century, thus performing a miracle acknowledged by the whole world," reads a page on the website of the Chinese embassy in the United States.

Any gains began to evaporate in the early 1980s, however. As China opened up to the outside world through economic and trade reforms, drugs poured into the country. Heroin use took off and continues to be one of the country's biggest public-health problems. It's mainly processed from opium grown in Myanmar. Meth too is largely sourced from Myanmar and other parts of Southeast Asia's Golden Triangle, though North Korea has also trafficked great quantities of it into northeastern China to subsidize its regime. Meth is a major problem throughout the Pacific region; it's not uncommon, for example, to hear about Indonesia seizing full tons or more. And China has meth labs of its own, supplying both the domestic market and other countries, including Australia and New Zealand. In 2017, Australian police seized about one ton of Chinese meth. Shipping methods are increasingly creative: "Australian authorities have found meth in Chinese shipments of garden hoses, handbags, lamps, aquarium pebbles, metal shafts, kayaks and 70 porcelain toilets," reported the *New York Times,* in 2015.

In at least one case, an entire Chinese village was devoted to meth production. Near the end of 2013, three thousand police officers, some arriving in helicopters and speedboats, descended upon the southern town of Boshe to break up a meth ring that consumed the village. According to Guangdong provincial police, one in five households was suspected to be linked to the drug's production or distribution, and officials from the local police chief to the party secretary were taken into custody. Three tons of meth were seized. Boshe had long been known for making drugs and for resisting government threats to its people's livelihoods. "The villagers would brandish replica AK-47s, lay nailboards on the road and hurl stones and homemade grenades at officers," reported the Associated Press.

The Guangdong province remains a busy region for trafficking, and the trade includes new drugs like fentanyl as well as fentanyl precursors. Adjacent to Hong Kong, on China's southeastern coast, Guangdong has ideal access to important shipping routes. Besides the meth company town of Boshe, Guangdong is also home to the world's most populated metropolis, which encompasses the Pearl River Delta and was formed by the growing together of already-enormous cities, including Guangzhou and Shenzhen. The US DEA announced in 2017 plans to open a new office in Guangzhou to battle the synthetic-drugs trade — a sign of how central China has become to drug trafficking.

Tian gao, huangdi yuan, goes an old saying in Chinese areas like Guangdong, far from the law-and-order-focused capital city of Beijing. "The heavens are high, and the emperor is far away."

China has responded to its renewed drug problem by executing hundreds of its own citizens. America's drug punishments, draconian in their own right, nonetheless pale in comparison to China's. Anyone found with fifty grams of heroin or meth (less than two ounces) could receive the death penalty there. "Drug offenders in China often call their participation in the heroin market as *ti naodai zou* (walking about with your head in your hands) or refer to the drug business as *shatou shengyi* (head-chopping business)," write Ko-Lin Chin and Sheldon X. Zhang, authors of *The Chinese Heroin Trade*.

Until fairly recently, executions were often public — the offender was shot in a field. Today lethal injection is administered in private. "On the day of the execution . . . we had breakfast together," reads a Brookings Institute interview with a convicted trafficker whose brother-in-law, the leader of their drug ring, received the death penalty. "None of us were interested in eating. My brother-in-law was calm. He talked to us as if he was leaving on a long trip, asking his children to listen to their mother, to look after each other, and to never ever touch drugs."

China uses propaganda campaigns to rally the public behind its drug-fighting initiatives, and the level of ceremony reaches a fevered pitch every year on June 26 — the

UN-designated International Day Against Drug Abuse and Illicit Trafficking. China takes the opportunity to execute a backlog of drug traffickers. Throughout the week, news viewers see armed units busting down doors, embarrassed perps hogtied, and videos of chemicals in plastic tubs. Bushels of drugs are publicly burned, and the government's website features photos of raging bonfires — with flames stretching toward the sky and officials posing like action movie stars. The China Post even issues a Day Against Drugs stamp, illustrated with doves and a giant rainbow.

June 26 also celebrates the opiate-battling tactics of a Qing dynasty official named Lin Zexu, who led the fight against the opium trade and banned the drug. Though he was harshly reprimanded after China lost the First Opium War to Britain, history was subsequently revised to paint him as a hero, and students are now taught about his excoriation of Queen Victoria, written in a letter: "Let us ask, where is your conscience?" Equally dramatic was Lin's destroying of more than a million kilograms of opium on a beach in Guangdong; his men mixed it with salt and lime and threw it into the ocean. A statue now commemorates him in New York's Chinatown.

Chinese children are taught that drug use will bring shame upon their families. College students are encouraged to run anti-drug campaigns in their neighborhoods over summer vacations. Neighborhood police go from house to house, asking residents to turn in users, including members of their own families. People who are suspected to be addicted are given urine tests, and those who fail are forced to register with the government and subsequently tracked for the rest of their lives. An alarm is triggered whenever they use their ID — to withdraw money at a bank or buy a train ticket — and if they have skipped rehab, the police will arrive to test their urine.

Repeat offenders are forced into rehab centers, and those who continue to relapse must spend between one and three years in labor camps, forced to dry out under draconian conditions with inadequate medical care. In the camps, some sort chili peppers into piles beneath the blazing sun, others tend to hog farms or polish gemstones, to be sent to Hong Kong. This is considered "treatment," but it more resembles hard labor on a farm or in a cramped factory — except the workers aren't being paid.

Some aspects of the culture are slowly changing in China. More methadone clinics are appearing, for example. But all too often addicted users are punished rather than treated. "At least in the US we know that detox isn't treatment," said Anna Lembke, an assistant professor at Stanford Medical Center who has studied heroin addiction in China. "There, they continue to think that if you just slap a person around a little, they'll stop using."

Chinese chemical companies selling drugs for illicit purposes to Western customers are based all over China but appear to be most common in the regions of Hebei (outside of Beijing), Shandong, Hubei, and Shanghai.

They can be broken down into three categories:

1) Companies that make drugs that are not just illegal in Western countries but illegal in China too, including MDMA, heroin, meth, fentanyl, and some NPS.
2) Companies that specialize in NPS that are illegal in the West but legal — *just* legal — in China, including synthetic cannabinoids, synthetic cathinones, and, until recently, exotic fentanyl analogues. They sell as much as they can before these

chemicals are scheduled in China, and then they move on to something else.

3) Companies that don't make NPS or any other drugs intended to get people high. Instead, they focus on items like fentanyl precursors and anabolic steroids that are illegal in Western countries but legal in China.

Companies in the first category are akin to illegal drug operations all over the world. They are forced to operate clandestinely, with the constant threat of police reprisal. The second and third, however, have been able to operate in the open, relatively speaking, in China for years. They pay their taxes and occasionally receive plaudits from the government.

This is part of what makes drug enforcement within China so difficult. "Many manufacturers of fentanyl and other NPS are legitimate companies legally producing chemicals," concluded a 2017 report about fentanyl commissioned by the US-China Economic and Security Review Commission. "Although some of these chemical manufacturers knowingly ship their products to the United States for illicit purposes,

Chinese chemical and pharmaceutical exporters continue to operate with little oversight."

Some labs are dirty and run-down. "Some of the pictures of these Chinese labs are sickening," Special Agent in Charge Dennis Wichern, of the DEA, told me in 2016. "It reminds me of the old meth-lab days when I worked in Missouri." Others are sparkling clean and clearly producing high-quality products. A knowledgeable participant on an Internet forum devoted to fentanyl, who asked not to be identified, spoke of the independent tests done on Chinese fentanyl and its analogues he has seen: "The purity is usually high, in the 90 percent range and regularly above 95%. These are real labs that make these substances for a profit, so they don't have much incentive to make inferior or impure products."

"They are clean," said American Dark Web dealer Desifelay1000, who traveled to China to meet a carfentanil supplier and see his lab, "and not very different from ours."

These Chinese chemical companies have little in common with backwoods methamphetamine cooks, the American Mob, or Latin American cartels. Shoot-outs and killings are extremely rare. Guns are uncommon throughout China, which has strict gun-control laws. When it comes to drug organizations, violence is simply not cost-effective. Instead, what drives the market is pure, unfettered capitalism.

"Unlike their counterparts in Latin America that are known for extreme violence and openly challenging the authorities," wrote authors Ko-Lin Chin and Sheldon X. Zhang in a Brookings Institution report, "Chinese drug trafficking organizations consist mostly of low-key entrepreneurs who are doing everything possible to avoid detection by and confrontation with the police or each other. Making money quietly is their motto."

For many years, Chinese organized-crime groups known as triads have been involved in the international meth trade. But experts familiar with triads say their influence appears to be waning in the fentanyl era. "They're a shadow of their former selves," said Justin Hastings, an associate professor in international relations and comparative politics at the University of Sydney, whose areas of expertise include China and drug trafficking. Though ad hoc criminal organizations continue to move drugs in China, major trafficking organizations are rare there, and cartels basically nonexistent. This leaves the market wide open for Chinese chemical companies, who benefit from an air of legitimacy.

Fentanyl-trafficking organized-crime groups with ties to China are active in Canada, however. In British Columbia, a province particularly stung by the epidemic, a gang called the Big Circle Boys has allegedly smuggled massive amounts of fentanyl from China, laundering profits through schemes involving real estate and casinos. The Big Circle Boys sprang from the Cultural Revolution and was originally formed by disenchanted Chinese emerging from reeducation camps who later migrated to areas including Hong Kong, New York, and Canada. They are now believed to have hundreds of members in Toronto and Vancouver, arranged in loosely organized, small cells. "The sophistication and complexity of the Big Circle Boys' structure, such as it exists, makes it extremely difficult to combat," wrote P. Wang in *Jane's Intelligence Review*.

The opium wars are still vivid in the Chinese public consciousness. The defeats brought shame upon the country, kicking off what Chinese call their "century of humiliation," which also included the Japanese invasion and occupation of Manchuria. The opium wars particularly resonate today, with China at the center of a new international drug crisis. Now, instead of Chinese citizens hooked on an opiate supplied by a Western power, the reverse is true: Westerners are hooked on drugs made in China. It's a turn of events that some commenters call the New Opium War.

"China has a deep, visceral understanding of how an Opium War can convulse a nation and collapse an empire," wrote journalist Markos Kounalakis. "Now the tables have turned. China has absorbed the Century of Humiliation's lessons of stealth attack and economic power and applied them globally." Some observers have called attention to a US Army Special Operations Command white paper report from 2014, called "Counter-Unconventional Warfare," which discusses "irregular threats" to the United States. It quotes two Chinese People's Liberation Army colonels articulating covert methods for attacking the United States, including "trade warfare, financial warfare, ecological warfare," as well as "drug warfare." While it's not clear that China is purposefully enabling its chemical industry to wreak havoc abroad, the historical parallels can not be ignored. That China takes severe measures to crack down on its own citizens' drug use but has tacitly allowed the production of massive quantities of NPS, exported around the globe, is deeply ironic.

"Whereas China has gone to war with other drugs that have a demand in China — such as methamphetamine — it has conspicuously failed to launch a similar crackdown on fentanyl, which has no demand in China," US representative Chris Smith, from New Jersey, said in October 2018, speaking about his proposed legislation that would specifically target Chinese fentanyl traffickers.

Countries like Mexico, Colombia, and Cambodia have fed America's drug habit for decades. Now China is front and center in a new quagmire, but its methods of production and distribution are much different from those of its predecessors. The Chinese drug industry is not run by cartels and criminal organizations, but by university-trained chemists who often play by their government's rules.

It dawned on me that there was only so much I could learn about this poorly understood industry from published reports. If I wanted to truly understand how synthetics made in China were causing a global epidemic, I needed to go to the source.

FIFTEEN

In the spring of 2017 I began making
contact with Chinese suppliers of NPS,
speaking with them over both the surface
web and the Dark Web, by Skype, e-mail,
and encrypted message. I started by creating a fake e-mail address, a fake name, and
a fake backstory, that I was in the market
for recreational drugs. The suppliers were
shockingly easy to find; I encountered most
of them through simple Google searches of
phrases like "buy drugs in China." Their
advertisements promised anything under
the sun (so long as it could be made in a
lab), including fentanyl and its analogues,
methamphetamine, ketamine, synthetic cannabinoids, N-bombs, and opioids I had
never heard of.

Most suppliers responded to my queries
quickly and spoke English proficiently. They
are well-accustomed to Western drug buyers, who are the bulk of their clients. I got

up well before dawn to catch them during business hours and peppered them with questions about their sales practices and manufacturing techniques. Some stopped responding when I didn't immediately place an order. Others, however, patiently answered my questions, and I eventually whittled down my contacts to a handful of promising leads who might be willing to show me their laboratories.

This is how I met a drug chemist and lab co-owner named Dowson Li — at least, that is how he signs his correspondence. He has a LinkedIn page under the name "Dowson Shanghai," which says he received his bachelor's degree in pharmaceutical engineering from Jianghan University in the Chinese city of Wuhan in 2001. Under "activities" it says, in English, that he took part in a "debate match held at the first grade of University, and won the champion in the Pharmaceutical Department." As this book went to press, his company still appeared to be operating normally.

Dowson's company is called Chemsky, and its official website dubiously claims it specializes in medical and pharmaceutical drugs. "[Chemsky] provides fine chemicals, natural products, pharmaceutical intermediates, and APIs [Active Pharmaceutical

Ingredients] for major pharmaceutical and biotech companies worldwide," it reads, next to a picture of a goggles-clad chemist handling test tubes. It adds that the company's international roster of clients includes Johnson & Johnson, but that is not true, according to Andrew Wheatley, a Johnson & Johnson spokesperson. The LinkedIn page for Dowson Li says Chemsky offers twenty thousand regular products as well as "custom synthesis from gram to kilogram tailored to our clients' specific needs."

In truth, Chemsky's bread and butter is NPS: synthetic cannabinoids, synthetic cathinones, novel benzodiazepines, fentanyl precursors, and fentanyl analogues, including the very dangerous 3-methylfentanyl, which is not a legitimate medical drug and has been a horrible scourge in places like Estonia. Many of these illicit drugs are advertised on Chemsky's official website, shchemsky.com, and others are for sale on ChemicalBook.com, a directory of chemical wholesalers.

In October 2017 I sent Chemsky an e-mail inquiring about fentanyl precursors. Dowson replied promptly and cordially, attaching a product list to the e-mail, which included a long list of NPS. We began chatting on Skype; clearly he was different from other overeager salespeople I had been talking to, no fly-by-night huckster hoping for a quick profit. A chemist with years of experience, he co-owned his lab and had been able, I surmised, to always stay one step ahead of drug laws. He had gotten it down to a science, literally. After I told him I would be coming to China, he said he would be happy to meet me.

With this promise, and the same from a few other illicit chemical industry employees, I bought a plane ticket to China. In January, 2018, I arrived in Shanghai. I was very nervous about this endeavor, considering no journalist had ever infiltrated a Chinese lab making fentanyls. I soon contacted Dowson, asking if he would be willing to take me to his company's lab. He said perhaps, but first we could talk at his company's office. Rather than giving me the office's address, however, he asked me to meet him outside a Shanghai subway station, and then we would head over together. Concerned for my safety, I arrived with a translator and researcher I'd met over the internet before my trip, whom I'll call Jada Li. I asked her to keep an eye on things. Since Dowson requested that I come alone, however, she monitored the situation incognito from twenty feet away, intending to follow behind us on foot at a distance when we went to his office. But Dowson unexpectedly arrived in a car, so that plan was abandoned.

It was pouring rain. I shook hands with Dowson and got into his Chevy. At the wheel was a beefy man who didn't speak English; Dowson identified him only as his driver, though the man also seemed as if he could be the operation's muscle. We drove off toward what Dowson said was his office, but actually turned out to be his apartment, a sleek flat on the top floor of a luxury high-rise in a gated community. From sixteen stories up we gazed through thick smog at ultramodern, pulsing Shanghai.

Dowson asked me to remove my shoes and gestured at three pairs of slippers that were reserved for guests. "Take the largest one," he said. "Now sit down please. I will make you some water."

People had cautioned me against visiting China in the winter, as hardly anyone seems to have heat, or at least most decline to use it. Even in restaurants, patrons huddle at tables in thick jackets, drinking soup and exhaling visible breath. To compensate for the discomfort, people offered me hot water everywhere I went, the way one might be offered coffee in the United States. In the chilly environs of Dowson's apartment, I could keep my rain jacket on without looking suspicious, allowing me to record our conversation on my smartphone, which I kept zipped up in a breast pocket.

We made small talk. Dowson suggested Shanghai tourist destinations I might enjoy — including the Jing'an Buddhist Temple and the famous Nanjing Road shopping district — and even volunteered to be my tour guide when it stopped raining. As a businessman he knew how to work the angles and to appeal to a prospective customer.

"You are so, how do you say, not old!" he said, as we sat down in his home office, in front of his desktop computer. I laughed and thanked him.

"I'm not too old, too. Thirty-eight," he went on. "I've owned the company for eight years. We do many chemicals, including a few of the chemicals that you asked about, such as MAF. I know it's not legal in several countries, but it's still legal in China."

MAF, also known as methoxyacetylfentanyl, is the fentanyl analogue also sold by Dark Web dealer U4IA. Though it had recently become a schedule I drug in the United States ("no currently accepted medical use and a high potential for abuse"), its legal status in China made it desirable, considering regular fentanyl and many other analogues were banned. MAF wouldn't be legal in China for long, but when the Chinese government outlawed it, Dowson would simply move on to new drugs that haven't yet been banned.

It is a never-ending cat and mouse game, and Chemsky thrives within this narrow window of legitimacy, which often lasts less than a year for any particular substance. During the brief period when a new drug has developed positive word of mouth on the Internet and is still legal in China, chemical companies like Chemsky produce and sell as much of it as they can.

I had a few sips of hot water, and then Dowson and I got down to brass tacks.

Many American politicians have found an easy scapegoat in China, including Chris Christie, who headed the Trump administration's 2017 opioid epidemic commission and called China's opioid export "an act of war." Some members of President Trump's cabinet have been more diplomatic. "China has been an incredible partner in helping stop the production of drugs like fentanyl in China," former Health and Human Services secretary Tom Price told the Associated

Press in 2017. Trump himself has at times sounded like both sides, alternately excoriating China for not doing more to stop the crisis and pledging to work with the country diplomatically.

Liu Yuejin, deputy chief of China's National Narcotics Control Commission, and other Chinese officials do not appreciate being blamed for the NPS crisis. Liu and others note that China has scheduled hundreds of new drugs, more than even the United Nations. In April 2019, at the request of President Trump, China said it would schedule "the entire class of fentanyl substances," effective May 1. Though it was far from clear if this new regulation would have teeth, many experts applauded it. "For the first time, China is expressing some responsibility for America's opioid crisis," said Katherine Tobin, former member of the U.S.-China Economic and Security Review Commission. This blanket ban of fentanyl analogues could potentially stymie companies operating in the legal gray area. The Dark Web fentanyl dealer Desife lay1000 said that some of his Chinese contacts are "jittery" because of the action.

Still, the United States has been burned by these types of promises from China before. In 2016, for example, China appeared to promise to crack down on exports of legal-in-China/illegal-in-America drugs but failed to do so. Experts say that, beyond grand pronouncements, China should focus on common-sense enforcement of its illicit industry, prosecuting violations of existing laws and targeting fentanyls with the same force the country has targeted methamphetamines. "China can develop human intelligence to identify drug flows before they get to the port of departure," said Vanda Felbab-Brown, senior fellow with the Brookings Institute.

Nonetheless, blaming China is a fundamental misunderstanding of the problem, insisted Liu Yuejin, of China's drug-control agency. The United States needs to work on scaling back its citizens' demand for these drugs. "It's common knowledge that most [NPS] have been designed in laboratories in the United States and Europe, and their deep-processing and consumption also mostly takes place there," Liu said at a June 2018 press conference. "The U.S. should adopt a comprehensive and balanced strategy to reduce and suppress the huge demand in the country for fentanyl and other similar drugs as soon as possible."

Indeed, most popular NPS were developed in Western laboratories, and China scheduled many of these chemicals not because Chinese people were excessively abusing them but because of US pressure. China now finds itself in an awkward position. When Western countries ban a drug, China eventually follows. At the same time, the country doesn't want to be told what to do.

The September 2017 US indictments of two Chinese nationals provides a good example: Jian Zhang, the Shanghai chemical manufacturer accused of manufacturing the fentanyl that killed Grand Forks teenager Bailey Henke and three other people; and Yan Xiaobing, from Wuhan, accused of operating "at least two chemical plants in China that were capable of producing ton quantities of fentanyl and fentanyl analogues," according to the US Department of Justice. This news was announced with great fanfare, and in October 2017 US deputy attorney general Rod Rosenstein held a press conference in which he noted that the two men were the first Chinese nationals to be placed on the Consolidated Priority Organization Targets list, the Justice Department's ranking of the world's most prolific drug traffickers and money launderers. The indictments "mark a major milestone in our battle to stop deadly fentanyl from entering the United States," said Rosenstein.

But China declined to hand the men over. Yu Haibin, director of precursor chemical control at China's National Narcotics Control Commission, said that while the country's law enforcement was investigating the men, it did "not have solid evidence to show that they have violated Chinese law." In the meantime, he added, the United States had only "made our investigation difficult."

The United States and China have collaborated in some instances. China's National Narcotics Control Commission said it regularly tips off the US government "to track NPS drugs and their buyers," and this works both ways. In September 2017, responding to a US tip that a Chinese citizen was smuggling fentanyl into the United States, Chinese police in Hebei province began investigating, leading to arrests of twenty-one people, including a Xingtai resident, Wang Fengxi, who allegedly created "a global NPS sales network" that trafficked new drugs including fentanyl to customers in the United States and other countries.

Because China's media is state controlled, getting reliable statistics about the country's volume of drug arrests and seizures is impossible, but China has made a number of high-profile NPS busts on its own, one of them a rogue chemistry professor named Zhang who earned comparisons to *Breaking Bad*'s Walter White in Chinese news reports. He first learned about NPS after a teaching stint in Australia. In 2005, Zhang — whose full name wasn't released to the media, though he doesn't appear to be related to Shanghai purported fentanyl dealer Jian Zhang — began making methylone, the popular ecstasy substitute. He and a partner named Yang made millions selling to Internet customers in the United Kingdom, Australia, and North America, but when the drug was scheduled in China in 2014 they appeared to have switched course. Zhang's Wuhan factory was soon busted for producing a "zombie drug," which appeared to have been MDMC, a Sasha Shulgin creation that is an inferior version of MDMA. The drug was already scheduled in China, and in 2017 Zhang received a life sentence, while Yang received a "suspended" death sentence, meaning that in all likelihood he will not be executed.

Wang Bo was a star chemistry student from a top high school near Wuhan, who, with his wife, founded a pharmaceutical company that employed thirty people and claimed to be performing "anti-cancer drug research." In reality they made NPS. "Bo had luxury products like a Mercedes Benz and a Jeep, and around $500,000 savings in foreign accounts," read a news account. In 2016 Wang was arrested for selling some fourteen hundred pounds of illicit substances, mainly to European customers. A seized package led to his downfall. Though investigators and even a chemistry PhD had a difficult time identifying his chemicals, they were eventually determined to include 3-MMC — which is similar to the stimulant mephedrone.

Hunan province resident Yao Xiao Dong was the first person convicted in China for distributing fentanyl, according to media accounts. A poorly educated man said to have committed crimes to feed his drug habit (though exactly what drug was not specified), Yao initially planned to make meth, but found fentanyl's synthesis easier. In 2013 he began buying precursor chemicals and processing equipment and soon had a client base. He employed a group of underlings, who called him "Dong Brother" (a term of respect, based on his name), and stashed his materials at friends' homes. After a raid, however, he and his accomplices were arrested. Yao's 2015 trial was challenging for prosecutors, who suffered from a lack of direct evidence, but Yao was nonetheless convicted of manufacturing and trafficking, received life imprisonment, and was stripped of his personal property and voting rights. Prosecutors gave the accused "a taste of their own medicine and penetrated Yao Xiao Dong and the others' lies, rationally and vividly exposing crimes and cracking down on their arrogance," according to a news account.

These arrests were possible because the traffickers sold drugs that were banned in China. Many drug manufacturers there, however, abide by the letter of their country's law. And because China has no extradition treaty with the United States, the country is under no obligation to respond to American complaints.

In such a situation, chemists like Dowson Li feel pretty comfortable.

SIXTEEN

At his apartment, Dowson handed me a computer printout listing his company's latest drugs. He enclosed it in a plastic sleeve and asked me not to remove it from the apartment. Compared to the previous list he had e-mailed me three months earlier, it had many changes, but in general the items listed remained obscure, little-known NPS with gibberish-sounding names, like AB-CHFUPYCA. I couldn't begin to pronounce many of them.

I recognized some fentanyl analogues, including MAF and BUF-fentanyl, also known as benzoylfentanyl, an obscure analogue with no data about human use available. As the print-out noted, one kilogram of benzoylfentanyl sold for $2,400. The bulk pricing indicated that the intended clients for these chemicals weren't individual users but drug distributors, such as I was pretending to be.

"What about ten kilograms, what would the cost be?" I asked.

"Ten kilograms, ten times [the price]," he said. "There is no discount."

Also on his product list were stimulants, depressants, and more than a dozen varieties of synthetic cannabinoids, with names like MMB-Fubica and AMB-Chmica. These were the next generation of fake marijuana products since the banning of John William Huffman's JWH series (China has scheduled at least nine JWH compounds) — or perhaps the next, next generation.

As I looked over the list, Dowson's expression became increasingly concerned. "We are afraid that a reporter come to our lab, to our country, to find out why we synthesize these chemicals, or why we sell these chemicals to your country," he said. "To let your people's health down. To harm your country's people. So, I wonder whether I should take you to our lab."

Still harboring doubts about me, he decided we should talk more over lunch. After I respectfully declined his offer to treat me to McDonalds, we settled on a local restaurant near Shanghai University. I discreetly texted Jada our location, as best as I could make it out. As we continued getting to know each other, our conversation sometimes veered in bizarre directions. "Why US government not bomb North Korea?" he said, apropos of nothing. "It is not good. And they have big weapon. The US government should bomb it. It's a responsibility. For the US, and also for China." Mostly he expressed admiration for the United States, including the leadership abilities of Donald Trump. The Chinese would always be grateful to the United States for defending their country against Japan in the Second World War, he noted.

He asked about my specific reason for meeting him. I explained that I was here at the behest of a friend from the States who was an NPS distributor. He was interested in making bulk purchases of fentanyl analogues and other drugs, and had asked me to visit Dowson's lab. If, according to my assessment, the lab had high enough quality standards, then my friend would go into business with him.

This explanation didn't entirely satisfy Dowson.

Why didn't he come himself?

"Because I was already planning to come to China, to visit a friend," I said, improvising.

A friend? Where?

"In Wuhan," I said, naming the city from

which I'd arrived the previous night.

I'm from Wuhan! What part of Wuhan?

Pretending not to understand what he was saying, I excused myself to use the restroom. When I returned, we got on to something else, and somehow, by the time lunch was over, he had decided that I passed muster.

"We have friendship, I trust you," he said, taking out his phone to call the beefy driver, who arrived shortly to take us to the lab. Soon we were back in the Chevy, speeding down a Shanghai interstate.

I was excited that he'd agreed to take me to his lab, but I was nervous that things might not go as planned. When I inquired about our destination, Dowson said only that the lab was "outside Shanghai." I began to sweat. My GPS wasn't functioning and the road signs were mostly in Mandarin, which I didn't speak. The driver wove between lanes while Dowson peppered me with more questions.

Where in the USA are you from?

Where are you staying in Shanghai?

I was from New York and I was staying at the Bund Hotel, I said, again improvising. I was actually staying at a youth hostel, but didn't want him to know my location.

In my anxiety I felt around for a seat belt,

but there wasn't one. I tried to track where we were going and surreptitiously texted the names of street exits and landmarks to Jada, in case something went horribly wrong. "Shangzhong Road Tunnel," I typed, and "Sanlu Highway." At one point I just typed, "Headed west I think."

Though our time together so far had been friendly, Dowson had an inquisitive manner and seemed to grow increasingly skeptical of my identity. He had his sun visor down and kept glancing at me through its mirror.

Are you a reporter?

No, I said, putting on my poker face.

In 2010, China passed Japan to become the world's second-biggest economy, along the way lifting hundreds of millions of its 1.4 billion people out of poverty. Its breakneck growth is revealed in everything from its bullet trains to its futuristic architecture. From China's tech and electronics wizardry to its fashion and tourism industries, it betrays a strongly capitalist mind-set, and initiatives like Belt and Road, a Eurasian–African infrastructure project, reveal its international ambitions.

Despite its problematic human rights record, including the internment of minority Uighur residents, the growth, innovation, and sheer magnitude of China's economic rise is unlike anything the world has seen, and a critical part of China's economy is its sprawling chemical industry. Its four hundred thousand chemical manufacturers and distributors (by US Department of State estimates) span the country, making everything from fertilizers to industrial solvents to antibiotics to psychoactive drugs. Most operate legally, some operate illegally, and others are in between. About 40 percent of the legitimate chemical industry worldwide is based in China, according to estimates, and it created $100 billion in profits in 2016, the most recent year for which statistics are available.

"Basically, almost any chemical that you want can be made in China," said Jean-François Tremblay, former Hong Kong–based senior correspondent for *Chemical & Engineering News.* He believes government subsidies, cheap land prices, and a lower standard of environmental and worker-safety regulations have fueled the industry over the years, buttressed by a plethora of skilled chemists and chemical engineers. And China's chemists have got an enormous market to sell to — the world's largest population. "For many years they had to produce their own drugs, until the end of the Cultural Revolution," Tremblay added.

Much of China's economic expansion in recent decades, however, has been driven by exports, which are seen as critical to the country's continued growth. It exports more goods to the United States than any other country — about $505 billion in 2017, over three times more than China imported from the United States — an imbalance that sparked President Trump's trade war with the country.

Driven in part by government subsidies and incentive programs, and fueled by exports, China's pharmaceutical industry has been growing at a breakneck pace for decades, especially since the normalization of US–China relations in 2000. Though previously the vast majority of medicinal and vitamin active ingredients came from the West and Japan, today China is known as the pharmacy to the world. But it's also been under fire for years for its record on food and medicine safety. Its medicines and supplements have been responsible for hundreds of deaths and thousands of hospitalizations around the world (exact numbers are unknown). The culprits have ranged from adulterated baby formula to fake glycerin used in cold medicine to contaminated herapin, a blood thinner. These adulterations are sometimes the results of company cost-cutting or corruption. Most dramatically, in 2007 China executed the former head of its State Food and Drug Administration, Zheng Xiaoyu, who was found guilty of accepting $850,000 worth of bribes from medical-device makers and drug companies. He approved more than one hundred drugs that were either entirely fake or hadn't been properly reviewed, including an antibiotic that killed at least ten people.

In 2013 the agency was restructured and renamed the China Food and Drug Administration. Corrupt factories were closed, and reforms were promised. But inspections remain sporadic, and American officials have not been satisfied.

For a variety of reasons, Chinese companies making medicines tend not to be inspected as thoroughly as those in Western countries. Though the US FDA has a presence in China, as it does in many other countries around the world, and is permitted to do some (though not all) of its desired inspections, it is, by all accounts, understaffed and underfunded. A report about drugs and China commissioned by the US Congress noted "several recorded instances of Chinese law enforcement and drug regulators delaying visa approvals for FDA officials and deleting laboratory test records."

China's clumsy, understaffed bureaucracy has a difficult time controlling the country's chemical industry, where legal and illegal elements bleed into each other. Different layers of government are sometimes at odds with one another, local officials are corruptible, and industry regulations are confusing and poorly enforced. Thus, dodgy companies that keep their heads down can often operate without problems. Many have websites advertising legitimate products, while also making recreational chemicals. Chemsky's home page, for example, focuses on its legitimate offerings, while its illicit offerings can be found by searching the site.

"Lack of coordination and competing regulatory oversight . . . creates opportunities for some firms to hide unregulated activities in plain sight," testified the RAND Corporation's Bryce Pardo, an expert on drugs in China, to Congress in 2018.

While American chemical and pharmaceutical companies tend to portray themselves as focused and streamlined, many of their Chinese counterparts offer an extraordinary range of products. Regulating this industry — where chemicals that speed up rubber manufacturing and those combating erectile dysfunction are peddled by the same people — is complicated by the fact that China's chemical bureaucracy involves at least eight different agencies, including its Food and Drug Administration, Ministry of Chemical Industry, and General Administration of Quality Supervision, Inspection, and Quarantine.

Because there are so many regulatory agencies, and because so many chemical companies make both legitimate and illicit products, the Chinese government has a difficult time finding and penalizing those who break the law.

"Many of China's chemical production facilities are described as 'semi-legitimate' producers, which are allowed to make chemicals but unlicensed to sell them to pharmaceutical companies," reads a 2016 report from the congressional US–China Economic and Security Review Commission. Being unlicensed doesn't necessarily stop these producers from selling to pharmaceutical companies, however. To further deceive the government, some companies set up "shadow factories," facilities shown to inspectors that are not actually where their drugs are made.

Fentanyl-precursor manufacturers, for

example, can evade scrutiny by labeling their products as industrial chemicals instead of pharmaceutical ones. "As long as, in China, you can produce chemicals without serious supervision," said Kai Pflug, a management consultant in the Chinese chemical industry, "the problem will persist."

Few people seem to understand the laws governing the manufacture and sale of Chinese chemicals. Long and complicated ordinances are enacted at the whim of the central government, and then enforcement often falls to regional agencies, who may not fully understand what Beijing has commanded or may have their own, competing interests. Chemical companies manipulate the large amount of gray area to their own advantage to reap profits.

His mood now improved as we approached our destination, Dowson sang John Denver's "Take Me Home, Country Roads" as we exited off the interstate. We had driven about a half hour south of Shanghai's center, and Dowson referred to our current location as the "countryside." The description didn't seem fitting; bare plots of land littered with garbage sat adjacent to clusters of colossal high-rises. Perhaps, given the frenetic pace of Chinese development, this location actually was the countryside not long before.

We eventually pulled into the parking lot of an office park, ringed by boxy, anonymous buildings a few stories high. A fountain sat in the middle. There was no way to tell, from the outside, that the building we were about to enter housed not a mail-processing plant or a grocery chain warehouse but a drug laboratory.

"Our lab is in here. We have arrived, man!" Dowson said, adding that I was not permitted to take pictures. I kept my smartphone recording inside my rain jacket.

We exited the car; the beefy driver stayed in his seat. The building's interior paint was blue and gray, and the stairwells smelled of concrete; the building seemed of fairly recent construction. Dowson said they had been at the facility for five years. He led me up two flights of stairs, ducking in for a quick word with someone in a room full of what looked like salespeople. The third floor harbored the laboratory — actually a series of lab rooms with chemical-processing equipment. Almost all the windows were open, but the frigid wind wasn't enough to dissipate the strong chemical smell.

Dowson introduced me to his partner,

whose name I didn't catch. Though Dowson himself seemed like a guy who would have been popular in school, his partner resembled a stereotypical science nerd, with broad gum lines and a slightly embarrassed manner. He was thirty and, like Dowson, wore glasses.

"We were at the same school, but not the same grade, in Shanghai," Dowson said. "He also liked the cannabinoid business. So we worked together."

His partner seemed suspicious of me but didn't object as Dowson showed off the facilities, which consisted of about a dozen rooms. Most were labs, full of the types of glassware and equipment that anyone who took high school chemistry would be familiar with: beakers, tubes, funnels, scales, and industrial-scale machines whose functions weren't immediately clear. Black lab tables sat in the rooms' centers, and fume hoods lined the walls. One machine, about six feet high, was used for drying the chemicals, Dowson explained. Posted signs, in both Chinese and English, warned the chemists to always wear gloves and protective eyewear.

The facilities might not have passed muster at some American academic or industry labs. Some of the equipment was rusting, and some of the glassware was dirty or coated with yellowing aluminum foil that was peeling off. "We have bought several older machines from other chemists, because it's cheap," Dowson apologized. That said, the facilities didn't seem unsafe. There was a level of professionalism.

"I seldom synthesize now, but five years ago, I synthesized," Dowson said, referencing the work of chemical manufacture. "I did the reaction. But the smell is bad when you synthesize." His partner, along with the four chemists they had on staff, did the bulk of the heavy-lifting in the lab these days. I didn't see anyone actively monitoring the equipment, but some of the machines were running. In the first room, a viscous, yellow, custardy-looking compound in an oversize, round-bottomed flask was being stirred by a mechanical arm. It looked to be, perhaps, three or four gallons of mixture.

"This is BUF," Dowson said, referring to benzoylfentanyl, the fentanyl analogue from the print-out he showed me in his apartment. "When this is finished we will get one kilo. It's legal in Europe, such as Belgium. Belgium customers need BUF. We wonder if Chinese will ban this, so we do not make too many stock. When it becomes a banned item, we will throw out the stock." Next to it whirred an identical machine, stirring an identical mixture.

Throughout our conversation Dowson, speaking for himself and translating for his partner, stressed that Chemsky preferred to operate within the boundaries of the law, both in China and the countries where they sent their drugs. Unlike other, illicit Chinese chemical concerns, they didn't disguise their chemicals with false packaging or label them with fake product names, he claimed.

In truth, though he knew Chinese drug law to the letter, the legality of the chemicals abroad didn't seem to concern him all that much. When we spoke about different synthetic cannabinoids and fentanyl analogues, for example, he often had no idea which ones were legal where. He asked me if MAF was legal in the United States, for example; it wasn't.

Dowson clearly understood the dangerous nature of these chemicals. At his apartment, he had spelled out, very plainly, what he thought of the compounds that were his livelihood, the ones that funded the posh abode we were then sitting in.

"These chemicals *harm* people," he said. "No safe. Because they are not green. They are synthesized by people in labs. They are harmful. They are drug. Every drug have harmful, and side effect. Right?"

As we entered the next lab room at the facility, I could hardly believe my eyes. Dowson covered his mouth and nose with his jacket to block fumes wafting from a yellow powder lying in big piles on the lab station island.

In the movie *Scarface,* near the end, Tony Montana, played by Al Pacino, powder on his lapel, sits at his desk before heaps of cocaine. That was child's play compared to this. The sheer volume had to be enough to get entire small countries high. The piles of compound were on sheets of aluminum foil, perhaps for drying; more mounds were on the floor, and small barrels were filled with one-kilogram ziplock bags of the substance.

"5F-ADB," Dowson said, identifying the yellow chemical, a synthetic cannabinoid that his printout noted sold for $1,000 per kilogram. ("Avoid from light, in cool and dry place," it advised.) This drug was popular in the Netherlands, he claimed. Presumably the buyers — or someone else further along the supply chain — would dissolve the chemicals in a solvent and spray them onto dried plant matter for smoking.

In the next room he showed off the equipment used for manufacturing the cannabinoid, huge, glass drums suspended in the air, each holding maybe twenty gallons. He pointed to a cardboard box filled with bags of a different compound, white with an orange tint. "These are 5F-MDMB-2201. It's famous in Russia. Russian customers like this." It hadn't caught on much further west, however, and curious Internet commentators complained about a dearth of available information. "It's highly potent, showing activity in sub-milligram dosages," wrote someone on Drugs-Forum.com. "Apparently this one becomes very intense and sometimes difficult and scary for the cannabinoid-naive or even more experienced individuals."

These new drugs become popular on the Internet in the same way many new products become popular — by word of mouth. The NPS landscape is evolving so fast that it's often hard to know where the new chemicals originate. Many are taken directly from legitimate academic research, such as the N-bombs developed by David Nichols and the synthetic cannabinoids conceived by John William Huffman. But New Zealand chemist Matt Bowden, who has made synthetic cannabinoids and other NPS, said that after he started manufacturing in China, his formulas were simply stolen by local chemists.

"You couldn't really protect the IP," he said. "We found a few times that if one guy was working on something, he'd go down the road to his friend from uni, and they'd have a go at it together. Then the guy down the road would think, 'Hey, that's a cool molecule, I'm going to start making this myself,' and he'd start selling it somewhere else." A chemist who designs new psychedelics said that, after he and other participants on a Russian-language psychonaut message board had too many of their new drug creations hijacked by Chinese labs and sold on the Internet, they closed the forum to outsiders.

The tour finished, we sat down at a table in a small, unadorned conference room. Another man came in with a plastic bag full of water bottles and Nescafe cans, the latter of which were, to Dowson's delight, warm. The man left the room and closed the door. Dowson, his partner, and I popped open our cans of sugary coffee and made more small talk. Finally, Dowson got down to business.

"We will find chemicals, new or old, that are suitable for USA. The work will be done by you and your workmate," he said, pausing to translate for his partner. "What quantity?"

"Maybe ten kilograms for some things, one kilogram for other things," I said, talking hypothetically.

They looked dubious. Then I remembered that, with some of these chemicals, one needed less than a grain of rice's worth to get high. "The ten kilograms per month is a lot of work," Dowson said.

"I will speak with my partner," I said, "and then we will speak again."

This seemed to satisfy them. "So, any questions? If you don't have any questions, we're done."

We walked outside to the hallway and waited for the elevator. After a few minutes it was still stuck on a floor labeled "−1," so we took the stairs down. The beefy man had the Chevy ready to go. While he drove us back to Shanghai, from the back seat I took notes about the visit and e-mailed them to myself. We wove back into the city center, and they dropped me off at the Bund Hotel.

Dowson said goodbye, repeating his recommendations for tourist spots. It was still raining, and he insisted that I take his umbrella. I watched the Chevy pull away, took a deep breath, and texted Jada that I was OK. Then I started figuring out how to get back to my youth hostel.

I soon stopped contacting Dowson, and he never pressed me about the order we discussed. Months after my trip when I was back home, however, he sent me a Skype message on my birthday with a cake emoji.

This infiltration helped me understand the scale and the scope of the NPS trade in China. A small company like Chemsky, with only a handful of employees, was producing chemicals on a large scale — compounds that, for the most part, didn't exist until recently, and about which little was known. And they were flying beneath the radar of law enforcement agencies everywhere. No government on earth would want these drugs in its country, and yet the latest technology was facilitating their creation, marketing, and distribution.

Despite the illicit nature of these drugs, Chemsky is a fairly credible business. It doesn't operate out of a disguised underground bunker but rather a traditional office park. Dowson and his colleagues understand chemistry, Internet advertising, and Chinese chemical law, and their output seemed especially large for a modest-size operation, if the piles of cannabinoids were any indication. They point toward a worldwide market for obscure chemicals that is bigger than I had even imagined.

And if the number of NPS ads on the Internet is any indication, Chemsky is just the tip of the iceberg. Hundreds more Chinese companies could be making these drugs in labs like this one.

Still, companies like Chemsky — which send NPS through the mail — are only part of the problem. Even if all of their drugs could be intercepted, this wouldn't stop the overdoses and deaths in the West, because literally tons of fentanyl is distributed on the street by Mexican cartels, an amount that is expected to increase in the coming years. This fentanyl is almost always made from Chinese precursors.

Experts agree that the precursors are key to the cartels' operations. "So long as the cartels can obtain the necessary chemicals, they will be able to synthesize the drugs that permit them to bribe officials, buy weapons and pay their gunmen," wrote Scott Stewart on the website Stratfor. And, unlike fentanyl analogues, all of which China banned in the spring of 2019, most fentanyl precursors remain perfectly legal in China.

I clearly needed to better understand the Chinese precursor trade. It had taken only a few keystrokes to find operations that were selling these chemicals openly on the Internet. But as I continued digging I realized that — unlike the NPS sold by Chemsky and others — the fentanyl precursors being sold to the cartels and others didn't seem to come from small to medium-size companies scattered around China.

The bulk of them seemed to come from a single corporation.

345

SEVENTEEN

Ye Chuan Fa works in a cubicle. His small station is indistinguishable from those of the hundreds of employees at his chemical company. The company is called Yuancheng — whose name in Mandarin means, roughly, "Extended Success Is Lasting Success." Founded in 1999, Yuancheng employs about 650 people and has branch offices all over China.

Ye works at the headquarters in Wuhan, a burgeoning industrial center of eleven million people in central China known for its spicy food. He isn't flashy and insists on flying coach, though he does favor an expensive brand of cigarette, Yellow Crane Tower 1916 — named for a popular Wuhan tourist attraction located nearby. He shows up in the morning wearing sneakers and casual clothes. "To quote the people around him: 'If our boss was sitting with his driver, you'd think the driver was the boss,' " read a 2007 *Wuhan Morning News* profile.

Ye is divorced, with four children. While most of his workers appear to be in their twenties, Ye is in his sixties, thin, with a sagging, falling face. He's a self-professed workaholic. "I get sick the minute I stop working," he said in the profile, which also referenced his great wealth, without putting a number on it. There are rumors around the company that he was once the richest man in Wuhan; even if that's an exaggeration, he has undoubtedly made a great deal of money over the years in varying business ventures, some more successful than others. But his only business today is Yuancheng, which sells chemicals both to other businesses and the general public. The company offers eleven thousand different compounds, a vast and head-scratching list of everything from food additives (including synthetic versions of cinnamon) to pharmaceuticals (including the drugs used in Viagra and Cialis) to collagen, pesticides, veterinary products, anabolic steroids, and precursor chemicals used to synthetize fentanyl.

A thriving company, it has been repeatedly praised by Communist Party officials. But understanding the company's full scope is difficult. It maintains countless subcompanies and websites, for example, some in

English and some in Chinese, which can be difficult to trace back to the parent company, called Yuancheng Group. The websites are tailored toward different products; some focus on steroids, for example, others on offerings like synthetic cinnamon. The fentanyl ingredients aren't mentioned at all on some sites, but receive prominent placement on others.

Everything Yuancheng sells is legal in China, according to the letter of the law. Some of the chemicals, like anabolic steroids and fentanyl ingredients, are not legal in Western countries like the United States, and the company is well aware of this fact. For that reason, its sensitive products are mailed to customers in phony packaging. The fentanyl precursors, for example, might arrive in bags labeled as dried banana snacks, so customs agents are less likely to examine them.

Since illicit use of fentanyl is uncommon in China, companies like Yuancheng selling fentanyl products focus on the export market. As worldwide demand for the drug has risen sharply since the mid-2010s, especially in North America, Yuancheng has sold untold quantities of fentanyl precursors.

When it's not being abused, of course,

fentanyl is an important medical drug. Legitimate companies like Janssen Pharmaceutical produce it using standardized techniques. Yuancheng, however, isn't focused on selling to hospitals or pharmaceutical companies. It takes orders from anyone. It accepts Bitcoin, Western Union, and direct bank transfers, and ships via companies like FedEx and UPS, promising "guaranteed 100% clearance" through customs. In the process, it has flouted the laws of the United States and other countries around the world.

Yet Yuancheng is no clandestine drug organization. Its contact information, including the company's address, is all over the Internet, and Yuancheng salespeople are available to talk about their products using whatever format the customer prefers; e-mail, social media, Skype, or even the telephone. When chatting online they use lots of emojis — rainbows, smiling faces, and shaking hands — and even send pictures of themselves in silly poses, with drawn-on bunny ears and whiskers, hoping to forge a connection.

When I first started researching the two most widely used fentanyl precursors, NPP and 4-ANPP, in May 2017, advertisements for these chemicals proliferated on the

Internet, from a wide variety of different companies. Later I determined that the majority of those companies were under the Yuancheng umbrella.

Posing as an interested customer, I messaged with or spoke to seventeen Yuancheng salespeople, sometimes conversing for hours at a time. These were wide-ranging conversations that touched on the company's products, practices, and working environment, and even the employees' philosophies about selling such destructive chemicals. The salespeople went by names like Julie, Sean, and Demi, and were recruited in part for their English abilities. One salesman, the director of Yuancheng's Shenzhen branch, told me that his Chinese name is Chen Li, but that as a salesman he goes by Abel, because it is "an English name." "Below 10 kg is express delivery, above 10 kg by air," he said, when asked how the NPP and 4-ANPP packages could be sent to the United States.

Salespeople offered to pick me up at the airport. They pledged friendship.

"Food additives officially," wrote a Yuancheng saleswoman named Alisa when I asked what products her company specializes in. "Steroids and 4-anpp npp underground."

These fentanyl precursors were available "for export only," a Yuancheng salesperson named Kay wrote — not to Chinese customers. The sizes of the orders they received tended to be, "50 kgs–100 kgs." Different salespeople quoted me different prices for the chemicals, ranging from $500 per kilogram (for NPP), to $2750 per kilogram (for 4-ANPP). Presumably, 4-ANPP is more expensive because it is easier to make into fentanyl.

According to the salespeople, their biggest markets are Mexico and the United States.

"Mostly shipping to Mexico," wrote Alisa.

"My friend we sold this product in large quantities, sent to the United States and Mexico," wrote a Yuancheng salesman with the Skype name Ian.Dang.

"Our products are sold to the United States less," wrote Chen Li. "More is sold to Mexico."

After almost two years of research I concluded that Yuancheng has likely sold more of the illicit fentanyl precursors used in Mexico, the United States, and other countries, than any other company. Yuancheng has done so not through secret underground networks or terrorist cells. It has done it over the Internet, using an army of young, perky sales representatives who live in a big hotel together. Posting cheeky job advertisements and offering employees free cell phones, it's a poison factory operating in plain sight.

China has pledged to help stop the export of fentanyl precursor chemicals, and yet it has failed to do so. In fact, quite the opposite: Through a variety of incentive programs, it has helped Yuancheng build an empire.

Stories of lawless Colombian and Mexican cartels and the rise and fall of renegade drug bosses like Pablo Escobar and El Chapo have by now been told countless times. But the story of Ye Chuan Fa is different. Having nimbly navigated the rise of capitalism in his country, his story is uniquely Chinese. And it brings into focus a wider story about how the country's chemical industry, powered by global capitalism, has become a Frankenstein's monster, powerful, destructive, and uncontrollable.

Ye Chuan Fa is an entrepreneur who has built a personal fortune by taking chances on emerging industries while staying in step with the government's priorities. In China, beyond savvy business skills, knowing which way the political winds are blowing is essential.

"Ye Chuan Fa dresses exceptionally plainly," read a 2004 *Chemical & Engineering News* article on prominent chemical companies in Wuhan, "a practice he adopted in the 1980s, when it was not clear whether China would embrace its new entrepreneurs or throw them in jail."

The profile makes no mention of steroids or fentanyl, the latter of which had not yet come into vogue when it was published. At the time, Yuancheng was based at an entertainment complex, adjacent to his restaurant and karaoke bar, and he owned companies that manufactured everything from industrial paint to sculptures for peoples' homes. "They had all sorts of businesses," remembered Jean-François Tremblay, the Hong Kong–based author of the piece. "They made these weird plaster garden statues."

Ye was born in Wuhan in 1953, the son of factory workers. After studying at a vocational school he began his career as a hospital pharmacist, before moving into business for himself. Ye Chuan Fa's entrepreneurial aspirations coincided with China's capitalist reforms of 1978, which began the country's transformation from a rural, farming society scarred by Mao's economic and cultural experiments into a global economic powerhouse. In 1979 Ye moved to the province of Fujian, where with a local partner he forged a business reselling goods. Fujian is near Taiwan, and his partner had friends from the country with access to goods that were desired on the mainland. "Everything was in demand: watches, stereos, leather. As long as you could get it, you wouldn't worry about selling it," Ye said. Ye invested in Wuhan real estate during the 1980s and amassed a fortune, before moving to Hong Kong near the end of the decade, "as insurance against a crackdown on the rich by Chinese authorities." Even today, Yuancheng's customers for fentanyl precursors are given the option of transferring their payments directly into Ye's bank accounts in Hong Kong, at either Citibank or Industrial and Commercial Bank of China. He also lists a home address in Kowloon, Hong Kong. When he speaks, his accent is part Wuhan, part Hong Kong, the unrefined diction of a self-made man.

Homesick, Ye returned to Wuhan in 1994 and began operating in the food and hospitality realms. The country's march toward capitalism continued, and the late 1990s saw the rise of reforms known as "retreating public sector, advancing private sector." In 2001 Ye invested millions to renovate and upgrade a hotel, which he named Jia Ye, after himself. Above its front door stood an elaborate, gold-plated likeness of Erato — the Greek muse of poetry — holding a harp. Ye also opened a theme restaurant of the same name, which was decorated like a jungle. "People who have eaten at Jia Ye are full of praise for its Amazon Rain Forest and Thai themes," read a *Changjiang Daily* story from 2006. "The enterprise promotes a 'human and nature' culture, letting people eat like a picnic."

The first years of the new millennium saw the government privatizing huge swaths of the economy, and Ye took advantage, buying state-owned factories and legacy companies, which he renovated and revamped. Soon his enterprises were selling machine parts, chemicals, furniture, decorative Roman columns, and many other products. Some of these concerns were still well-known, if fading, brands in Wuhan, and Ye did his best to repurpose them as dynamic private companies. "The biggest opportunities in China lie in buying state-owned companies on the cheap, something that foreign investors rarely do," he said in 2004.

Ye soon began focusing more on the chemical industry, selling everything from aspartame to melatonin to chemical coatings. The 2004 *Chemical & Engineering News* article noted that Yuancheng had "nearly completed building a plant to extract up to 150 metric tons of natural vitamin E per year." That year Yuancheng also placed a big bet on synthetic-cinnamon products.

Natural cinnamon comes from cinnamon tree bark and is most commonly used as a spice, but its synthetic derivatives have a wide variety of uses, including as candy flavorants, insecticides, corrosion inhibitors that slow the breakdown of metals, and traditional Chinese medicines said to help with asthma, hernia pain, impotence, and even "cold uterus" (a Chinese term referring to infertility). According to its press materials, Yuancheng was the first Chinese company of its kind to obtain a production license for these chemicals, and later became the "largest supplier of cinnamon products in the world."

The company increasingly sought market share outside of China. After the country's admission to the World Trade Organization in 2001, Yuancheng received state permission to begin exporting its goods. "People in the company told us that Yuancheng acquired the export business license very early on," read the *Changjiang Daily* story. "Some of their subsidiary companies even exclusively focus on the European and

North American markets. We see in their HR department that new employees of Yuancheng all need to have strong English skills for sales."

It's unclear whether Yuancheng was selling steroids or fentanyl ingredients at this time but, then as now, the company maintained a reputable public profile. According to company literature, it collaborated with Wuhan University — one of the country's most prestigious colleges — to develop its products and management systems. Yuancheng was firmly in the government's favor. In 2007, after being nominated by readers of the *Wuhan Morning News* for something called an "entrepreneurial spirit" award, Ye Chuan Fa was publicly commended by the local Communist party as one of the top business leaders in the community.

Yet, the company often stumbled. In particular, its cinnamon business was dealt a major blow. In early 2013, Ye Chuan Fa held a press conference to announce that Yuancheng's intellectual property regarding its cinnamon line had been stolen, to the benefit of a rival company called Xin Gan, in the nearby province of Jiangxi. The rival had begun producing similar cinnamon products and distributing them at a lower price, he claimed.

The Chinese news outlet reporting this story was not able to reach the allegedly infringing rival for comment. But in an intriguing twist, the man responsible for leaking Yuancheng's synthetic-cinnamon secrets — the former factory manager — was on hand for the press conference. Named Zhu Ru Hui, the man said the head of Xin Gan promised him 300,000 yuan (about US$44,000) and a stake in its own cinnamon business if he stole the information from Yuancheng.

"In September 2011, after receiving the promised 300,000, he divulged the blueprint, equipment and other essential information," read the news account. "Xin Gan also recruited many sales representatives from Yuancheng, acquiring their customer resources." Eventually, Xin Gan "streamlined the entire production."

Upon realizing proprietary information had been compromised, Ye went to the police, and after a lengthy investigation Zhu Ru Hui was arrested and admitted to his crimes. "After this, I wanted to jump off a building," he said, although the account did not explain why he was at the press conference instead of in prison.

Nonetheless, the damage was done. Having invested, by his count, 30 million yuan (US$4.4 million) in synthetic-cinnamon products, Ye said he was forced to cut back on Yuancheng's staff and production of cinnamon chemicals. "This caused our company grave losses," he said.

Yet, Ye Chuan Fa remained diversified. For years he had opened businesses in a variety of fields, trying everything, to see what might stick. Around 2007, he opened a resort called the Jia Lun River Hot Springs Villa. At a time when "countryside tourism" had become trendy in China, the resort was billed as a weekend sanctuary for residents of crowded Wuhan. Located on hundreds of acres on the outskirts of the city — abutting both the Jia Lun River and a busy highway — it had a Vegas-style "Five Thousand Years of the World" theme, housed in gaudy architecture topped with domes and Roman-style statues, which were undoubtedly made in-house. The facility featured a hotel, restaurant, spa, conference rooms, movie theater, and even bungee jumping. Its centerpiece was a massive outdoor hot springs area with baths and pools surrounded by trees and rock structures. Promotional materials gushed about its baths, which they said were sourced from naturally occurring carbonated springs, rich in vitamins and nutrients. "After soaking in a hot spring like this, your mind will be calmed, the body heat will be cleared, the physiological network will be connected, your blood will be alive, the toxins will be taken away, and your muscles will be revived."

With a reported price tag of 150 million yuan (US$22 million), the resort was launched with great fanfare and a promotional blitz. Unfortunately, many visitors found that it didn't live up to expectations. Some believed that Jia Lun didn't have natural hot springs at all but rather "boiled water," as alleged in critiques. Indeed, the resort's claims were deemed "deceptive" by the Trade and Industry Bureau of Hubei Province. Even worse, only about two months after the announcement that Yuancheng's cinnamon secrets had been stolen, Ye's resort also suffered a terrible blow. In the spring of 2013, a massive fire, reportedly caused by students barbecuing under a wooden roof, consumed a large portion of the resort. A strong wind fanned the flames. There were no casualties, but the blaze took hours to contain, by firefighters using water from the pools themselves.

The resort suffered great damage. Some of the charred remains were never cleared away, and though sections of the facility remained in use, before long the entire resort closed permanently. Felled trees from the property were carted away on a large truck, and a military-run job-training program took over one of the buildings. Area drivers can still see the resort's decaying, blue and gold shell from the highway. It's a scene like something out of a postapocalyptic movie: the hotel rooms have been ransacked, the restaurant's windows are smashed, and the outdoor baths are returning to nature.

It seems likely that the failings of Ye's hot springs and the theft of his synthetic-cinnamon secrets had enduring financial repercussions for his business interests. Nonetheless, he was able to rebound.

It helped that his children were moving up in the ranks. In 2014 Ye Chuan Fa's daughter, Ye Si, took over for her father as Yuancheng's legal representative. This is a powerful position without a clear Western equivalent; the legal representative acts on the company's behalf in legal agreements and is ultimately held responsible by the Chinese government if it breaks any laws.

In the ensuing years Ye Si worked her way into a top managerial position at her father's company. A 2016 Yuancheng press release read, "Comrade Ye Si will be the leader of the new economy of the city, and a leader in the innovation field." ("Comrade" implies she is a member of the Communist Party, along with nearly ninety million other Chinese.) It appeared that she was being groomed to take over the company when her father retired, but in February, 2019, Ye Chuan Fa said that his son, Ye Jia Ren, who had recently graduated from university and was "training" at Yuancheng, was next in line. (Ye Si, Ye Chuan Fa said, was now focused on the company's real estate holdings.)

Ye Chuan Fa's son will inherit a thriving company. Since the cinnamon secrets theft and the hot springs fire of 2013, Yuancheng has experienced a period of dramatic growth. This period corresponds with the explosion of the illicit fentanyl market.

EIGHTEEN

According to the DEA, the two most commonly used precursor chemicals to make fentanyl are NPP (N-phenethyl-4-piperidone) and 4-ANPP (4-anilino-N-phenethylpiperidine). The DEA says the Siegfried method is the easiest and most common technique: NPP is reacted with a compound called aniline and then "reduced" (wherein another compound is used to add electrons) to form 4-ANPP, which is then reacted with another compound called propanoyl chloride, to form fentanyl.

Precursors aren't intoxicants in themselves, but they are the most important ingredients used in drug making, because they are the most essential to the process, and the most difficult to obtain. Most famously, pseudoephedrine was used by American backwoods chemists to cook meth, before pseudoephedrine's sale was regulated in the United States, pushing the industry into Mexico. There, cartels began purchasing pseudoephedrine (and another meth precursor, P2P) from Chinese companies, and the meth crisis continued.

China has been supplying Mexican drugmakers with fentanyl precursors for well over a decade. In 2006, a clandestine chemist named Ricardo Valdez-Torres was caught making fentanyl for US export at a lab near Toluca, Mexico. He admitted buying NPP from Kinbester, a chemical company based in Xiamen, China. The drugs used in this collaboration seem to have been largely responsible for a rash of American fentanyl deaths from 2005 to 2007, when about a thousand people died in cities including Chicago and Philadelphia.

This was, essentially, the first wave of our current fentanyl epidemic. After this bust, in 2007 the United States placed NPP on its schedule I list ("drugs with no currently accepted medical use"), requiring all US transactions involving the chemical to be submitted to the DEA. Not long afterward, 4-ANPP was added to the schedule II list ("drugs with a high potential for abuse"). Neither have any use beyond making fentanyl or fentanyl analogues. "I am not aware of any other product for which you would reasonably require NPP and 4-ANPP," said

Martin Raithelhuber, an illicit-synthetic-drug expert with the UN Office on Drugs and Crime. Further, there would be no legitimate reason for anyone in the United States to buy these chemicals from a Chinese company, said DEA spokesman Melvin Patterson. "The U.S. doesn't import fentanyl because we have plenty of domestic companies that provide it. Which means anything coming from China would be illegally exported and/or imported." He added, "The same is true for the precursors as well."

China wouldn't schedule these precursor chemicals until ten years after the United States began doing so. As a result, when the current fentanyl crisis began to gain speed in the 2010s, Yuancheng and other Chinese companies were well-positioned for legal NPP and 4-ANPP sales, with virtually no oversight from the Chinese government. "There was little scrutiny on their manufacture, and producers faced little, if any, reporting, production, or exporting restrictions," RAND Corporation associate policy researcher Bryce Pardo testified before Congress in September 2018.

This coincides with what Yuancheng characterizes as a successful period, according to its own promotional materials. A recruitment advertisement said that in 2013 the company "achieved 300 million platform transactions" and the following year "achieved 500 million." (It's unclear what exactly constitutes a transaction.) A company website claims: "In 2015, the export volume reached 2 billion yuan [US$294 million]. The development of Yuancheng also witnessed the rapid growth of China's economy and opened a window for global understanding of China. . . . In 2015 the total sales exceeded 5 billion yuan [US$736 million], contributing tens of millions of dollars to the country every year." Another company website says Yuancheng has established "good business relations" with "Europe, the United States, Asia and other continents."

Though Yuancheng had been selling fentanyl precursors for years, business heated up in the mid-2010s as the crisis accelerated. By mid-2017 the company was advertising them on scores of search-engine-optimized Internet websites. At that time, Google search terms like "buy NPP in China" or "4-ANPP China" turned up pages and pages of results for companies selling the precursors. While some links led to organizations that aren't affiliated with Yuancheng, the majority led to companies that are. Their names include Shenzhen Sendi Biotechnology, Zhuhai Wumei Technology, Chembj, Wuhan Hezhong Bio-Chemical Manufacture, Wuhan Hengwo Scien-Tech Co. Ltd. [*sic*], Hangzhou Fuluo Biological Technology, Zhuhaishi Shuangbojie Technology, and Guangzhou Huao Chemical. All were selling fentanyl precursors, and careful reviews of their sites, as well as analyses of bank account information and interviews with employees, indicate that they are all under the Yuancheng umbrella, with payments received directly by Ye Chuan Fa.

The company knows these precursors are used to make fentanyl. Ye Chuan Fa himself admitted as much, and marketing materials make this clear. A website featuring products for Yuancheng affiliate Wuhan Hengwo Scien-Tech Co., for example, lists NPP as "a precursor in the synthesis of fentanyl and related opioids" and 4-ANPP as an "intermediate in the synthesis of fentanyl."

The company's salespeople claimed to sell more of these precursor chemicals than anyone else in China. "Most the NPP and 4-npp [*sic*] are sold from my company," said one saleswoman, who asked to remain anonymous. "Friend, our company is the only manufacture of this product in China," said the Yuancheng salesman Chen Li, referring to a different fentanyl precursor called N-phenylpiperidine-4-amine dihydrochloride.

Salespeople are paid to trumpet their company, of course, and it's impossible to know exactly how much of the world's fentanyl precursor supplies are sold by Yuancheng. In 2016, then US secretary of state John Kerry wrote a letter to the UN secretary-general, Ban Ki-Moon, requesting that NPP and 4-ANPP be regulated internationally; documents attached to the letter indicated that the United States had identified "at least 178 suppliers of NPP and 79 suppliers of ANPP globally, more than half of which are located in China." The methodology for determining those numbers isn't clear, nor are the identities of the suppliers; the US State Department declined to provide the details, and a Freedom of Information Act request had not been fulfilled at press time. Yuancheng's affiliates likely accounted for many of those suppliers, although some may have come from India, and some may no longer exist today.

Yuancheng, however, appears to dwarf all other sellers. Though it's difficult to know for certain, it appears that, if the size of its salesforce, the quantity of its shell companies, and the strength of its advertising are any indication, Yuangcheng has sold more of the NPP and 4-ANPP used illicitly than any other company. Thus, it bears an enormous responsibility for fentanyl's explosion.

Fentanyl is permitted for medical use in China, and medical-grade fentanyl is legally manufactured there, as well as in other countries, including the United States, Belgium, and India. When this fentanyl is exported, it's tightly controlled and accounted for — down to the microgram — by the International Narcotics Control Board (INCB). The INCB oversees United Nations drug treaties, including the one under which fentanyl is controlled, the Single Convention on Narcotic Drugs of 1961.

Fentanyl precursors are under the auspices of the INCB as well. In March, 2017 — following John Kerry's request — NPP and 4-ANPP were added to the list of internationally controlled drugs as part of the 1988 United Nations Convention Against Illicit Traffic in Narcotic Drugs and Psychotropic Substances. As with the 1961 treaty, the United States, China, Mexico, and most major European, Latin American, and Asian countries are signatories. The treaty requires strict protocols for the trade of NPP and

4-ANPP. "Exporting governments have to send pre-export notifications about each individual shipment," said Reiner Pungs, a member of the Precursors Control Section of the secretariat of the INCB. The company exporting fentanyl precursors is required to inform its government of the sale, and the exporting country is required to log the transaction, using an online system administered by INCB, which alerts the government of the importing country.

The amount of fentanyl precursors legally exported each year is tiny compared to other precursors under international control. Companies synthesizing legitimate fentanyl tend to make the precursors themselves. "The international trade is very small," said Pungs. "It's for research and for standard reference material for laboratories." As of February, 2019, his agency had only seen ten legal shipments of NPP and twelve of 4-ANPP since the chemicals were controlled in 2017.

The entire time it was selling NPP and 4-ANPP, Yuancheng was exempt from the INCB's monitoring system. It didn't have to report its fentanyl precursor sales. That's because, despite NPP and 4-ANPP's international scheduling in March, 2017, China did not follow suit until November 2017.

This was not out of the ordinary, as countries are given a grace period to comply; Mexico scheduled NPP and 4-ANPP in July 2017, for example. When China scheduled these fentanyl precursors, Yuancheng stopped selling them and began selling different fentanyl precursors that were still unscheduled in China.

Before China scheduled NPP and 4-ANPP, however, Yuancheng's salespeople made it clear to me that they were fully aware that the precursors were scheduled in most (if not all) of the countries they were exporting them to. In fact, the salespeople described the ways they smuggled their products through the United States customs process. Their salesman Chen Li bragged of a "double-western route from China to the United States which can guarantee 100% clearance. . . . Shenzhen to all the cities of the United States. . . . It means that we have a line with special people in charge of customs clearance in China and the United States."

On Skype, the company's salespeople were happy to show off examples of their fake packaging, to ensure that their sensitive products — fentanyl precursors and steroids — arrived intact. The fake packaging included bags marked as dog food and small boxes with photos of bread, labeled "High-Gluten Wheat Flour." All looked perfectly legitimate. A Yuancheng saleswoman named Julie offered "tamper evident" bags, tape, and labeling, as well as "hologram labels" to help undermine the customs process.

"You won't get in trouble," said an anyonymous Yuancheng saleswoman, speaking about shipping NPP and 4-ANPP. "We will keep eyes on the package after it is sent out, if we see any troubles for the customs, we will tell you don't contact the [shipping company], then the customs won't find you. If you think it is not safe, you can also give me a fake receiver name. And also find a shipping address which you don't live there."

In 2011 Yuancheng was honored by the economic commission of the province where it is located, Hubei, with an "Economic Construction Leading Enterprise" award, for "contributions to promoting the rise of the central region," an honor bestowed by ranking province Communist Party members. That year the company was also certified by the government as an official "New and High Technology Enterprise" — a critical designation toward receiving financial incentives — and in 2012 was chosen "by experts and the public" as one of Hubei's top 10 "innovation companies," in a province-sponsored competition. In 2016 it was a finalist in a contest honoring Wuhan's best entrepreneurs, in which it was called a "successful model for the establishment of high-tech enterprises."

It seems strange to call Yuancheng — which makes and sells chemicals — a "tech" company, but the term *tech* is used differently in China. "It's not just those that make computers or chips or semiconductors," said Lucy Lu, research analyst for the Washington, DC–based Peterson Institute for International Economics. "If you're a chemical company and, say, invent some new chemicals or new drugs, you will be considered a tech company in China."

China's biotechnology industry is roaring, in part owing to government rule changes in recent years making it easier for new drugs to get approved and allowing emerging companies to raise money on China's stock market. There are a host of incentives for these types of companies, and, as a result, many established enterprises have shifted their missions — as well as changed their names, adding the words *technology* or *biotechnology.*

For more than a decade, China has been

encouraging its chemical and pharmaceutical industries by offering companies lucrative tax incentives, subsidies, and direct financial support. The government has devoted enormous resources to the task, and these incentives have driven innovation and helped expand these industries. But the rise of dangerous NPS has been a terrible side effect. Quietly, money intended to spur legitimate innovation has gone to companies exporting fentanyls, fentanyl precursors, synthetic cannabinoids, and other dangerous products. It's unclear how aware the Chinese central government is of this. Neither China's National Narcotics Control Commission nor the Chinese embassy in Washington DC responded to my requests for comment. What is clear is that Yuancheng is a major case in point. Even as it has sold chemicals driving the fentanyl epidemic, the company has received vast amounts of government assistance.

Being named an official New and High Technology Enterprise (NHTE) in 2011 greatly aided Yuancheng's fortunes. It qualified because of its chemical innovation work. According to the company, this has included 180 "self-developed products" and more than fifty patents over the years, including a preparation method for a flavor agent called cinnamyl cinnamate and many chemical extraction processes.

Its NHTE status entitles Yuancheng to preferential tax policies and also makes it eligible for various rebates and reimbursements related to research-and-development efforts and staff training. "Since China's new Enterprise Income Tax Law took effect in January, 2008, the country's national and provincial governments have implemented a series of tax incentives for [NHTEs]," reads a briefing by the Asian business advisory firm Dezan Shira & Associates. "A hugely profitable industry in China, proactively applying for the different subsidies, tax exemptions and government funding schemes can significantly reduce a high tech company's tax burden and improve its market position."

Beginning in 2012, Yuancheng was sponsored for three years by an initiative called the Torch Program, which is run by China's Ministry of Science and Technology and delegates resources to technology companies, helping establish special industrial zones, as well as assisting with marketing and personnel training. "In size, scale and commercial results China's Torch Program," wrote the *Huffington Post,* "is the most successful entrepreneurial program in the world. Of all the Chinese government programs, the Torch Program is the one program that kick-started Chinese high-tech innovation and start-ups." Yuancheng has also been a beneficiary of the Spark Program — which according to the Chinese government's website is "aimed at popularizing modern technology in rural areas" — as well as something called the Innovation Fund, both of which are also administered by the Ministry of Science and Technology. The Innovation Fund has "channeled 3.5 billion yuan of investment into more than 3,000 projects in emerging industries," and in 2012 granted Yuangcheng an award of 500,000 yuan (US$79,000) for a project entailing the "oxidation of cinnamic acid (crystalline) with a new silver/copper catalyst." A year later the company won 50,000 yuan for a particular patent through a technology innovation program hosted by Hubei's Xiaonan district.

Some of Yuancheng's sub-companies list an address in a special industrial zone, the kind which seek to promote Chinese businesses, through subsidized land, subsidized rent, shared manufacturing infrastructure, and other resources. "China has been very generous in building these industrial parks as attractions for companies," said Gary

Hufbauer, a trade expert at the Peterson Institute for International Economics. "It's a nice break, certainly on the land, and maybe even the building." The benefits of operating in these zones can significantly impact a company's bottom line. "The high-tech zones have become a major engine to China's economic growth," said Zhang Zhihong, director of Torch High Technology Industry Development Center, of the Ministry of Science and Technology.

"I think the government, when they approve the company's application for the subsidies, sometimes just don't know the real things the chemical companies are producing," said Lucy Lu, research analyst for the Peterson Institute for International Economics.

Yuancheng isn't the only rogue Chinese chemical company taking advantage of programs created to bolster science and technology, and to promote the country's economy. Other companies allegedly making NPS and precursors have also been incentivized by the government.

They include 5A Pharmatech Co., led by Yan Xiaobing, one of the Chinese nationals accused by the United States of distributing fentanyl, and placed on the Justice Department's list of most prolific international drug traffickers. Indicted in September 2017, Yan, who is based in Wuhan, stands accused of conspiring to manufacture a host of NPS, including Flakka, N-bombs, synthetic cannabinoids, methylone, fentanyl and fentanyl analogues, and then distributing them in the United States and twenty other countries. China has refused to extradite him to the U.S. 5A claimed to make legitimate chemicals for export, and to work with large firms including Johnson & Johnson and Pfizer, but representatives from both companies denied this. Nonetheless, 5A — which is a subsidiary of Wuhan Livika Technology Co., and until early 2016 was known as 9W Pharmaceutical Technology Co. — had the support of the Chinese government, from which it received financial incentives. According to a company profile on Hubei Province's official website, the company was located in an economic development zone. (The company also claimed to have received certification as an NHTE, but this could not be confirmed.) The authors of a *Bloomberg* story published in May 2018 caught up with Yan on the twentieth floor of his Wuhan high-rise. The story quoted Yan saying that his company served only as a broker — selling chemicals manufactured by other labs — and that he closed his company because business was slow. His wife, Hu — named in documents as the owner of 5A — continued to run her tutoring business. "This is horrifying," said Yan, of the US charges. "Their investigation must have gone wrong."

Zaron Bio-Tech (Asia) Limited is the company whose leader, Jian Zhang, was charged in 2017 with operating a drug ring that made and sold fentanyl, fentanyl analogues, and fentanyl precursors all over the United States, including the fentanyl that killed eighteen-year-old Bailey Henke of Grand Forks. Zhang has also been identified as an international kingpin by the US Department of the Treasury; even so, China refuses to extradite him. Zaron Bio-Tech was engaged in the tech sphere and claimed to sell a wide variety of legitimate chemicals. (It's unclear whether the company still operates.) Company materials said it "engaged in manufacture and sales of food additive such as soy products, multiple sugar, alcohol, spice and others products." Like Yuancheng, it also sold body-building chemicals, including a human-growth hormone called Jintropin. According to the US Department of the Treasury, Zaron Bio-Tech was registered in Hong Kong and operated out of Shanghai, and the company claimed to have factories all over eastern Asia, with more than one thousand employees.

It's not clear whether Zaron Bio-Tech received subsidies or government incentives, but at least one of Zhang's indicted colleagues appears to have been involved with a company that did. In early 2018 a new US federal indictment charged four of Zhang's employees with international money-laundering conspiracy, accusing them of helping Zaron Bio-Tech in its fentanyl distribution operation. One of these employees is Cuiying Liu, who was sixty-two at the time of the indictment. Along with the three other employees, she stands accused by the Department of the Treasury of being a "key financial associate" of Zhang's, who "conducted financial transactions through money service businesses to launder illicit narcotics proceeds for Zhang and his organization." Cuiying also appears to be connected to a company called Dezhou Yanling Bio-tech Co., Ltd. That company lists a woman named Cuiying Liu as its legal representative and majority shareholder. (I was unable to confirm definitively that the two Cuiying Liu's are the same person, though this seems likely, especially considering that the company is located in the Shandong province city of Dezhou, which is the indicted Cuiying Liu's birthplace. The company did not respond to multiple requests for comment.) Dezhou Yanling Bio-tech, which was formerly known as the Yanling Honey Wine Factory, sells varieties of mead, alcoholic beverages made with fermented honey. Dezhou Yanling Bio-tech was certified as a New and High Technology Enterprise (NHTE) in 2017 and thus is entitled to preferential tax policies. It has also won numerous local and national honors for its products, and company materials cite its award-winning "temperature-controlled pure fermentation process technology," as well as its export sales to "seven countries," including the United States. Cuiying Liu is also the primary investor in two other honey-wine companies, both established in the mid-2010s, with earnings of around 8 million yuan (US$1.2 million) according to public records.

It is possible that Communist Party officials don't realize companies they support are exporting illicit fentanyl products and other NPS. Then again, it's possible that they do, considering that the Chinese tax code directly encourages the export of these chemicals.

NINETEEN

When one buys a children's toy or piece of clothing, its label will likely say whether it was made in China, but when one buys medicine the label most likely won't. It's extremely difficult to find out which household drugs come from China. A bottle of generic pain reliever I purchased recently, for example, is sold under the brand name TopCare. Its active ingredient, acetaminophen, is likely manufactured in China (as is the case with most acetaminophen), but there's no way to tell. The bottle lists only a distributor, Topco Associates, based in Elk Grove Village, Illinois, and the company did not respond to my requests for information. This is not unusual. Companies selling medicines on American shelves aren't required to list the manufacturers of their drugs' active ingredients on their packaging.

While the US pharmaceutical industry

makes expensive, patent-protected, brand-name drugs, China specializes in cheap generic drugs, which is why its legal, above-board chemical revenue is smaller than America's, despite greater output. In 2017, Chinese companies received thirty-eight approvals from the US Food and Drug Administration for generic drugs, up from twenty-two the previous year.

China is trying to change this, however. A countrywide initiative called "Made in China 2025" seeks to upgrade the country's manufacturing status, to move it up the "value chain," using policy changes and government investment. The Chinese pharmaceutical industry is a major part of this initiative, and the government has moved to incentivize increased spending on research and development, and to promote industry consolidation. The goal is to produce higher-quality, more expensive medical drugs, for use at home and abroad. Already, Chinese medical scientists have developed promising new cancer drugs, and experts believe it's only a matter of time before Chinese pharmaceutical companies are among the world's biggest. "It's not whether they are going to," said Jonathan Wang, senior managing director of health-care fund OrbiMed Asia. "They are going to."

One way China has sought to develop its industries and expand its exports is by offering tax reimbursements via the value-added tax, or VAT, rebate. Companies are reimbursed for tax money they have already paid in the process of making their products — for example, taxes they paid when they bought the ingredients needed to make a certain chemical compound.

The VAT rebates go as high as 16 percent; a 16 percent rebate means the exporters receive a full tax reimbursement. Not every exported chemical gets one, but thousands do, and the rebates vary wildly. According to China's State Administration of Taxation website, aspirin and sildenafil (the drug in Viagra) get no VAT rebates. Melamine, the industrial chemical used to adulterate milk powder products that was linked to infant deaths in 2008 — but which also has safe uses — gets a 10 percent rebate. Yuancheng products like the aforementioned cinnamyl cinnamate, and potassium cinnamate also receive a 10 percent VAT rebate. So does fentanyl. And beyond that at least ten fentanyl analogues — including 3-methyl-fentanyl, which is not used for legitimate medical reasons, anywhere — get a 13 percent rebate. The best-known fentanyl precursors, 4-ANPP and NPP, get 13 percent rebates, as does the John William Huffman-created synthetic cannabinoid JWH-018. In September 2018, China announced it would raise VAT rebates on about four hundred different products for export, from chemicals to semiconductors, in what Reuters described as "a bid to boost prospects for shipments amid its trade war with the United States." Also in 2018, the VAT rebate for fentanyl was increased, from 9 percent to 10 percent. It was not one of the four hundred products from the September announcement, and it is unclear when exactly in 2018 this occurred — or whether it was also in response to Trump's trade war — but the elevated rate remained in place as this book went to press.

China began issuing VAT rebates in 1985, to make its exports more competitive. The rebates are big business, having had "a large and significant positive impact on Chinese export growth," according to an academic paper on the subject. China doesn't explain why particular chemicals get the rebates they do; one possibility is that products with a "value add" get higher rebates, while generics get lower rebates or nothing.

VAT rebate rates go up and down regularly. This is, to other countries, a problem. Though China is far from the only country that gives VAT rebates, others have static rebate rates. The fact that China's fluctuate makes some countries believe it's unfairly promoting certain export products. The United States has been particularly concerned, despite the fact that China's rebates do not violate World Trade Organization rules. In 2012, the US Department of Commerce announced that, in response to China's VAT rebates policy, it would begin calculating certain duties differently, penalizing Chinese exports it believed benefited from subsidies, an approach that continues.

There is no doubt that if a particular chemical's VAT rebate rate is higher, companies are more likely to export it. "Even small variations in these rebates can have a big impact in the profitability of exporting," wrote researchers in the *Oxford Review of Economic Policy*.

Among the beneficiaries of these rebates are legitimate Chinese companies legally manufacturing fentanyl for medical use. Though only five are permitted by the government to do so, it's big business. In addition to selling the drug to Chinese hospitals — where fentanyl is a dominant painkiller — some also export. The largest of these five companies, Renfu Pharmaceutical, based in Hubei province, sells more than 2 billion yuan (US$290 million) worth of fentanyl per year. It exports to countries including the Philippines, Turkey, Sri Lanka, and Ecuador. (None of these companies export fentanyl to the United States.) US President Donald Trump's December 2018 meeting with Chinese President Xi Jinping in Buenos Aires — in which China first promised to control all fentanyls — was big news in China, and it was the first time many citizens there learned about the American fentanyl crisis. It also stirred panic within China's pharmaceutical-fentanyl industry, causing Renfu to issue a statement saying that the company did not sell fentanyl to the United States. The company's chairman, Wang Xuehai, noted that the illicit fentanyl used in America "is illegally processed and smuggled by underground factories, and has nothing to do with the five regular manufacturers."

Only three types of fentanyls are legally permitted to be manufactured in China for domestic medical use or export: fentanyl, sufentanil, and remifentanil. It's unclear why at least eight other fentanyl analogues get VAT rebates. And while it's also unclear how many Chinese companies exporting fentanyls or fentanyl precursors for illicit use are receiving these tax rebates,

Yuancheng is included among them. Ye Chuan Fa said his company takes advantage of VAT rebates for every chemical it sells.

There is little doubt that China is under-cutting its publicly stated goal of stopping the export of dangerous drugs for illicit use. That's because the country actively encour-ages the export of fentanyls and fentanyl precursors — and even synthetic cannabi-noids — through its tax code and high-tech subsidies. Further, it has been ineffective at ensuring such exports don't end up in the wrong hands.

"If China had a subsidy on lead, you'd probably see a lot more bullets coming out of China, and that's what's happening here with the precursors. They're just subsidizing whatever is a high-value commodity, and in this case it just happens to be really potent synthetic opioids or opioid precursors," said RAND's Bryce Pardo. "The Chinese gov-ernment doesn't have a good capacity for regulating its own industry. At the same time, it wants to export and make as much money as possible. They're getting ahead of themselves and causing a lot of harm in the process."

What's unclear is if China realizes its poli-cies spur the international drug trade.

"As with many of China's policies, the aid

in fentanyls export is myopic," said Justin Hastings, an associate professor of international relations and comparative politics at the University of Sydney, whose areas of expertise include China and drug trafficking. He speculates that these policies were developed to encourage chemicals and industries deemed important to the country's national development. "It's also a lackadaisical approach to enforcement of Chinese companies' behavior outside of China and in doing business with foreign companies that are not explicitly on sanctions lists," he went on, adding that "some genuine corruption" of Chinese officials may be at play as well.

Appointed by former Senate Democratic leader Harry Reid, Katherine Tobin served as a commissioner on the US–China Economic and Security Review Commission until the end of 2018. The bipartisan panel advises Congress on matters including drugs, and Tobin said my findings fit with a pattern of Chinese government activities that the commission has long been tracking.

"The primary incentive, particularly for local-level Chinese government officials, is to support economic growth," Tobin said. "Therefore, it is likely Chinese regulators and policymakers have chosen to look the other way regarding the production and export of fentanyl products. This incentive structure persists despite the Chinese government's repeated promises to crack down on narcotic flows, a sign that Beijing is guilty of gross negligence in enforcing its chemical regulations, bad faith in its negotiations with the United States, or both."

Tobin added that the government's promises to control fentanyls are meaningless until regulatory reforms and rigorous inspection systems are implemented. "The Chinese government's promises have not been fulfilled until US officials and law enforcement on the ground in China — such as the DEA and FDA — observe these controls being implemented in a manner consistent with Beijing's pledge to crack down on flows of fentanyl, as well as fentanyl analogues and precursors."

Occasionally, Chinese officials have spoken candidly about the country's out-of-control drug industry. "My feeling is that it's just like a race and I will never catch up with the criminals," said Yu Haibin, of China's National Narcotics Control Commission, in 2017. It's clear to see that, whatever one thinks of China's efforts, reigning in such a large chemical industry is extraordinarily difficult. It might be easier to stymie a small company like Chemsky — one clearly focused on making illicit chemicals for recreational use — than a large one like Yuancheng, which employs many people and wields a great deal of local influence. "For them to shut down an entire legal pharmaceutical company comes with many, many problems," said Vanda Felbab-Brown, an expert on illicit economies, of the Brookings Institution.

China's President Xi Jinping has sought tighter regulations in drug production and increased penalties for rogue actors, and in March, 2018, it was announced that the Chinese FDA was once again being reorganized to strengthen its oversight capabilities, which involves being absorbed into a new overarching organization called the State Administration for Market Regulation. Yet whether China is putting forth its best effort in this herculean task remains a matter of some dispute.

"If the Chinese government pursued drug smugglers the way it crushes dissident Christians, labor activists, lawyers or feminists, those drug exports would end," wrote *New York Times* columnist Nicholas Kristof, who has reported on China extensively.

On the other hand, Reiner Pungs, of the

secretariat of the International Narcotics Control Board, feels China has been reacting quickly to the NPS crisis. "Every time a new substance falls under international control, they put it under control nationally," he said, noting that in 2017 China scheduled 116 NPS at the same time. Martin Raithelhuber, an illicit-synthetic-drug expert with the UN Office on Drugs and Crime, concurred, saying he believes China is playing a very active role.

If that's true, it was perhaps not always the case. Roumen Sedefov of the European Monitoring Centre for Drugs and Drug Addiction believes China was likely shielding its illicit chemical industry in the past. "I think they used to turn a blind eye for quite some time," he observed.

In 2015 the former Mexican ambassador to China, Jorge Guajardo, said the Chinese government had been actively undermining Mexico's efforts to control synthetic drugs. "They just didn't see what was in it for them to look into their own industries exporting these chemicals," said Guajardo, who served as ambassador from 2007 to 2013. "In all my time there, the Chinese never showed any willingness to cooperate on stemming the flow of precursors into Mexico." The Chinese foreign ministry denied failing to cooperate. In 2016 the *Wall Street Journal* paraphrased an anonymous "Mexican official" as saying that Mexico's government "was hesitant to press China too aggressively on the fentanyl trade as leaders there seek greater Chinese investment to boost the Mexican economy."

China has undoubtedly stepped up its efforts since then. Narcotics-control officials have installed thousands of machines at shipping companies to check for drugs in outbound parcels to "high-risk" locations, and they have targeted those who import magnetic resonance spectrometers, which are often used by drug labs.

Despite the recent blanket ban of fentanyl analogues, China still doesn't have an analogue law for other drugs, including fentanyl precursors, and thus it is forced to prohibit most new drugs piecemeal. This can be a slow, bureaucratic process, and it is often not accomplished until long after the new drugs have been popularized on the Internet.

Some experts say that, although China doesn't want to be directed by the United States — and told whom to arrest — the country cares deeply about its image and doesn't want to be seen as the world's drug pusher. "The drugs . . . exploit the differences in drug policing in different countries, in turn severely affecting our national image," reads a 2017 report about NPS, entitled "Third Generation Drugs — New Psychoactive Substances," published by a police department in Sichuan province.

Ultimately China is no "narco-state," like the small West African country of Guinea Bissau, where cocaine-related corruption reached the top levels of government in the 2000s. Corruption is certainly common in China, but drug-related bribery is less tolerated than other types. Being convicted of drugs sales — along with arms dealing — is among the rare crimes that could get a public official executed. For this reason Chinese officials, particularly high-level ones, are less likely to enrich themselves through drug production and trafficking, though they are often successfully bribed by drug traffickers seeking to receive lesser sentences.

And those quick to blame China should bear in mind that the American government doesn't have its hands clean. Decades of War on Drugs practices have failed to promote policies experts believe will help addicted users break their habits, all while resulting in the needless incarceration of generations of nonviolent offenders.

But there is no doubt that China has made grave errors in its haste to promote its pharmaceutical and chemical industries. Whether or not the intention was to do harm, China's manipulations of its tax code and the launching of incentive programs have directly fueled the rise of companies making NPS for export.

Just like Britain's East India Company two centuries ago, today the world's two biggest superpowers are producing opioids by the ton. The U.S. generally does so legally, as medicine, while China also does so illicitly, as drugs, but the damage from each country fuels the other. Neither is taking sensible means to stop it. While they focus on blaming each other, the contagion continues to spread around the globe.

TWENTY

Yuancheng lists its address on its websites and invites interested customers to come by for a visit. In January, 2018, while I was in China, I did exactly that.

Some five hundred miles west of Shanghai, bisected by the Yangtze River and formerly known as an agricultural hub, Wuhan is expanding rapidly, even for booming China. Blanketed by dense smog, full of college students, and featuring a wide array of industry and manufacturing, it's not picturesque, but its sheer scope inspires awe, in particular the ubiquitous clusters of identical high-rises, dozens of stories tall. Wuhan is home to a large chemical industry; the official website of its province, Hubei, describes the city as the "capital of petrochemical equipment and fine chemicals in China." Wuhan benefits from a symbiotic relationship with the local universities, which spawn talented chemists and affiliated research labs. Government-sponsored development zones help foster the local chemical industry as well. Some of these companies are found in gleaming industrial parks; others in disguised residential facilities. Yuancheng, it turns out, operates out of a hotel.

Posing as a buyer, I answered an online advertisement for fentanyl precursors and was put in touch with a Yuancheng salesman who called himself Sean. We arranged to meet at the company's main office in Wuhan, in the Wuchang district near a busy subway station in a blue-collar neighborhood. The posted address put Yuancheng at the corner of a chaotic intersection. No large sign announced the company's presence, however, only a small one in an alley not visible from the street. Reached by cell phone, Sean said that he was not actually available but that a colleague who called herself Amy would be waiting in the lobby of the Home Inn at that intersection.

Yuancheng's Wuhan operation is based in this dilapidated eight-story edifice, sharing the space with the operating hotel, the same facility Ye purchased in 2001. The facility was formerly known as Jia Ye, and while Ye Chuan Fa still owns the building, now the hotel is run by Home Inn, a Chinese budget hotel chain. Erato the Greek muse is still there, but the hotel, with its crumbling windowsills, cracked paint, and stained floors, has seen better days. A room without a window costs as little as seventeen dollars per night.

After about fifteen minutes Amy arrived in the lobby, along with another young woman, who with a laugh introduced herself as Amy as well. They were friends since their school days, who had studied English together and had been selling chemicals at Yuancheng for three years. Neither spoke particularly strong English, but both were exceedingly friendly. They led me down a back hallway, up an elevator, and then past a locked gate into the company's offices, which were partitioned off from hotel guests.

We sat down in a small meeting room, and one Amy offered a steaming cup of hot water, while the other got to work taking my order. "How many do you want?"

Before discussing fentanyl precursors, I claimed to be interested in chemicals including a steroid called nandrolone decanoate, which is illegal to possess in the United States without a prescription. Amy was eager to comply, noting that it sold for $1,800 for one kilogram. Selling controversial drugs designed to help athletes and others gain muscle is one of Yuancheng's primary businesses. The company maintains many different websites focused on anabolic steroids, including supplysteroids. com and anabolicsteroidssupplements.com. When asked to name the most popular products her company sold, another Yuancheng salesperson responded, "Steroids." The salesman Sean is listed on Skype under the handle, "Sean SteroidHormone." The Chinese government provides incentives to companies exporting these products. Nandrolone decanoate, in particular, receives a 16 percent VAT rebate, the highest available. Other Chinese companies advertising anabolic steroids on the Internet appear to be taking advantage of government benefits as well; a company called Hugeraw Health Technology Co., Ltd. ("a profession well-known company in the steroids&bodybuilding field," reads its website) lists its address in a medical-focused industrial zone in the city of Taizhou.

The Amys were happy to comply with my requests for steroids, and asked whether I was interested in anything else. I inquired about the two most popular fentanyl precursors, NPP and 4-ANPP, but I already knew that my timing was bad. On November 6,

2017, China scheduled both of them, and Yuancheng immediately stopped selling them.

"It is illegal in China now," one of the Amys said, regretfully. "We do not sell it, because we are legal company in China."

I said that I nonetheless remained interested in making fentanyl and wondered whether they would be able to sell me other chemicals for this purpose. There was a pause, followed by a short conversation between them in Chinese. One Amy left the room to get more information. Eventually she returned and said that, yes, Yuancheng would be happy to sell me these chemicals. "You can ask Sean to find similar products for you," she said.

After our discussion I requested a tour of the Yuancheng facilities, which the Amys, amused, were happy to provide.

Two floors of the facility were crammed with salespeople, perhaps two or three hundred, most in front of desktop computers in cubicles that were red and gray on one floor, green and gray on the other. It was a bustling place, with cold-calling, deals being struck, and money being made. Salespeople offered to speak with potential customers on just about any app or platform they desired, fitting for a company that calls itself "the first e-commerce conglomerate in the chemical industry."

Many employees seemed to be fairly recent college graduates, and most were wearing thick coats. As in other places I had visited in China, it was cold inside. The facilities were a bit drab but had plenty of natural light, and the environment wasn't unpleasant. Employee cubicles were filled with plants, stuffed animals, and other personal tokens familiar in Western offices.

Other aspects of the working experience differed sharply, however. As confirmed by numerous employees, Yuancheng salespeople work nine hours a day, six days a week, though this is not particularly unusual in China. About 20 to 30 percent of their salary — at least for some employees — appears to come from commissions. As for the pay, one Yuancheng saleswoman, who requested anonymity, said, "New staff is not high wages," but some employees made a decent salary.

Ye Chuan Fa was right at his own cubicle, also wearing a thick coat. As the Amys introduced him, he stood up and stuck out his hand. He didn't speak any English, but smiled and offered a chair and his business card, which had his information in Chinese characters on one side and in English on the other. He didn't seem suspicious or ask any personal questions — he had surely dealt with plenty of Westerners engaged in shady chemical-trade business over the years.

"This is our head office," he said. "We have thirty branch companies in China." (In February, 2019, he said that number had risen to forty-one.)

He spoke for a few minutes about his business, but the Amys' translation skills quickly petered out, and I was not able to understand the details about who manufactures the chemicals that Ye's company sells. He later said that although Yuancheng had four factories operating as recently as 2016, "at the moment, our factories are all just rented out. We ourselves only do sales." Other Yuancheng salespeople told me in 2018, however, that Yuancheng maintained two factories, one in Shenzhen and one in Wuhan. "Most of the steroids we make at our own factory," said one of the Amys, during my office visit. "Not all, most of." It was off-limits, however. "We can not go into the laboratory. Our boss say, for safety."

"For security," added the other Amy.

One of the company's websites says it has a thirty-thousand-square-meter plant, built to "GMP standard," referencing Good

Manufacturing Practices, a universal system used for regulating pharmaceutical-manufacturing techniques, including working conditions and product testing, which is required for drugs that are to be sold on the pharmaceutical market. An employee of the Shenzhen branch named Julie, however, had told me earlier that not all of their products met GMP standards. "To be honest," she said, "it's not GMP."

We said goodbye to Ye, and the tour continued downstairs. There the Amys offered a surprising revelation: the workers live on the premises — in dormitory-style hotel rooms housing between four and seven people, on average. In fact, the Amys were roommates. They presented the personnel department and then, on the bottom levels, a pair of canteens where employees take meals. Inside the kitchen the Yuan-cheng company chef chopped up meats and vegetables for that night's dinner with a cleaver.

Dorm environments like these are not uncommon at Chinese companies, and the free room and board is part of Yuancheng's sales pitch. The company's ads promise that successful employees will be able to "buy a car within ten years and a house within twenty" — considered particularly desirable traits among singles — and many ads mention a variety of perks, including free cell phones, a pension, the possibility of domestic and foreign travel, "occasional dinner parties," and "six types of insurance."

All in all, it would be an appealing offer for a recent college graduate, most of whom have no idea they may be selling ingredients for the world's most lethal drug and have little idea what they are actually offering. "I don't know buyers usage," Sean wrote on Skype. "I don't care about it."

"NPP is a sensitive products. Why you buy it?" one Yuancheng saleswoman asked me on Skype, before the product was scheduled in China. "I know many people buy it. But I don't know what it is used for."

I explained that it was used to make fentanyl.

"I know fentanyl," she continued, "but why people use it? We Chinese don't use it."

"It's highly addictive," I said.

"Yes, I know it is a bad products to person," the saleswoman admitted, "but I still sell it, so sometimes I feel guilt. NPP is not forbidden in China, so we can sell. I sell it, because I want earn money, earn a living."

After the tour, the Amys led me out of the building through a back-alley exit and walked me to the train station, avoiding the treacherous intersection out front. They laughed at my jokes and attempted to guess my age. "Not over thirty," one of them insisted, suspiciously off by a full decade.

A few weeks later, after I was back home in the United States, Yuancheng posted a notice on one of its websites that read: "All products can only be sold to companies or institutions, and not to private clients." This seemed to be an abrupt change in policy, and one explicitly and clumsily designed to insulate Yuancheng's legal liability. "If any legal problems arise from staff selling products to single clients, the company will not be implicated," it added.

If this was, in fact, the new policy, the employees apparently didn't get the memo.

"May I still do the order?" I messaged Sean, over Skype.

"Yes," he wrote back. For the other sales-people, it was also business as usual.

The impact of China's scheduling of NPP, 4-ANPP, fentanyls, and other NPS is not yet known. If these changes succeed in substantially shutting down the supply of these chemicals, perhaps India will step in to fill the void. India has a robust chemical industry of its own and is second only to China when it comes to supplying the world with generic medicine and active pharmaceutical ingredients. It manufactures fentanyl and fentanyl precursors in both their legitimate and illicit forms, and the country's chemical industry is already fueling an international drug crisis involving an opioid called tramadol. Tramadol, which is weaker than fentanyl but nonetheless powerful and addictive, is wreaking havoc in Africa and the Middle East. Made in India, it is smuggled by terrorist groups including ISIS. Kids are particularly affected — the former director of Nigeria's drug enforcement agency estimated in 2016 that 70 percent of boys in northern states were taking drugs like tramadol — but its abuse is widespread. In 2013, researchers from a French university reported the startling news that a sub-Saharan African plant named *Nauclea latifolia,* used by locals to treat pain and disease, naturally produced tramadol. This finding was soon debunked, however; it turns out the chemical was being absorbed by the plant through soil that had been contaminated by human and cattle excrement. Farmers were giving their beasts of burden tramadol to get them to work harder and longer, and took the pills themselves for the same reasons.

Up until now, India's output of NPS has been significantly smaller than China's. But that may be changing. Like China, India has many knowledgeable drug chemists. In September 2018, Indian authorities seized about ten kilograms of fentanyl from a clandestine lab in the city of Indore. The lab was allegedly run by a chemistry PhD named Mohammed Sadiq. He was arrested by Indian police, along with two other men, a local businessman named Manu Gupta and Mexican national George Solis, who allegedly had come to India for the purpose of picking up the fentanyl shipment. Three months later Indian police arrested four men in Mumbai, seizing one hundred kilograms of fentanyl; it was reportedly being prepared for shipment to a Mexican cartel. The country has also been producing large quantities of synthetic cannabinoids and mephedrone, the latter of which had become a tremendous public-health problem there by the mid-2010s, with people addicted to "meow meow" flooding rehab centers. NPS and "research chemicals" are sold openly on web marketplace IndiaMart, based in the northern Indian state of Uttar Pradesh.

Should the NPS industry migrate from China to India, the epidemic could get even worse. Whereas China has been at least somewhat responsive to American requests to control its chemical industry, India has trailed when it comes to scheduling NPS and fentanyl precursors. Further, Indian government bribery is rampant — the highest in the Asia Pacific region, according to Transparency International — which helps facilitate the country's illicit drug exports.

Most likely, in the face of competition from India, China will continue doing what it has always done: adapt. The country's illicit chemical industry has been resilient, even as its drug laws have shifted.

Almost immediately after I arrived home, in mid-January, 2018, Yuancheng employees began making a new push. Now that the old fentanyl precursors NPP and 4-ANPP were scheduled, they had new alternatives I might be interested in. The advantage of these chemicals, of course, was that they were still unscheduled in China.

"Hello! How are you doing friend!" Kay wrote. "We recommend another stuff that similar to NPP or 4-ANPP. It is: N-phenylpiperidine-4-amine."

"Can these two products replace 4-ANPP?" wrote Chen Li, from Yuancheng's Shenzhen branch, listing N-phenylpiperidine-4-amine dihydrochloride, as well as one called 4-anilino-1-benzylpiperidine. These two chemicals can also be used to make fentanyl and its analogues, and the latter precursor is eligible for a 13 percent VAT rebate.

It seemed unlikely that Kay and Chen Li — whom I first contacted long before my China trip — were trying to poach me from Sean. Instead, their outreach seemed to be part of a larger, coordinated Yuancheng sales strategy, an attempt to proactively meet the needs of those interested in making fentanyl. It confirmed that Yuancheng wasn't planning to let China's prohibition of NPP and 4-ANPP slow their business.

Fentanyl is slower to make with these new precursor chemicals, because extra steps are involved, but the Yuancheng staff believed they were the next best thing. And it appears they are right. When I checked in with Sean a year later, in late January, 2019, he told me that N-phenylpiperidine-4-amine dihydrochloride was doing tremendous business for the company. "It's very hot . . . it sells a lot," he wrote over Skype. Almost all of the business for this chemical — "nearly fentanyl," as he called it — was coming from Mexico, as much as 50 kg per order, a quantity that would cost me "$82,080 by airshipment," he added. Chen Li, however, said that export business for N-phenylpiperidine-4-amine dihydrochloride was still strong in the U.S. Yuancheng now had "overseas warehouses," including in America, where they regularly send "batch[es] of products" including fentanyl precursors. From these warehouses — including one in Chicago — the precursors could be delivered directly to American customers, he added. (I could not confirm the existence of these warehouses.)

These new fentanyl precursors will likely be scheduled before long, first in the United States, then internationally, and then, finally, in China. But that wouldn't be an insurmountable problem for Yuancheng either; according to the DEA, there are sixteen different known precursor chemicals that can be used to make fentanyl, most of which remain unscheduled worldwide.

In February, 2019, I called Ye Chuan Fa, speaking to him through an interpreter. Revealing my identity as a journalist, I told him about my findings. Though I expected him to hang up on me, he was cordial, if sometimes evasive. I began by asking him which of Yuancheng's chemicals were their best sellers.

"That depends on the year," he said. "Perhaps this year one product is very popular, and next year it's another one that jumps out."

I asked him if he was, as rumored, the wealthiest man in Wuhan. "Very early on," he said. "A dozen years ago." (This timeline corresponds with the opening of his hot springs resort, which would go on to fail.)

The conversation soon moved to fentanyl precursors. He didn't deny selling them. "Anything that the country schedules, we don't sell. As long as it's scheduled, we won't sell it. If it's not scheduled, we can sell it."

He did claim, however, to be uninformed about these chemicals' use. "I don't know much. It was only reported in the news last year that these things are meant to make fentanyl. Back in the day we had zero idea what these chemicals are used for. No clue. Right now, it's still not clear."

I pressed him further, noting fentanyl's danger, and the crisis it had caused in the U.S. and other countries. "We don't know much about these things," he said. "We

412

make raw materials. Not finished products. We are factory-to-factory." I disputed this assertion — that his enterprise only sold to other companies — noting that numerous Yuancheng salespeople had tried to sell me precursors, as an individual. I asked him if he worried that criminal organizations were buying his chemicals. "I think not," he said. "We are not under criminal suspicion. It's not possible to know what other people do."

He was claiming ignorance. On the topic of his company's good fortune in recent years, however, he seemed to have more information. Yuancheng's standing as a New and High Technology Enterprise gave them "help with income tax," and the company took advantage of all available Value Added Tax export rebates, including those for fentanyl precursors and steroids.

He said Yuancheng began selling NPP and 4-ANPP "many years" ago, though he didn't know how much the company had profited off of their sales. He sounded defensive. "Back in the day we had no clue about these things. Their usage is really wide. It's not just one domain," he said, implying (incorrectly) that the chemicals have other uses than as fentanyl precursors. He added that his company has sold more than "30 plus products" in the fentanyl precursor "category."

"And then it was listed. And then we can't sell them anymore, and it's taken off the shelves."

I inquired about the other, still-unscheduled fentanyl precursors Yuancheng salespeople were still trying to sell me, but he denied knowledge of these chemicals. He also denied that Yuancheng had sold more fentanyl precursors that any other company, pointing instead toward Renfu Pharmaceutical, a fellow-Hubei province company that "made it big" selling "finished" fentanyl. Indeed, Renfu's parent company, Humanwell Healthcare, is listed on the Shanghai Stock Exchange. But what Ye declined to mention, or didn't realize, was that Renfu has explicit permission from the Chinese government to manufacture fentanyl, and that, unlike Yuancheng, it didn't smuggle chemicals into other countries for illicit use.

When I asked him why Yuancheng mailed some of its chemicals in disguised packaging, with the promise to evade customs, he went uncharacteristically silent. My final question, about anabolic steroids, he didn't understand at first, until I described them as the "chemicals for making big muscles."

"Oh I got it," he said with a chuckle. "We

sell a lot. This stuff, our country doesn't regulate."

■ ■ ■ ■

PART IV:
A NEW APPROACH

■ ■ ■ ■

TWENTY-ONE

The War on Drugs was launched during Richard Nixon's first term. "Public enemy number one in the United States is drug abuse," the president said, at a 1971 press conference. "In order to fight and defeat this enemy, it is necessary to wage a new, all-out offensive."

Using public resources to battle drugs — no matter whether or not doing so benefits the public — goes back much further. The 1909 US law banning opium took aim only at the kind favored for smoking by Chinese immigrants and not the "medical" type sold in stores, which was also commonly misused. Harry Anslinger, the commissioner of the Federal Bureau of Narcotics, set back opiate-addiction therapy by pushing to criminalize users. Nixon himself, in the recollections of top adviser John Ehrlichman, said the target of his drug war was hippies and blacks. Nixon specifically targeted LSD, and the DEA's establishment in 1973 was right around the time of the arrests of members of the Brotherhood of Eternal Love, purveyors of Orange Sunshine.

President Reagan doubled down on Nixon's drug war, and First Lady Nancy Reagan coined the phrase, "Just Say No," which became ubiquitous in American society in the late 1980s. The Reagans' legacy is not one of eradicating America's drug problem, however, but of enacting harsher penalties for drug crimes, including mandatory minimum sentences. Democratic president Bill Clinton doubled down in turn, signing a 1994 crime bill that featured a "three strikes" law. These zero-tolerance policies helped crowd prisons around the country with nonviolent drug offenders, disproportionately black and Latino.

American policies for countries producing our drugs have also been problematic. The United States has pushed for eradication and targeted kingpins — at a huge cost, in terms of both dollars and lives lost. The DEA-assisted killing of Pablo Escobar in 1993 did not curtail Colombia's cocaine industry, and El Chapo's capture has not slowed the Mexican cartels. "In terms of taking down kingpins and burning heaps of their narcotics, [the War on Drugs] has been a stunning success," wrote *New York Times* contributing opinion writer Ioan Grillo on the eve of El Chapo's 2018 trial in New York. "In terms of reducing the number of Americans killed from overdoses or Latin Americans murdered over smuggling profits, it has been a resounding failure." Indeed, cartel battles and security actions have resulted in nearly 120,000 Mexican deaths in the last ten years.

All of this costs US taxpayers about $58 billion a year, according to the Drug Policy Alliance. In the views of many, these efforts not only have been futile in reducing drug abuse but have actively aided the suppliers. "See, if you look at the Drug War from a purely economic point of view, the role of the government is to protect the drug cartel," conservative economist Milton Friedman said in 1991. "That's literally true."

Today, US drug policy is in shambles. Our laws — and those in countries around the world — simply weren't ready for the NPS revolution. These laws stem mostly from the UN's Single Convention on Narcotic Drugs, a treaty that was ratified in 1961, a time when the drug landscape was very different. "We have a regulatory system that's designed for plant-based drugs," said RAND's Bryce Pardo. "The 1961 convention was based on a collection of earlier international agreements and resolutions governing poppy, coca, and cannabis, and their derivatives. We barely had an understanding of neuropharmacology back then."

Dennis Wichern is a St. Louis–area native with a flat Midwestern accent, rimless glasses, and a seemingly unflappable demeanor, befitting a man who takes on the world's most dangerous criminals. He began his DEA career tracking heroin dealers and helping bust meth rings run by biker gangs, and has been on the front lines of the War on Drugs for more than thirty years.

Wichern is proud of the work he and his colleagues have done. He mentions crackhouse busts in which neighbors gave officers standing ovations because they were tired of chaos on their block. He has arrested drug offenders who thank him for intervening in their spiraling-out-of-control lives. He notes the agency's success in tamping down specific drugs. "I know there's still ecstasy out there, but we don't see it near in the amount," he said, adding that another party staple of the early 2000s, GHB — also known as the date-rape drug — is much less common as well. "DEA controlled many of those things, made them illegal. I was on the ground floor."

Besides St. Louis, Wichern has also worked in Indianapolis and Washington, DC, before rising to become the top DEA official in Chicago. When I first spoke to him in June 2016, he was concerned about the influx of fentanyl and other NPS. "Whereas we only had a handful of drugs back ten years ago, now we got a witches' brew of death," he said.

He achieved the rank of special agent in charge before retiring on the last day of 2017. To the end, he believed in the DEA's "three pillars" philosophy for how society should stop drug problems: "enforcement of laws, prevention, and demand reduction." Upon his retirement Wichern was lauded for his efforts, including work on the case that brought down El Chapo.

One of Wichern's last major cases was a huge fentanyl sting in Chicago that was months in the making. Chicago is a national distribution center for fentanyl, and the case provided insight into what has — and hasn't — changed during his three-decade tenure.

Interstate 290 cuts past Chicago's Rush University hospital and then through the city's near Southwest Side. Adjacent to the expressway, homeless people and others suffering from opioid-use disorders do deals and shoot up, and the highway also provides quick access for affluent people from the suburbs. "They serve you in your car, quick-out in under a minute, and you're back home in Hinsdale before the kids wake," Jack Riley, ex–special agent in charge of the DEA's Chicago office, told *Rolling Stone*. "That's why gangsters kill for those corners. They're the Park Place and Boardwalk of the drug game."

To Chicago residents, 290 is better known as the Eisenhower Expressway or, to many, the Heroin Highway. Chicago's famously high murder rate, which police say is driven by drug dealing on the West Side, all comes to a head near the Heroin Highway, in drug markets on streets like Independence Boulevard.

"The people that are dealing this are street gang members, and they're dealing the drugs to fund the gangs and that's what puts guns on the street and what leads to all the violence," Anthony Riccio, chief of the Chicago Police Department's organized-crime bureau, said about the area.

There's just one problem with the nickname Heroin Highway: these days what is sold is almost all fentanyl or a mixture of heroin and fentanyl. Fentanyl sold at the street level goes for about the same price as heroin — around ten dollars per bag — and looks similar, which sows confusion. The Chicago DEA office calls fentanyl the area's "most serious" drug threat. "Chicago's street gangs have likely been more inclined to involve themselves with fentanyl distribution due to its close association with heroin and increased profit potential," said Chicago DEA public information officer Sharon Lindskoog.

Chicago had encountered fentanyl before, but in the middle of the 2010s the problem began spiraling out of control. Cook County had 103 fentanyl deaths in 2015, and the next year the number shot up to 562. In contrast to the demographics in much of the rest of the country, those who died in Chicago were disproportionately African American. "The epidemic in Chicago is not the national epidemic," said Amanda Brooks of the local PCC Community Wellness Center, which offers health care services to the disavantaged. "The Chicago epidemic is affecting 45- to 65-year-old men on the West Side. Most of our patients are not intentionally taking fentanyl." Instead, they believe they are taking a less powerful drug, like heroin.

Local and national law enforcement agencies have collaborated to fight the rising tide. In the spring of 2016, Dennis Wichern and the DEA's Strike Force and a Chicago police team called the High Intensity Drug Traffic Area task force began organizing a massive sting. These efforts culminated on September 22. In a series of quiet West Side busts during daylight hours, thirty-three suspected dealers were arrested and charged with selling fentanyl. Nearly all of them, police said, had ties to gangs and had previous felonies.

The Chicago bust received a lot of media coverage. Some of it focused on the law enforcement techniques used, which went beyond undercover buys and leaning on informants. The operation also employed something called a "strategic subject list," a Chicago Police Department algorithm employing suspects' background information to identify individuals "200 or 300 times more likely than the average person to be prone to violence, either as a victim or perpetrator." The Illinois State Police crime lab also helped the operation generate "heat maps" showing where, specifically, the fentanyl was being distributed. Wichern noted that they even tracked emergency medical service runs — specifically, ambulance and fire department calls that resulted in the use of Narcan, the opioid antidote that can save the life of someone having a heroin or fentanyl overdose. "We get their data, where they're using Narcan the most, and then we'll target that area."

Less publicized was that very little actual fentanyl or heroin was seized. "We were targeting the street dealers, so the seizures were small, if any," Wichern acknowledged. Also, for all the razzle-dazzle of the law enforcement techniques, none of them were specifically designed to target fentanyl. James Jones, DEA special agent for the Chicago field division, noted the organization's strategy for fentanyl was exactly the same as for heroin. "There's nothing unique about how we work these," he said, in November 2016. "All the stuff you see on TV, the agents use all those techniques. We don't attack these any differently." ("Investigations geared towards the cyber realm as well as the recently passed scheduling regulations for fentanyl-related substances will become important tools for stemming the flow of these substances," added Sharon Lindskoog in August 2018.)

Since 2016 there have been more local–national collaborations to fight fentanyl on

Chicago's West Side, including an investigation called Operation Sweet Dreams, which came to a head in March, 2017, and another called Operation Full Circle, which culminated in June 2018. The latter resulted in the arrests of fifty-seven people and the seizure of seventeen illegal guns, three hundred pounds of marijuana, one kilogram of heroin, one kilogram of fentanyl, and $8,000 in cash. The operation featured wiretaps and undercover work and included the Chicago police, the DEA, the IRS, and the Bureau of Alcohol, Tobacco, Firearms and Explosives. The arrested include a man accused of agreeing to perform a kidnapping in exchange for money and drugs, and an alleged wholesaler who trafficked fentanyl between Mexico and Chicago.

US Attorney John Lausch said the suspects were "mid-level" distributors. "Everything that we do makes a dent," he said. "We have a long way to go, and that's one of the reasons why we're here: to let you know that we're going to continue to be here."

Despite the huge amounts of local, state, and federal resources being used to fight the problem, Cook County fentanyl-related deaths have continued to rise, from 560 in 2016 to 650 in 2017 (the most recent statistic available). Without question, the problem is enormous and has hit Chicago particularly hard. With so many people dying from opioids, with so many families torn apart, the impulse to hit back with as much force as possible is understandable. And yet, at a certain point, one wonders whether these investigations are, in fact, making a dent.

A year after Chicago's big 2016 bust, upon the occasion of his retirement, Dennis Wichern was asked for his takeaway from three decades on the job. "With the addition of fentanyl from China, I'd say there's more death and destruction now than there was 30 years ago," he lamented.

In Chicago, shows of force have been accompanied by some progressive changes. Police there have been arresting fewer heroin users, for example, and many nonviolent drug offenders are receiving treatment rather than prison. The arming of first responders with Narcan is estimated to have saved the lives of perhaps thousands of Chicago-area opioid overdose victims in recent years. In 2017, Chicago EMS crews administered naloxone ninety-six hundred times. The opioid crisis has led many police departments around the country to believe that we can't arrest our way out of the problem. For this and other reasons, many cities are slowly learning to treat addiction as an illness, rather than a crime.

On the federal level, Health and Human Services secretary Alex Azar has signaled that treatment is preferable to lockup and seeks to provide greater access to medications like buprenorphine, which is used to treat opioid dependency. "At HHS and across this administration, we know that we need to treat addiction as a medical challenge, not as a moral failing," he said. Former US attorney general Jeff Sessions sought to distinguish between dealers and users, saying that the latter would not be targeted but that the former would receive the stiffest penalties permitted.

In October 2017, President Trump officially labeled the opioid crisis a public-health emergency and a year later signed legislation pledging $6 billion to the problem. The money gives first responders better access to Narcan and opioid users better access to treatment, as well as increasing funding for law enforcement and border control agents working to stop the influx of fentanyl into the country. The bill received bipartisan support, though critics contended that much more money was needed; rival legislation cosponsored by Massachusetts senator Elizabeth Warren would have dedicated $100 billion to the crisis. Trump has also publicly mused about executing drug dealers. "Some countries have a very tough penalty, the ultimate penalty, and they have much less of a drug problem than we do," he said, in March 2018.

Yet this attitude belies a fundamental misunderstanding of the situation, considering that many addicted users become dealers simply to support their habits. "These aren't two distinct sets of people," said Maryland public defender Kelly Casper. "They want to charge all of these people with drug dealing, when in fact the core of the problem is that they're users." Criminal justice reform legislation, signed by President Trump in December 2018, reduces some drug sentences, but it specifically excludes fentanyl offenders.

Meanwhile, states like Ohio and Maryland seek to impose tougher sentences on fentanyl dealers, and the US Sentencing Commission has urged raising federal sentences for dealers marketing fentanyls as other drugs. Yet dealers themselves often have no idea whether the heroin, pills, cocaine, or methamphetamines they're selling are actually unadulterated, or if they are laced with fentanyl. And around the country, friends and partners who got high with people who ended up dying are increasingly being treated like drug dealers — charged with homicide and sent to prison.

It's clear that, despite the best efforts of agents like Dennis Wichern, massive federal spending in the billions of dollars, and unparalleled resources given to local enforcement, the War on Drugs — with the goal of eliminating drugs from American life — has not worked and will not succeed. Focused on a top-down solution, it has failed to address the root causes of abuse, addiction, and overdose.

One group of people, however, is approaching the increasingly complex problem of new drugs in a fresh way. They are not policy wonks, academics, or law enforcement officials. They are young people, by and large; many are dance-music enthusiasts. They aren't trying to discourage drug use — some are recreational drug users themselves. They understand that drug use isn't going away. They understand that the fight is going to be won on the ground. They see the drug war differently, because they themselves are immersed in it.

TWENTY-TWO

In the United States, vanquishing enemies, be they geopolitical foes, plagues, or diseases, is a common goal. We tend to prefer "cure" over "care" and to start a "war" on a disease to eliminate it instead of treating the social factors that cause disease and thereby reducing its incidence. Our most famous nontraditional war has been the War on Drugs, whose stated goal is to eradicate them, rather than accepting that they are inevitably part of our lives.

"Now is the first time in history that people are beginning to truly reckon with how impossible it is to continue the War on Drugs," said *Vice* synthetic-drugs expert Hamilton Morris. "Because the number of emerging psychoactive substances, it's truly exponential."

Harm-reduction activists seek a new approach. They believe "Just Say No" is as ineffective as abstinence-only sex education.

Commanding children to avoid drugs and sex doesn't work — it never has. If young people are going to indulge, they argue, we shouldn't judge them. Rather, we should teach them how to do so responsibly. Rejecting the law-and-order approach of the War on Drugs, these activists have pioneered new methods that are especially applicable to NPS. But their efforts are being stymied by legislators and law enforcement officers — and even by rave promoters.

The Electric Forest music festival is held every summer deep in the Michigan woods. It's equal parts scenic natural getaway and illicit chemical extravaganza. After sunset, the forest is lit from within in psychedelic colors, and whimsical giant owls carved from wood dot the grounds. The musical lineup splits between popular DJs like Skrillex and jam bands like String Cheese Incident. Electric Forest mixes the artistic spirit of the old raves with the big budgets of the new ones. Forty thousand attendees include raver girls in tutus, bearded bros in tie-dye, and older, unwashed drug dealers. Most people camp, and many are content to while away afternoons stretched out on hammocks beneath mammoth pine trees while tripping.

At the time of the 2015 festival, Michigan

cops were targeting anyone who looked like they were headed to the forest, pulling over cars to search them for drugs. A flagged vehicle resembling the *Scooby-Doo* van, inhabited by San Diego residents Tyler Stinson and Nathan Strickland, was pulled over on Michigan highway 31 in Allegan County. The men say that nine police cars surrounded them and searched their van, finding two grams of marijuana, for which Stinson spent the night in jail. "When I have two grams of weed, I'm considered 'out of weed,' " he said.

Just outside the festival's gate, Michigan State Police on horseback kept order, and both uniformed and undercover cops roamed the premises inside.

Despite the law enforcement presence, drug use inside was widespread; during String Cheese Incident's set that year, one young woman standing near the stage collapsed and was carted away by medical personnel. The music didn't stop, and no one looked overly alarmed, as this was not an uncommon occurrence.

A wide array of drugs was for sale, but buyers didn't necessarily know what they were getting. The Denver-based harm-reduction organization DanceSafe, focused on the intersection of dance-music culture and drugs, was there to help anyone who wanted to understand the hodgepodge of NPS on hand. Since its founding in 1998, DanceSafe has helped tens of thousands of ravers navigate the world of recreational substances. The group's Day-Glo yellow tent sat not far from one of the main stages, and its twenty- and thirty-something team members — also clad in bright yellow — handed out water, earplugs, prophylactics, and informational postcards explaining the effects of various drugs. The brightly colored cards contained unbiased scientific information about recreational chemicals and their effects, the kind of information that was difficult to access in decades past. For example, the card labeled "Cathinones" explained that drugs like methylone and mephedrone will "likely be strongly felt for 1–3 hours before gradually coming down for another 1–2 hours."

Former and current club kids themselves, DanceSafe volunteers also act, pro bono, as psychedelic counselors, guiding nervous users down from bad trips. "People trust us," said Tre Meisel, who was the cohead of DanceSafe's Midwest branch. "They're worried that if they talk to EMS [emergency medical services] they'll get reported to the police."

At some festivals DanceSafe works with organizers to monitor which drugs are floating around the festival and coordinates with medical staff to be prepared for overdoses. The group also sells its own drug-checking kits, which can determine the presence (or lack) of dozens of drugs — and help fund the organization — and even provides free snorting straws to help prevent the spread of hepatitis C when users do drugs like cocaine.

But at the 2015 Electric Forest, those interested in DanceSafe's services arrived on the festival's second day to find that the booth had been mysteriously shut down. Told to vacate, along with its yellow tent, DanceSafe had departed overnight. Electric Forest officials had taken issue with its drug kits, it turned out. "DanceSafe was actually participating at the festival as a nonprofit information booth," said festival representative Carrie Lombardi, and Electric Forest's guidelines mandated that this distinction meant the organization couldn't sell anything. (Despite the fact that sales of drugs were happening all around.) DanceSafe denied that their contract prohibited selling items, but Electric Forest's actions meant that festival-goers who wanted to check their drugs — to see if they were about to ingest, for example, actual MDMA or something that could potentially kill them — were left in the dark. This was a strange position to take, considering six people have died from drugs at the festival since it began in 2008.

Electric Forest's issue with DanceSafe was likely owing to a federal law called the Illicit Drug Anti-Proliferation Act, usually referred to as the Rave Act. Though the law was intended to curb the abuse of ecstasy and other drugs, it alarmed companies like Insomniac — America's biggest rave promoter, which puts on Electric Forest with a company called Madison House Presents — because the Rave Act made it a crime for concert organizers to host events where controlled substances are knowingly used or sold. (The law was passed in 2003, at a time when American interest in electronic dance music was small, but as the scene grew, companies became increasingly paranoid.) As a result, Insomniac and other promoters often ban groups like DanceSafe from selling drug-checking kits at their events. They fear this would amount to admitting substance abuse takes place on their grounds and thereby make them criminally liable. "Promoters' feel their hands are tied due to the Rave Act," said DanceSafe's founder

Emanuel Sferios, adding that he believes this feeling is misplaced, since the act has not led to prosecutions in many years.

"Fan safety is our highest priority," said Insomniac spokeswoman Jennifer Forkish. "We go to great lengths to keep illegal substances out of our venues and educate fans about the dangers of drug use. Unfortunately, there is a limit to what we or anyone can do to protect people from the bad choices they sometimes make."

Insomniac's founder, Pasquale Rotella, arrived at the 2015 Electric Forest shortly after the festival began, with his then wife, Holly Madison, and their two-year-old daughter, Rainbow, in tow.

Rotella, who had sold half of Insomniac to Live Nation for $50 million in 2013, has faced criticism from harm reduction organizations who believe Insomniac could be doing more to prevent drug overdose deaths at its events. Critics include the Drug Policy Alliance, a nonprofit focused on reforming drug policies, which has partnered with Insomniac at some of its festivals to provide a booth, under the banner "Project #Open-Talk," where educators dispense "honest, unbiased information about drugs, sex and mental health concerns."

"While progress has been made, Insomniac is still a ways away from a full embrace of drug education and harm reduction at their events," said Stefanie Jones, Drug Policy Alliance's director of audience development. "The idea of drug checking on-site is a nonstarter. The best we've done in that area is be allowed to message an alert when a particular substance was determined to be the cause of several medical incidents."

At Electric Forest in 2015, after DanceSafe had departed, a curious masked man was spotted roaming the grounds. He wore a T-shirt with an image of a beaker on it, a matching baseball hat, and sunglasses. A bandana hung around his neck, and he held a laminated placard with the names of recreational chemicals, both synthetic and natural, and colorful illustrations. Also in big letters were the words "Ehrlich," "Marquis," and "Mandelin."

Pulling his bandana up over his nose to hide his appearance, the man declined to be interviewed. But his T-shirt revealed his affiliation with a drug-checking group called the Bunk Police. Like DanceSafe, the Bunk Police were focused on harm reduction and weren't permitted to sell their drug-checking kits at Electric Forest. Unlike

DanceSafe, however, they had gone rogue.

When the Bunk Police learned they wouldn't be allowed to sell their drug-checking kits, they decided to operate clandestinely. Sometime in the middle of the previous night, they had put a few hundred of their kits into a giant bag and tossed it over the fence into the festival. They retrieved it the next morning so they could sell (and give away) kits to attendees who needed them. "Ehrlich," "Marquis," and "Mandelin" refer to reagents in kits that test for different types of drugs, to see if they had, for example, actual ecstasy or some dangerous knockoff.

The founder of the Bunk Police is a mysterious activist and entrepreneur pseudonymously named Adam Auctor, an Eagle Scout from the Houston suburbs who went to business school. Auctor lived in Denver and was inspired to enter his unusual line of work in 2011, he told me, when he attended Nocturnal, a massive electronic dance music festival outside Austin, which had featured some of the biggest names in electronic music, including Kaskade and Paul Oakenfold. What happened in the audience, however, left the biggest impression on him. He was shocked to witness kids overdosing around him. Some convulsed with seizures — "One was a young girl, and she looked really frightened" — as EMTs fought their way through the crowd.

The overdose victims survived, but as Auctor continued attending EDM events he began noticing more erratic behavior — from ravers grinding their teeth so hard they appeared to be damaging them to "almost tic-like behaviors that seemed, at least to me, to point to deep psychological turmoil." Many claimed they had taken ecstasy, but they weren't behaving the way people on ecstasy were supposed to. "I had been a bit of a drug nerd for several years, not taking them, just studying user reports and evaluations online out of curiosity," Auctor said. "So I knew what most substances were supposed to do. This wasn't it."

Also around that time, Auctor had a near-death experience. After nicking himself shaving, he developed a bad staph infection known as methicillin-resistant *Staphylococcus aureus,* a "superbug" largely resistant to traditional antibiotics. It nearly escalated into a brain infection before it was finally contained. Majoring in business and Mandarin, Auctor was on his way toward a marketing job in China, but witnessing the rave overdoses and his health scare changed his trajectory. "It made the idea of moving to China and working with marketing firms seem really empty," he said.

Instead, in 2011 Auctor dropped out of college, though he had only a semester left. He received his $9,000 student loan and used it to purchase drug-checking kits for MDMA, methamphetamine, and other substances, which he found on forensic-supply websites used by law enforcement. He took the kits to music events, offering to check attendees' drugs for them, and found that very few ecstasy tablets or Molly doses had any MDMA at all. "I was really surprised to see that somewhere in the neighborhood of 90 percent–plus of the MDMA was testing negative for MDMA." Indeed, a formal study conducted by DanceSafe, in which volunteers tested samples of drugs from music events held between 2010 and 2015, also found that ravers weren't getting what they thought they were. Only 60 percent of Molly and ecstasy had any MDMA at all, much less "pure" MDMA. Instead, the study discovered a wide range of adulterants: everything from the ingredients of Tylenol and Robitussin to cocaine and PMA, the extremely dangerous compound that, along with its cousin PMMA, has been linked to more than a hundred deaths.

Courtney Pero, a narcotics sergeant in Plano, Texas, has been following this transition. Plano is a suburb of Dallas, which has been ground zero for ecstasy use ever since the mid-1980s, when it was still unscheduled. A twenty-two-year veteran of the force, Pero was as recently as the first decade of the 2000s regularly seizing thousands of ecstasy tablets — real ecstasy, containing MDMA. Yet in 2016, he acknowledged, "I don't recall the last time we seized pure MDMA."

Both Auctor's investigation and DanceSafe's study found that among the most common ecstasy adulterants were synthetic cathinones, the stimulants made to resemble the effects of the khat plant. These included mephedrone ("meow meow") and methylone. "These cathinones were being marketed as 'plant food' and 'bath salts,' " Auctor said. "You could buy them at truck stops and smoke shops. People were just switching them out and selling them as MDMA."

With the help of a chemist, Auctor began adjusting and modifying reagents to produce new kits that checked for these drugs. Today Auctor's company, Bunk Police, makes eight different kits, including test strips for fentanyl. It sells tens of thousands of its kits every year, giving away almost as many. Auctor

444

and his cohorts travel to music festivals but are almost never permitted in. "We use secret compartments in cars," he said. "Sometimes we'll have food-truck owners put them under their produce to bring them in." At Bonaroo, the massive rock and alternative-music festival held every June near Manchester, Tennessee, Auctor conspires with food-service vendors, but one year they got caught, and police confiscated thousands of kits. It didn't deter Bunk Police from returning the following year.

At the 2018 Lost Lands music festival in Thornville, Ohio, Bunk Police showed up ready to help prevent overdoses; the rave was being held in the heart of fentanyl country, after all. Indeed, two attendees died over the weekend (the causes of death weren't immediately known), and others appeared to have overdosed. "People were dropping like flies," Auctor said. "I watched one girl get strapped to a gurney screaming that she was going to die and another incident where this guy was running through the crowd yelling for help carrying his unconscious girlfriend." Festival organizers, however, shut down Bunk Police's operation and threatened to confiscate its supplies. "We were treated like criminals, by security guards wearing riot-like equipment," Auctor lamented.

Another of the group's biggest challenge is attempting to stay ahead of drug manufacturers and dealers profiting from knock-off synthetics. At first Auctor was not subtle about attempting to undercut dubious drug sales. "I would walk up, get in the middle of the transaction, have them test their products right there," he said. "That definitely garnered attention from some of the higher-level drug dealers, because they were losing a lot of money." But his efforts paid off, and his tests began discovering potentially fatal drugs, like PMA and PMMA. He has also developed a communication system, called Bunkbot, which alerts festival attendees of adulterated drugs via text message.

Bunk Police now has about ten employees as well as a large "street team" that distributes test kids, like the masked man at Electric Forest. Auctor describes the organization as both a business and a harm-reduction organization. Starting at twenty dollars, its kits usually include a small plastic container with a skull-and-crossbones poison symbol, a plastic vial, and one or more small bottles of liquid reagent. (The reagents themselves are toxic and can burn your skin.) The more advanced kits include UV flashlights and other instruments to test for multiple drugs mixed up in the same batch. Though they've inspired a rash of imitators, Bunk Police kits are the most advanced on the market for the general public, able to test for hundreds of drugs.

Now in his early thirties, Auctor is sinking his money into drug-checking, developing new kits to test for the ever-increasing amounts of substances coming out of China. He employs pricey chemistry consultants to help with this task. Some of the fentanyls are active at such tiny amounts that it's easy to accidentally dose oneself. When Auctor or his employees test them they wear full hazmat suits, with face masks.

But fentanyl testing is worth the effort, Auctor believes. "That's how we can save the most lives," he said. Indeed, a 2017 study carried out at a supervised-injection site in Vancouver, British Columbia, found that those who discover fentanyl in their drugs are ten times likelier to lower their dose, which makes them 25 percent less likely to overdose. A 2018 study released by Brown University found that among Rhode Island users whose drugs tested positive for fentanyl, 45 percent reported using a smaller amount, 42 percent proceeded more slowly during their use, and 39 percent used with someone else present, who could give them Narcan if they overdosed or call 911.

"Drug users are far more rational than we make them out to be," said Dan Ciccarone, a University of California, San Francisco, doctor, who is an expert in this field. If people all over the country begin using these types of kits, Auctor and many others believe, rates of overdoses would dramatically fall.

"We can't keep drugs out of solitary confinement in a federal prison," Auctor is fond of saying. "How are we going to keep them out of festivals or off the streets?"

Still, drug checking is controversial. Elinore McCance-Katz, who was made assistant secretary for mental health and substance use by President Trump, has come out against fentanyl test strips. "We cannot guarantee that the strips will always have 100 percent accuracy," she wrote, in an October 2018 posting on the Substance Abuse and Mental Health Services Administration site. "We can't afford to create a false sense of security. . . . Let's not rationalize putting tools in place to help [drug users] continue their lifestyle more 'safely.' "

Australia has similar restrictions. There, a dozen rave deaths have occurred since 2013, all confirmed or suspected drug overdoses. As of this writing, the law did not permit drug checking, though some politicians said they were willing to consider changing it. "Unfortunately, we know that pill testing won't work," said New South Wales premier Gladys Berejiklian, "because it will give people the green light to take substances which in the end could still kill them."

Though Auctor's test kits themselves are legal under federal law, he can't legally develop them in the United States, because to do so Bunk Police needs to possess the drugs the kits are made to test for, a process that requires soliciting small amounts of illegal new substances from drug manufacturers all over the world. Therefore, in 2016 he started working in Europe, where harm-reduction methods are more commonplace, prosecution is less likely, and the rate of deadly overdoses is quite low. In 2017, the most recent year for which statistics were available, the United States, a country of 326 million people, had seventy thousand drug overdose deaths. The European Union, which has 510 million, had seventy-six hundred.

Auctor set up at a satellite office in an unlikely corner of the continent — Ljubljana, the capital of Slovenia. In addition to drug laws that are considerably more lax than those in the United States, the country also has a low cost of living, natural beauty, and cheap shipping to other countries in Europe. Furthermore, Slovenia is also home to an enlightened harm-reduction scene — a loose collective of casual and addicted users and dealers, public-health workers, and activists, who understand this scourge better than anybody, because they are right in the eye of the storm.

TWENTY-THREE

I knew little about Slovenia before arriving there, except that it was the birthplace of Melania Trump. In my ignorance I half-expected a war-torn Balkan wasteland. In truth, the 1990s Yugoslavian conflict barely touched Slovenia, which won independence through the short-lived Ten-Day War in 1991, and nowadays the capital, Ljubljana, gleams. Surrounded by mountains and forest and overlooked by a medieval castle, the city has buildings hundreds of years old, and its denizens shop on traffic-free cobblestone streets in the city center. There are very few homicides, and the city feels clean and tidy.

Most of the same drugs are scheduled in Slovenia as in the United States, but, per a 2008 law that made sharp distinctions between drug use and drug trafficking, possession of a small amount for personal use is punishable by only a small fine, ranging from 40 to 200 euros, though even the fine can be waived if the individual is willing to enter a drug-treatment program. Those engaged in drug manufacturing and dealing are still subject to incarceration. The country is focused not on locking up users but on helping minimize harm associated with drug abuse. Adam Auctor said, "The Slovenia government is one of the most liberal, when it comes to substance abuse, in the world." The country is home to cutting-edge harm-reduction groups like Drogart, an army of gung-ho young volunteers, who call themselves "peers" and are well-respected on the nightlife scene. In bathrooms at music events, they set out papers that can be rolled to snort cocaine and offer counseling and drug checking, though they don't push their services on anyone. They have also created harm-reduction-themed compilation albums, featuring songs with such titles as "Drink Water" and "Eat before Rave." The model is practiced in an environment much different from that of US electronic dance music events, where practically anyone could be an undercover cop. Because Drogart members engage openly and honestly with them, users are more likely to follow advice about how to take drugs safely.

Slovenia has also been particularly successful at containing the scourge of dangerous drugs. In 2016, the most recent year for which statistics were available, only forty overdose deaths occurred — in the entire country of two million people — a per capita overdose death rate far smaller than that of the United States, where more than four times as many people died from drug overdoses *every day* that year. Slovenia is aggressively concerned with helping problem users, approaching drugs from a public-health perspective rather than a strictly law-and-order one. Even the Ljubljana police support these efforts. In fact, drug checking involves the police directly: users drop off samples of their substances at Drogart's offices, whereupon police pick them up, check them for purity, and then send back the results. No harm, no foul.

In 2016 Adam Auctor moved to a house on the outskirts of Ljubljana that doubled as the Bunk Police's lab and production center. Accessed through a separate door on the ground floor, the modest lab facility has a low ceiling, fluorescent lights, a big orange cabinet of chemicals, respirators, and an emergency eye-wash station; it looks not unlike a typical laboratory at a university, even as it analyzes the newest, most powerful drugs in the world. "That cost six times more than my car," Auctor said, pointing to a fume hood, a type of workstation capable of quickly eliminating noxious gases. "You could explode a bomb in there, and it would suck it away."

In recent years Bunk Police's efforts have gone largely into creating a new and extensive reference booklet. Each page reveals different drugs' reactions to reagents that Bunk Police sells. Resembling time-lapse photography, the reaction pictures are taken from video stills, which show — second by second — what colors the drugs turn when hit by the reagents. The booklet covers hundreds of different chemicals, many of which are obscure. There isn't a greater resource in the world, if you want to know whether the drug in hand is 5-APDB or 5-DBFPV. Videos of these reactions are also available online. "While my peers were putting a down payment on their houses, I was making these booklets," Auctor said. "These things cost me about three years of my life. Close to $100,000 dollars." He's currently focused on developing highly specialized strips that quantify the amount of fentanyl in mixtures; users don't need to know just whether their drugs are adulterated with fentanyl — they need to know how much is in them.

Good help is hard to find. "It is so easy for people to be tempted," he said, noting that after he spent months tracking down a rare sample of pure heroin, one of his employees used it to get high.

Auctor was convinced to come to Slovenia in the first place by psychonaut and new-drugs expert Julijan "Sidney" Picej, who later served as Bunk Police's head of European operations, though he has since left the company. A millennial who, with his wild, uncombed brown hair, resembles a Deadhead, Picej is willing to risk his health for the sake of new thrills and has taken just about every drug in the book — not to mention plenty of new chemicals that aren't in any books. He's something of a psychedelic historian, diligently cataloging hundreds of psychoactive drugs that have come onto the market in recent years.

Over lunch in Ljubljana, between eating and blowing big plumes from an electronic nicotine pipe, Picej explained how he went from high school dropout to landing his job with Bunk Police. He smoked marijuana and ate mushrooms as a teenager but at age seventeen found his real passion — mephedrone, the synthetic cathinone — when a girlfriend introduced him to it. At that time mephedrone was unscheduled in Slovenia and sold over the Internet by Hungarian labs. Buying drugs over the web seemed too good to be true, however, so Picej regularly trekked to Budapest, a scenic four-hour car ride, to acquire kilos of mephedrone, which he sold to his high school classmates. No drug kingpin, he just sought to support his habit. His father was absent and his mother not around much, and so, when he should have been studying, Picej was binging on mephedrone or roaming the city with his girlfriend.

Picej doesn't take much mephedrone anymore, because it's hard to find. After it was scheduled in Slovenia in 2011, a close analogue took its place, known as 3-MMC (short for 3-methylmethcathinone; mephedrone is 4-methylmethcathinone). The analogue was designed to evade the mephedrone ban and provide similarly stimulating and euphoric effects while still remaining technically legal.

Though Picej didn't like 3-MMC quite as much as mephedrone, many people found it just as satisfying. White crystals that could be snorted or eaten, the drug was reportedly first seen in Sweden in 2012 but soon began to take off in Slovenia. A survey of students at the University of Ljubljana in

2015 found that it was by far the most popular of the new drugs; 6.6 percent of students said they had tried it, followed by 4.1 percent who had tried methylone, and 3.9 percent who had taken mephedrone. Little was known about 3-MMC; no human studies had been done, though scientists had tested it on pigs. "During the pig studies the authors reported no treatment-related mortality and morbidity was observed and no gross pathological findings were detected," summarized the World Health Organization in a report.

Along the way, 3-MMC acquired a curious nickname — "ice cream." In fact, when I was in Slovenia, "ice cream" was all anyone in drug circles was talking about. I soon learned that 3-MMC is a perfect example of how brand-new chemicals can enter countries and immediately take hold. Its story is one not just of law and chemistry but of savvy marketing.

Picej knew the drug dealer who had popularized it. His name was Vlad, and Picej warned me that he was in bad shape because of heroin addiction. Nonetheless, Vlad was willing to talk, perhaps because his weird local celebrity hadn't been publicly acknowledged before. He had a bedraggled, Bobcat Goldthwait air about him, down to the shaggy hair and high-pitched, off-kilter voice. His English was limited, but he got his point across. There was still a light in his eyes; heroin had not defeated him, though he looked a decade older than his twenty-eight years. He was friendly and not suspicious or paranoid, though he did ask to use a pseudonym.

"I get addicted to everything," he said. "To cigarettes, to coffee, to everything" — most detrimentally, to heroin. Vlad had previously excelled in his studies, but around 2012, not long after he started university, he and his girlfriend got heavily into heroin, and at one point he was doing five grams per day, he claimed. This interfered with his schoolwork, and his life began to go off course. He was currently on something called substitution therapy — taking twelve methadone pills and two hundred milligrams of morphine almost every day. It was enough for him to achieve a daily general feeling of "below average," as he described it — not great, but better than withdrawal.

Though he had stopped taking heroin, Vlad still indulged in other drugs. Like Picej, he had tried almost everything, natural or synthetic, including, he said, as many as ten drugs at the same time. He knew a little chemistry and had made the ultra-powerful psychedelic DMT with a friend. Though people who have done DMT describe it as a face-melting, life-changing experience — many claim to meet God — Vlad did it almost casually. "I like to ride my bike when I'm on it," he said.

The sudden popularity of NPS earlier in the decade had benefited Vlad's drug-dealing business, and he began to specialize in semi-obscure synthetics, including the psychedelics 2C-B and 25I-NBOMe. "I just went to parties and gave out free samples, and people were interested. I got it so cheap." He ordered these chemicals off the Dark Web or bought them from other dealers. Police caught him a number of times; around 2011, he said, cops stopped him with fifteen or twenty grams of methylone, but he managed to talk them out of arresting him for dealing by insisting (accurately) that it was unscheduled and therefore legal.

He and his girlfriend stayed together despite their heroin abuse, and in fact she was behind his most famous drug — "ice cream." Vlad sold mephedrone until it was scheduled, and then soon afterward began selling its close analogue 3-MMC. He didn't invent this new drug but, after hearing about it online, began purchasing it from anonymous sources — first on the surface web and then on the Dark Web. It was a powerful stimulant and inexpensive. Vlad heard it described as "Chinese cocaine," although it lasted longer than cocaine.

Sales were fine, but 3-MMC really took off when, around 2013, Vlad's girlfriend had the idea to cut it with vanilla protein powder. It was extremely successful branding. Diluting drugs with other, cheaper substances is common. But it's rare that the cutting agent becomes a main selling point. She thought the powder might give the drug's users — who often binge and go without eating for extended periods of time — some necessary calories. But neither of them anticipated just how much buyers would appreciate the vanilla flavor when they snorted the drug, which they could taste in their mouths as well. The vanilla taste earned the drug the nickname "ice cream," and before long it was in great demand, not just in Ljubljana but all over Slovenia and in parts of the Czech Republic and Austria as well. At one point Vlad removed the vanilla flavoring. He'd had a change of heart about selling adulterated products to his customers, he said. But they complained, so he added it back.

Dare Kochmur, the director of Stigma, a Slovenian harm-reduction organization dedicated to fighting drug addiction, said "ice cream" is dangerous because, as with cocaine, when its effects wear off users feel a strong urge to take more. Thus, it can become habit forming.

Perhaps this explained why Vlad's customers kept returning. He said he made a lot of money during his time selling "ice cream" — maybe 5,000 euros a month, quite a lot in an inexpensive country. He noted that most of his profits were spent on his drug habit. Another run-in with police, in 2015, convinced him to stop dealing entirely. Vlad has since revived his pursuit of a university degree and is trying, not always with success, to limit his drug use.

"Ice cream" has nonetheless marched on without him. In fact, he said, a host of knockoff stimulants are currently being sold in Slovenia as "ice cream," even some that don't have the vanilla powder or even the same active chemical.

TWENTY-FOUR

"Harm reduction" means different things to different people. Matt Bowden, for example, believes himself to be a pioneering figure in the field for his work developing safer chemicals in New Zealand. Even the Dark Web fentanyls dealer U4IA embraces the harm-reduction mantle, claiming that his cheaper products benefit society at large by reducing his clients' costs and making it less likely they will have to rob or steal to feed their addictions.

I asked those I spoke with — including academics, activists, substance-abuse counselors, elected officials, law enforcement officers, drug manufacturers, traffickers, psychonauts, and chemists — what they believed to be the best methods for stopping NPS overdoses and limiting the deadly march of drugs like fentanyl. The majority spoke to the necessity of harm reduction, including a surprising number of law enforcement officers and drug dealers alike. Very few were prohibitionists; almost all had their eyes open and agreed that limiting the negative effects of NPS rather than imprisoning their users was the most important goal.

No matter how harm reduction is defined, it springs from the understanding that preventing the use of drugs is impossible and that making sure they are used as safely as possible is a necessity.

Most harm-reduction policies seem like common sense — and an easy way to save lives — but many governments don't see them in that light. In November 2018, a Russian harm-reduction organization, the Andrey Rylkov Foundation — which provides clean needles and other services — was ordered by a court in Moscow to pay a fine of 800,000 rubles (US$12,000) for an article advising synthetic-cathinone users about how to take the drug safely.

In the United States, with the War on Drugs still looming large, few harm-reduction tactics have been attempted on a widespread scale. Organizations like Dance-Safe and Drug Policy Alliance, while effective, operate on extremely limited budgets. In Europe, however, a number of efforts have made breakthroughs, including government programs providing heroin directly to addicted users. In Switzerland, for example, users can receive prescription-quality heroin from a clinic for free, as long as they are eighteen, have been addicted for two years, and have failed at more conventional treatments. They must use the heroin in the clinic, rather than taking it with them.

Taken in the proper quantity, heroin itself usually does not kill people — rather the killers are adulterants like fentanyl or dirty needles or other problems resulting from behaviors while high or violence resulting from street life. The Swiss program has led to drops in deaths, drug dealing, and crime in the country — since enrolled users no longer have to steal or deal to pay for their habits. Those in the heroin-prescription program committed 55 percent fewer auto thefts and 80 percent fewer burglaries and muggings, and were almost 95 percent less likely to sell drugs. This program has also been successful in the Netherlands, where heroin use by people under forty has fallen dramatically. It even has precedent in the United States: when the government banned heroin in 1914, the law still permitted doctors to administer it to people who were addicted; only after doctors were forced to stop doing so did crime rates and health problems begin to spiral upward.

In Europe, a number of groups are doing cutting-edge work in harm reduction, including the Netherlands' Drug Information and Monitoring System, Switzerland's Safer NightLife, and the Austrian organization CheckIt!, which boasts some of the most sophisticated drug-checking technology in the world. These programs provide a wide variety of services, including educating users about new drugs; providing clean needles, contraception, water, and other safety supplies; and sending out updates about adulterated drugs being sold locally, often in real time.

Spain in particular stands out for its creative, forward-thinking measures to stop drug overdoses, which combine government efforts with private ones. For instance, a Spanish harm-reduction group called Energy Control is allowed to order new drugs from vendors on the Dark Web for the purposes of analyzing them and understanding their potential to cause problems. In fact, when Adam Auctor and Bunk Police need to confirm that their sample of a new drug from China is "pure," they send it to Energy Control.

"Energy Control is the best in the world," according to Auctor. "They're what Dance-

Safe could be if they didn't have all kinds of regulations covering them."

The scope of Energy Control's operations, and what the group is legally permitted to do, is staggering. On an annual budget of 640,000 euros (US$720,000) — about 60 percent of which comes from regional and national government coffers, with most of the rest raised by the organization itself — it provides counsel and information to drug users and those who are curious. Working with state-of-the-art mass-spectrometry and gas-spectrometry equipment, the organization will test anyone's drugs. The service is free for Spanish nationals. Others can pay for it, even Dark Web vendors, who are known to send in their wares and then post Energy Control's analyses showing the purity on their vendor sites. The only comparable system is the website Ecstasydata .org, run by American drug-information database Erowid, which the DEA permits to receive drugs in the mail, test them, and post the results. But Energy Control is better funded and, according to the organization, processes results faster.

Energy Control's outreach prowess is on display each year at the Own Spirit music festival, set in the Spanish countryside.

Located an hour and a half from Barcelona by train and nestled in a rocky, forested area surrounded by mountains, the event is small by mega-rave standards, drawing perhaps a few thousand people. There are no superstar DJs or major corporate sponsorships. You can purchase beer only if you've got a reusable cup for it.

Occasional cops wander the premises. But because Spain — like its neighbor Portugal — has largely decriminalized recreational drugs, attendees are unafraid to light up a joint or deal chemicals. LSD is sold openly, ten euros per drop. Nobody seems out of control. However, nobody is assured that what's purported to be LSD actually *is* LSD, and that's where Energy Control comes in. For the festival's April 2017 iteration, the group arrived just before sundown, setting up its black tent near a main stage. ENJOY THE PARTY, read its banner, in English, with the *N* composed of images of tablets, pills, and blotter papers.

The Energy Control crew attends parties or concerts every week. This night, as the festival began, it numbered about ten people, including both staff and volunteers. The drug checking was helmed by Energy Control's twenty-six-year-old lab technician, Cristina Gil, a chemical analyst who had traded her white lab coat for a hoop through her nose and gray lipstick. She's equally at home, she admitted, scrolling through gas-chromatography-analysis graphs at the lab and feeling the bass in her face. Of course, said bass doesn't make for ideal lab conditions, but the group had jury-rigged a serviceable setup at the back of the tent, with a lab station made from a folding table, lit by floodlights powered by extension cords.

Almost immediately, people started queuing up. One young woman, wearing green and orange makeup, arrived with a small metal tin of various substances, asking for a test of what she believed was speed. She was followed by a British guy in a bright orange winter hat, who had purchased two ecstasy pills on the festival grounds. One was silver, while the other was stamped with the logo of Chupa Chups — a brand of Spanish lollipop. Both attendees were given numbers and told to return in about an hour for their results. A thirty-year-old man from France, wearing gauged earrings and a hooded sweatshirt, approached the tent cautiously, first asking whether the testing was authorized. Upon assurance, he removed three stashes from his camouflage-printed fanny pack: a dropper bottle of LSD, ketamine powder, and some cocaine. He was a dealer, he sheepishly admitted, adding that he was seeking Energy Control's stamp of approval to help sell his wares at the festival. This revelation didn't faze Energy Control's staff. "As long as the overall purity and information is increasing, it's a benefit," said Rafael Sacramento, who was coordinating the group.

Energy Control used a technique called thin-layer chromatography. A volunteer helped scrape off a tiny fraction of a pill — or spooned a bit of the powder — into a small vial. Gil or her colleague then added a solvent, shook it up, and placed drops from the mixture onto a testing strip, followed by a small bit of the reagent. After the combined liquid spread across the test strip, they compared it with samples brought with them, of known drugs like MDMA, cocaine, amphetamine, and ketamine; and a host of adulterants, including N-bombs. Different drugs present different colors; MDMA turns dark purple, but some others are hard to track with the naked eye — for such cases Gil strapped on eye-protecting sunglasses to examine the samples under a UV light. There are limits to this type of testing, and she couldn't identify everything. "In that case it's better not to take it, since nobody knows what could happen," she advised.

Later in the evening, the handwritten results of the first ten tests were posted to the tent's wall, drawing an anxious crowd. The woman with the green and orange makeup had amphetamine, as she expected, although it was cut with caffeine, which is common. The British guy's ecstasy pills were indeed MDMA. The dosages for these particular types of pills are often very strong, however, so Sacramento cautioned he might not want to take an entire pill at once. The drug dealer from France had legitimate LSD and ketamine. His cocaine, however, was cut with levamisole, an animal dewormer used by veterinarians, which produces an effect that weakly mimics cocaine. Relieved, he headed off into the night to hawk his wares.

"Everything is pretty normal," Gil concluded, after completing a few more rounds of testing. "But that's good."

"Pretty normal" is typical at Spanish music festivals, where the ecstasy tends to be genuine. In fact, in an Energy Control study, about 80 percent of samples analyzed contained only MDMA. Though Dance-Safe's American study, by contrast, found only 60 percent of samples had *any*

MDMA, and Bunk Police found even less than that.

With fewer large-scale safrole oil busts in recent years, and the emergence of a viable synthetic precursor called PMK-glycidate, which is often made in China, the pure-ecstasy supply has rebounded. Though American dealers still commonly attempt to pass off adulterated ecstasy, this is much less common in Spain, and the same is also true with LSD. Though Energy Control has seen some adulteration from drugs like 25I-NBOMe, aka N-bombs, those instances have been decreasing as well. "One of the reasons is that we have several drug-checking services around the country," said Mireia Ventura, Energy Control's coordinator of drug-checking services. "It's the same in other countries that have them. It's a type of quality control. We are totally sure that we have some influence in the market." Logically, drug dealers are less likely to sell drugs that are filled with adulterants if they know their customers will be checking them.

Though many consider Dark Web drug markets a dangerous gathering place for the deviant and immoral, Ventura feels differently, noting that the marketplaces' vendor ratings also serve as a form of quality control, as bad Dark Web reviews will quickly have an effect. Energy Control also works with a Madrid doctor named Fernando Caudevilla, who, as "DoctorX," for years on various Dark Web sites has been candidly answering questions on recreational substances, ranging from how long MDMA is detectable in your system for a drug test (forty-eight to seventy-two hours) to how to store one's amphetamines ("in a dry, dark place, out of direct sunlight") and whether or not taking Advil will counteract memory loss from smoking too much marijuana (it will not).

Energy Control and other harm-reduction organizations believe in candid drug talk. "If you overemphasize the negative effects, they don't believe you," said Steve Mueller, director of the Vienna-based CheckIt! program. "We talk about the positives too."

Though Energy Control can't provide many statistics to validate its harm-reduction tactics, Spanish authorities believe in the organization's work. Despite close association with drug users and even dealers, Energy Control isn't controversial. Part of the reason has been its rapid response to emerging drug crises.

Stamped with the famous *S* logo and bearing a pink hue, the "Superman" pill was blamed for the deaths of four people in England during late December 2014 and early January, 2015. The users apparently thought it was ecstasy, but the pills were found to contain the toxic knockoff PMMA. The Superman pills continued to circulate, however, making their way around the European continent. Many feared they would continue wreaking havoc.

Nearly a week before the first of the British deaths, however, scientists at a Utrecht laboratory uncovered the actual contents of the pills, which were believed to have been manufactured in the Netherlands. The authorities organized a national, televised alert, which appears to have been successful — no one died in the Netherlands. The relevant English authorities received the information too, but tragically failed to sound the alarm, reportedly because they didn't think the Superman pills had arrived in England.

Energy Control received the alert through the Trans-European Drug Information project, which pooled information supplied by drug-checking programs all over Europe. Energy Control acted quickly, asking users in its network to bring in for testing any Superman pills they came upon. Dozens did exactly that, and Energy Control determined the batch to indeed be toxic.

It immediately issued a "red warning," sending out e-mail, Facebook, Twitter, and WhatsApp messages to anyone who might be at risk, targeting university groups, festival owners, hospitals, college students, and others. They also got the word to journalists, and soon stories on these dangerous Superman pills were all over the Internet, TV, and radio. In the end, there were no deaths in Spain, and the pills promptly vanished. "Some dealer was like, 'Well, we can't sell these in Spain!' " commented Núria Calzada, Energy Control's national coordinator.

Since so many NPS — including N-bombs, fentanyl, and the more nefarious ecstasy substitutes — have potentially fatal effects, a key strategy is to convince people not to use them. And this is exactly what they've been able to do in Spain. Since Spanish users won't get busted for using traditional drugs (which tend to be safer than NPS) most choose from among those options. "NPS is not an issue here," said Mireia Ventura. "Most people prefer classic drugs."

That's not to say Spain doesn't have its issues. It is located on major smuggling routes; cocaine from Colombia and hashish from Morocco have overwhelmed authorities in recent years, and drug traffickers in the southern part of the country have been known to attack police who try to seize their shipments. Rates of cocaine use, and trafficking arrests, have soared. But Spain boasts a very low rate of overdose deaths, only about 1 in 120,000 in 2015 (the most recent year for which statistics were available), one of the lowest rates in the world. That year in the United States, the number was about 1 in 6,100.

As shown by Energy Control and other organizations, some of the best solutions to the NPS crisis are coming out of the rave scene. But many of the services provided by Energy Control are illegal in the United States. Organizations that want to test drugs at raves aren't showered with government funds — they're sent home. Right now there doesn't seem to be much political will to overturn the Rave Act, which threatens promoters of events where drugs are consumed. If the bill were changed, however, big raves would quickly become safer. "I definitely know that if we could do harm reduction, and it was allowed, we would do it," said promoter Gary Richards, who puts on an enormous annual southern California electronic dance music event called Hard

Summer. "I've been to other festivals in Canada where they do it, and I know they find all kinds of things in those pills. We would love to be able do that if we're allowed to, but we can't."

The musicians performing at these festivals tend to feel the same way, even those who are sober, like Kaskade, a celebrity DJ who is also a devout Mormon. He emphasizes that these events can be enjoyed by teetotalers, but he's not deluding himself. "I think a lot of kids are going to take drugs no matter what we say," he said. "If you're going to take stuff, have it checked. These guys can check this stuff out to make sure it's not going to kill you."

At the very least, just about everyone — from both sides of the political spectrum — agrees that disseminating information about NPS is critical and that users need to understand the dangers of NPS, even compared to traditional drugs. For kids who are experimenting, the educational aspect might be their only protection.

Suburban Dallas, an area where teenagers, including Montana Brown, have died from new drugs, has since found some success by getting the word out about them. Grace Raulston, a substance-abuse counselor from Collin County — which contains a section of Brown's hometown of Frisco — said that the K2 menace in the area was significantly reduced after an information campaign about synthetic marijuana. "The biggest thing we're fighting now is education. The majority of people out there — parents especially — do not have *any* idea the scope of the problem we're dealing with today," said Courtney Pero, the narcotics sergeant in nearby Plano, Texas. Parents need to believe that an overdose could happen to their kid, because it can happen to any kid.

TWENTY-FIVE

The majority of NPS overdose deaths don't come from party drugs and knockoffs. They come from opioids, which, unlike ecstasy and hallucinogens, can be deadly addictive. Combating them requires specially tailored initiatives.

Americans take more opioids per capita — legitimate and illegitimate uses combined — than any other country in the world. Canada is second, and both far outstrip Europe. Americans take four times as many opioids as people do in the United Kingdom.

Many factors contribute to this disparity. A BBC investigation into the issue highlighted the overprescription of pills, driven by a lack of universal health care, the advertising of prescription drugs on television (which is legal only in the United States and New Zealand), poor medical training, and "a culture of medication."

Many experts believe, however, that abruptly cutting off addicted patients' access to pain pills is not the right solution, either, as sufferers of chronic pain may well be pushed toward illicit heroin and fentanyl.

"Making it harder for people to get pain medication legally will most likely drive many to seek relief from far more dangerous and superpotent synthetic opioids," wrote Richard A. Friedman, director of the psychopharmacology clinic at New York's Weill Cornell Medical College. A flurry of new regulations designed to lower patients' dependence on opioids are nonetheless going into effect. In Colorado, some doctors require their patients to take special classes before they can receive their medication. The classes suggest a variety of alternatives for battling chronic pain, including yoga, acupuncture, and dietary supplements. However well intentioned, such requirements have caused some pain patients to feel as if they were being reprimanded or worse. "I am uncomfortable with this approach because it feels like my care is being undermined, and my condition discounted," said a Fort Collins, Colorado, patient named Shelley Neth, who suffers from conditions including osteoarthritis and was told by her doctor that she would have to attend classes to continue receiving her Vicodin. "Now I'm considered a 'person on opioids.' " She added: "The punishment for the overdose epidemic is being exacted on chronic pain patients."

Curbing the tide of US opioid deaths will require sweeping new public-health initiatives, including treatment programs and campaigns to educate everyone, from users and medical providers to teachers and police, about the drugs' dangers. First responders, police, firefighters, and others who encounter overdose victims need to be better supplied with naloxone, which should be available and affordable to anyone who could benefit from it. Nonetheless, naloxone (including Narcan, the best-known brand) has faced controversy in some communities around the country. Butler County, Ohio, sheriff Richard K. Jones has declined to equip his officers with Narcan. "All we're doing is reviving them, we're not curing them," he told NBC News in 2017. "One person we know has been revived 20 separate times." (He added that police nonetheless don't let people die, and that paramedics can instead administer Narcan.)

Some argue that naloxone enables drug abuse and express concern about so-called

Lazarus parties (named for the biblical figure Jesus brought back to life), in which fentanyl users push the limit, confident that an acquaintance standing by will revive them with naloxone if they overdose. "I know it is not uncommon for users and their friends or fellow users to have Narcan available for that exact reason," said Grand Forks, North Dakota, police lieutenant Brett Johnson.

Simply reviving overdose victims is no solution by itself. Stopping opioid overdoses will also require giving users access to drug-checking kits, like those made by Bunk Police, so they can find out whether their heroin contains fentanyl. This idea is making some headway domestically; in 2018 a Rhode Island state representative announced a bill that would cement the legality of drug-checking kits, specifically mentioning fentanyl test strips. California's public-health department now also provides fentanyl test strips to needle-exchange facilities there, as do public-health departments in a number of US cities, including Columbus, Baltimore, and Philadelphia.

Others would take this idea much further.

"I would set up free drug-purity testing sites, that are anonymous, where people could submit samples of their drugs and then get a chemical analysis breakdown," said Dr. Carl Hart, chairman of the psychology department at Columbia University. Hart is one of the most outspoken proponents of radical harm-reduction practices in the United States, also advocating for pharmaceutical-grade heroin to be dispensed to addicted users.

Supervised-injection sites are another form of harm reduction. Located in a dozen or so countries around the world, including Canada, France, Norway, the Netherlands, and Switzerland, they are clinics where people can use drugs like heroin and fentanyl free of legal repercussions. Doctors and nurses monitor them, providing counsel, care, and clean needles. Often funded by governments, the clinics have been found to provide dramatic societal benefits, including helping to reduce HIV transmission and fatal overdoses.

As of this writing, however, the United States has no officially sanctioned supervised-injection sites, although at least one has operated secretly in recent years. "In an undisclosed location in the US, a social services agency has secretly overseen more than 2,500 injections by around 100 people who take drugs — in an effort to fight the overdose crisis," wrote *Vice* in

August 2017. A planned site in Philadelphia drew a lawsuit from the federal government in February, 2019; its fate was unclear.

Canada has clinics across the country, including in Vancouver, Toronto, Montreal, and its capital, Ottawa. After the opening of Vancouver's first facility, InSite, in 2003, overdose fatalities dropped significantly, though the center has since been hard hit by the rise of fentanyl use, and administrators hope to increase its annual $3 million budget. In recent years proposals for supervised-injection sites have been considered in US cities including Seattle and San Francisco, and New York City mayor Bill de Blasio has supported the idea, but opposition has been too fierce to overcome. As this book went to press, Denver's city council had approved a pilot program for a site (which would include testing of users' drugs for fentanyl), but approval by the state legislature was still required.

In March, 2017, when officials in the Seattle area were considering approving a pair of supervised-injection rooms, Lisa DuFour, a lawyer, published an editorial in the *Seattle Times* with the headline, "I Lost My Son to a Drug Overdose: Say No to Safe Injection Sites." Her piece was powerful, and it raised a number of objections to the proposal: "Heroin is illegal. Will the police allow illegal drug use at a 'heroin house' and yet arrest people elsewhere who use the same drug? . . . A major cause of overdose is the different strengths of drugs and the combination with other drugs like fentanyl. Will the staff test drugs for purity or safety? And why should taxpayers be burdened with the costs of providing a 'heroin house' and paying for the lawsuits when we cannot solve our homeless problem?"

While legitimate questions, asked in good faith, they overlook the fact that well-regarded supervised-injection rooms, such as Baluard in Barcelona, are having a huge impact.

Baluard is housed inside a giant medieval stone fortification known as the Wall of Drassanes. It is located near the Port of Barcelona, is part of what was once the Barcelona Royal Shipyard, which dates back to the thirteenth century, and once served as a bulwark to defend against intruders. The symbolism is not lost on anyone.

Opened in 2004, Baluard was the first center of its kind in Barcelona. At that time, the city was overrun by people using heroin in public places. Some twelve thousand used syringes were collected from city streets and parks that year; by 2016 that figure had dropped to one thousand. Today more than a dozen similar facilities can be found in the area — and eighty in the encompassing Catalonia region, including mobile buses. There are even needle-exchange programs in prisons. Baluard itself is close to tourist spots like Las Ramblas, the famous strip of eateries and shops, but it feels a world apart. In the grassless park in front of the facility, men lie on benches, and transients mill about, their dogs and plastic bags of belongings near at hand. Baluard has become the center of their universe, even when they are not in the facility.

Inside, the staff members wear lab coats but interact casually with patients, while upbeat Spanish pop plays over speakers. A calendar of events advertises movie nights for the users, as well as museum visits, table tennis (*entrenamiento de ping-pong*), and theater classes. Also advertised are workshops on how to administer Narcan and how to convert cocaine to crack, so it can be smoked instead of shot up, which has some health benefits. (Baluard does not provide recreational drugs.)

The shooting-up room looks surprisingly antiseptic and clinical, like a hospital room, with blue dividers separating spaces at a table that holds five users at a time. There are fresh supplies of needles, tourniquets, antiseptic wipes, and sterile water in which to dissolve heroin. The users inject themselves, but staff is on hand if someone overdoses, ready to assist in the small infirmary nearby. The staff also helps users ensure their heroin is pure, with the assistance of Energy Control.

The facility's smoking room has six chairs, and on a day in 2017 was overseen by a chipper staffer named Anna. A posted sign says the maximum amount of time to smoke heroin is thirty minutes, and crack forty-five. Pipes cannot be shared. The room is also used for smoking meth and cannabis. Anna, a former Energy Control volunteer, sat just outside the room, on the other side of a window, operating a pass-through tray (like at a bank), through which she handed out paraphernalia, including nontoxic aluminum foil for heating up heroin and special inhaling straws. She also provided crack vials and special crack pipes made of glass that resemble small bongs.

Whenever someone entered the room, Anna input the person's information into a computer, which contains their substance abuse history. "Hola!" she said as a man entered, asking if he was there to smoke heroin. "Sí!" he responded. She passed him a sheet of foil and a straw, and he sat down at the table, unwrapping a small blue piece of paper holding his bit of "brown sugar" heroin. He put the heroin on the foil and, from below, heated it with a lighter. As the smoke billowed up he sucked it through the straw. The man was perhaps forty-five, had close-cropped hair, and wore orange and blue shoes and an almost-trendy, long-sleeved button-down shirt. After his hit, he lit a cigarette, which he puffed momentarily before setting it in a filtered ashtray, where it slowly burned down while he finished his heroin. "Adiós!" Anna said as he left, smiling. All told, he had been in the room for maybe five minutes.

Another man soon entered. He was scruffier and had come to use both oral methadone and heroin. "Hola, hombre!" Anna said. Her familiarity with her patients spoke to their health and relative longevity; with the aid of supervised-injection sites, they can more safely manage their addictions. Ideally, they would kick the habit. In reality, however, that can be incredibly difficult. Fortunately, even those who are addicted to opiates and opioids can potentially live long, productive lives, provided they have access to clean needles, care, unadulterated drugs, and safe spots to shoot up.

Baluard's coordinator, Diego Arànega, has a shaved head and a talent for maintaining perspective amidst chaos. "The target group here is problematic users," he said, speaking in rapid Catalan. "People who are basically in a big mess."

A psychologist by training, Arànega directs the center and acts as a social worker here, his responsibilities varying depending on the moment. Baluard also provides free drugs for substitution therapy, to try to wean people off opiates. "The methadone is sometimes the hook, to stay in touch with the users every day," Arànega explains, which also allows the center to treat them for infections and other maladies and to provide counseling.

Substitution therapy appears to be a breakthrough in the fight against the problems associated with heroin and fentanyl addiction — not only overdoses but HIV, criminal activity, and other abuse-adjacent personal issues. Substitution treatments use drugs like methadone, naltrexone, or buprenorphine and are "associated with substantial reductions in the risk for [overdose death] in people dependent on opioids," according to a 2017 study led by Spanish doctor and public-health expert Luis Sordo del Castillo. According to the European Monitoring Centre for Drugs and Drug Addiction (EMCDDA), Spain now has just about as many people using facilities like Baluard (around sixty thousand) as it has high-risk opioid users in the country as a whole. These clients aren't coming in just for clean needles and to get high, they have a support system, and their addictions are controlled and monitored. This may not have solved Spain's homeless problem — a concern voiced by the *Seattle Times* opinion writer — but the people who have started free substitution therapy at facilities like Baluard are no longer on the streets committing crimes to make money for their next fix.

Not everyone is interested in quitting heroin. About twenty-five hundred injections per month take place at Baluard, Arànega told me. No one has ever died inside the facility and, to date, there are no reports of anyone ever dying inside one of these types of centers worldwide. In 2016 in Barcelona, according to Arànega, only seventy people died from opioid use, in a city of nearly five million. The center's clean-needle program also seems to be working. More than half of its clients have hepatitis C, and about one in eight are HIV positive, but according to the EMCDDA, HIV diagnoses "attributed to injecting" have plummeted in Spain in recent years, down from 300 in 2009 to 113 in 2016, the most recent year for which statistics were available. As a result, the public costs associated with treating HIV have gone down; when added to the money saved due to reduced crime and to other health-care savings, the financial benefits to the public are substantial, addressing another of the Seattle writer's concerns.

Arànega dispels another common fear about these centers: that they encourage addiction. The people his clinic sees are not first-time users, he said, but those with opioid-use disorder, who long ago chose this life. Now they're trying to get well. "If they're here, they're not in the parks, in the streets, with children. If you are offering not just an injection room but access to psychologists and doctors, you're doing good work."

Officials in countries that have had success with these types of injection rooms, such as Switzerland, now see them as benefits not just to addicted users but to the population at large. "The consumption room is the best tool I have to ensure public safety in Bern," said the police chief of the Bern region, Manuel Willi, using another term for the sites. The trend seems to be growing worldwide, as numerous sites opened across Canada, Europe, and Australia in 2017 and 2018.

Stigma, the Slovenian public-health group focused on opiate addiction, operates needle-exchange centers in Ljubljana, including one in the city center, located near a bridge guarded by a dragon sculpture. It's a small room inhabited by people quietly drinking coffee or juice. Near the front sits a table blanketed with plastic-wrapped needles — hundreds of them, in different shapes and sizes.

Though possessing the stale air of a homeless shelter, it and similar centers across Slovenia are making an impact. The country has very few opiate or opioid deaths, and its HIV rate has dropped and is now among the lowest in Europe. This is undoubtedly aided by government-sponsored efforts to reach out to addicted users. Stigma's director, Dare Kochmur, admitted his organization literally pulls them in from outside. "By moving people from the streets inside, you eliminate the unseen population. We don't judge them. We don't encourage [drug use], but our goal is to eliminate unnecessary harm." The United States has perhaps a few hundred needle-exchange centers scattered around the country; it's difficult to know how many, because more are opening all the time. Kentucky, New Mexico, and California each have more than forty, and New York and Washington have at least twenty each. Many states, traditionally, have been reluctant to embrace the concept, but an omnibus spending bill signed by President Obama in 2016 allowed states and municipalities to use federal funds for these exchanges in some situations, and the movement is gaining steam. Despite scattered local resistance, officials in some states have marshaled resources for these exchanges, including Republican governors in Kentucky and Indiana.

Fentanyl is barely visible in Slovenia. Harm-reduction efforts get some of the credit, according to Kochmur. Slovenia's methadone program started in the mid-1990s, and opiate addiction rates have since fallen. The country currently boasts twenty-two methadone-substitution clinics, and Kochmur has lobbied for more. Baluard and the other European supervised-injection centers don't see much fentanyl, either. "There's no fentanyl here in Barcelona, because you have greater availability of heroin, and users prefer heroin," said Energy Control's Mireia Ventura.

Experts on both sides of the Atlantic agree that it would be easy to establish supervised-injection facilities for opioid-ravaged communities in the United States, to create one-stop shops where people could test their heroin for fentanyl, exchange needles, and shoot up safely. On-site help would be ready with Narcan, and users could also receive counseling, information, and medical assistance, likely slowing the opioid crisis wherever such practices were administered. These facilities already have a long track record of success. However, big barriers remain because the United States has not decriminalized drugs; in Canada, for example, the government had to provide supervised-injection sites with an exemption. But continuing on the current path would likely be much worse.

"Harm reduction is the only answer," Kochmur said, offering advice to the United States. "You can't just do primary prevention in the schools. You can't get all the addicts clean in the health-care system. And you can't arrest all the drug users."

The tension in the United States is encapsulated in an October, 2018 exchange, when former Pennsylvania governor Ed Rendell announced that he had incorporated a nonprofit seeking private funding to open a supervised injection facility in Philadelphia, which at that time had the highest opioid death rate of any major U.S. city. This despite threats from US deputy attorney general Rod Rosenstein that if one opened it would be immediately shut down by federal authorities. "I've got a message for Mr. Rosenstein," Rendell said. "They can come and arrest me first."

EPILOGUE

In 2017 American life expectancy declined for the third consecutive year, something that hadn't happened since the 1940s. The Centers for Disease Control and Prevention attributed the drop in part to fentanyl, which also appears to be driving down life expectancy in regions of Canada. Solving this crisis will require us to change some of our most basic assumptions about how we perceive drug abuse. We need to treat it as a disease, not a crime, and understand what causes it, rather than simply trying to eradicate it. There are indications that this might be happening in parts of the United States, and the results are encouraging.

Initially, New England states were most severely hit by the fentanyl crisis, but in 2017 Massachusetts, Rhode Island, and Vermont saw their drug overdose death rates decline, likely thanks in part to increases in addiction treatment programs and public-health campaigns. "It could be an indication that increased access to treatment, safer use practices, and prevention methods are working," said Mario Moreno, former press secretary for the White House Office of National Drug Control Policy. A hallmark of Rhode Island's strategy is providing access to opioid replacements for incarcerated people with addictions, which appears to stop them from overdosing upon their release. The program has already saved lives, state officials say. Ohio, a state whose Medicaid expansion in 2015 has given many users access to addiction and treatment programs, has also seen its overdose death rate drop dramatically in some of its hardest-hit areas. On the national level, the SUPPORT for Patients and Communities Act, signed by President Trump on October 24, 2018, was a step in the right direction in its provisions for better opioid treatment options, though greater resources are needed.

As with almost any major social movement, change needs to happen at the local level first. Thankfully, even in opioid-ravaged areas like St. Louis, there is hope. After her most-recent fentanyl relapse, during the second trimester of her pregnancy, East Alton resident Bree felt an urgent need to turn her life around and discovered the WISH Center, a St. Louis substance-abuse clinic tailored to pregnant women and infants.

Traditionally, more men die from drug overdoses than women. Women, however, are equally likely to develop drug and alcohol addictions and may be more sensitive to the effects of opioids than men. Withdrawal can be more intense for women, said Robert Glatter, an emergency physician at Lenox Hill Hospital in New York City. "Data indicates that women run a higher risk of drug craving and relapse, which are important stages in the addiction cycle," he said.

The WISH Center is run by Dr. Jaye Shyken, a maternal-fetal medicine subspecialist who previously worked with pregnant women addicted to cocaine. Now, at the WISH Center, almost everyone she sees has opiate- and opioid-use disorders. Shyken would argue that the way the United States treats opioid dependence is all wrong. "There's money for in-patient stabilization, three- to six-day detoxes, then they're discharged, with a telephone number for chemical-dependency treatment," she said, a quick release that fuels a high recidivism rate. She advocates a type of addiction care called medication-assisted treatment, similar to Baluard's substitution therapy, which treats people with opioid dependency with replacement drugs, like methadone or buprenorphine. In combination with traditional therapy, this approach gets to the core of the issue for most people: a physical dependence combined with personal problems spiraling out of control.

Opioid addiction is often portrayed as an irreversible rewiring of the brain; the common perception is that once one becomes addicted to these drugs it's impossible to break free. But according to Shyken's experience, those able to fix major problems in their lives often break the cycle. The problem for many is that expecting them to get their lives in order and go through withdrawal at the same time is asking too much. At the WISH Center, Shyken prescribes buprenorphine, which is sold as Suboxone or Subutex. Studies have given medication-assisted treatment credit for reducing overdose deaths, and it is frequently described as the gold standard for treating opioid addiction.

Buprenorphine and methadone are controversial because they are opioids, although less powerful than heroin, fentanyl, and other opioids of abuse. Still, methadone dependence is a problem in itself; it is frequently sold as a street drug and causes thousands of overdose deaths per year. Many believe buprenorphine to be a better solution, and it is undoubtedly safer, though it has traditionally been difficult for doctors to prescribe, as it requires a special license from the DEA. The benefits of buprenorphine and methadone are that these drugs prevent debilitating physical withdrawal symptoms — which many often compare to a terrible flu — without (usually) getting the average user high. This helps users get their opioid compulsions under control and their lives in order while, ideally, helping them slowly taper off opioids altogether.

"When people say, 'Dr. Shyken, aren't you just substituting one drug for another?' I say, 'Yes, what's your point?' It's saving lives."

Though this philosophy is disputed by some treatment providers, who stress the importance of abstinence-based recovery, many doctors and addiction experts support it. The renowned Hazelden Betty Ford Foundation, for example, once took an abstinence-only approach, but in 2012 began providing medication-assisted treatment. The WISH Center opened in 2014, and demand for its services has been overwhelming. "The word of mouth is just amazing," Shyken acknowledged. "It's not like we're doing a lot of advertising."

She also believes that a spiritual approach can be helpful in some instances, a possibility that has been recognized in academic literature. "Spirituality for some people produces chemical changes in the central nervous system that we seek with medication and self-efficacy," she said.

Opiods are often abused in company with other drugs, however. Bree overdosed on fentanyl and the benzodiazepine Xanax, passing out in her van at a gas station, and had to be revived with Narcan. Benzodiazepine and opioids can be an especially deadly combination, since both drugs slow down the central nervous system, which affects breathing. Indeed, the National Institute on Drug Abuse says that more than 30 percent of overdoses involving opioids also involve benzodiazepines.

"We have this whole infrastructure set up now to prevent overprescribing of opioids and address the need for addiction treatment," said Dr. Anna Lembke, a researcher and addiction specialist at Stanford University. "We need to start making benzos part of that."

Exclusively focusing on the chemical

aspect also overlooks another important factor. "One hundred percent of my patients have experienced childhood trauma or have a mental health disorder, which are tied in," Shyken said.

Bree, who in her three decades has faced a host of traumas, was prescribed Subutex at WISH, which she takes orally. For the time being at least, she has been able to stay off fentanyl. "We made a promise to ourselves we would never do it again," she said, looking at her boyfriend, Mike, who has had his own problems with fentanyl.

Six weeks later, she gave birth to their baby, a healthy girl.

Jack Sanders, the fentanyl dealer from suburban St. Louis, was able to find redemption. Before he could escape his nightmare, however, he had to hit rock bottom. After his friend Marcus, who gave him all the heroin he could use in exchange for serving as the muscle on drug transactions, went to prison, Jack lost his heroin connection, even while his habit remained in full force. Broke and suffering from withdrawal, he did the only thing he could think to do: he brandished his .38 and started robbing people, preferring drug dealers.

"I'd look into your eyes, I'd see if you were

a killer or not. And if I didn't think you were a killer, I'd put a gun to your head, and I'd fuckin' take all your shit," he said. Guns, cash, drugs — everything. Even, sometimes, shoes, so his victims couldn't run after him. This was how Jack fed his habit for more than a year. But he was living on borrowed time. The world of St. Louis drug dealing is small, and he eventually robbed the wrong man, someone who came back at him with force. Fearing for the safety of his family, Jack traveled about two hours south to a city called Cape Girardeau, where he lived in a homeless shelter for almost a year.

Cape Girardeau, a pretty river town, held an added benefit for Jack — he didn't have any heroin connections. So, around 2015, he dried out. It was painful. When he heard that the man stalking him had been murdered, he finally returned to St. Louis and found a psychiatrist who helped pull him out of the pit. "She found out the right medications I needed, antidepressants, stuff like that, and I've taken those ever since," Sanders said.

He's not kidding himself into thinking that he's going to shake his past anytime soon. He's committed too many crimes, hurt too many people, and spread too many dangerous drugs for that. "Now that I'm clean, I have nightmares all the time. I don't know which ones are real, and which ones aren't. I see ghosts of people I've hurt."

Jack got out, and is now gainfully employed in his hometown. But the scourge of fentanyl remains, and St. Louis heroin products continue to be manipulated. When fentanyl packages first began arriving from Mexico, Jack and his crew used one part fentanyl for every seven parts heroin. As fentanyl caught on, dealers began competing with each other to offer a stronger product. Before long, said Jack, the ratio was one to six, and then one to four. Today it might be one to two. A higher concentration brings a much greater mortality risk.

Even while Jack and Bree are recovering, fentanyl deaths in the St. Louis area remain on the rise.

In Grand Forks, North Dakota, the college town by the Red River where this story began, the tragic fentanyl overdose death of eighteen-year-old Bailey Henke served as an alarm bell for the members of the community, almost all of whom, in early 2015 when Henke died, had never even heard of fentanyl. The city has taken a multipronged approach to confronting the epidemic, enlisting the mayor's office, the police department, the public-health office, addiction counselors, and doctors. In one of the most conservative states in the country, on both the city and state level, people put aside politics to confront the quickly rising toll of fentanyl and opioid overdoses.

"Bailey's death shocked us to our core and caused the community to look deep within itself," said Grand Forks' mayor, Michael R. Brown. "Because we're in the Midwest, we think we're isolated from these types of things, but I'm very proud of our response."

Brown is a part-time mayor and a full-time obstetrician-gynecologist. His background as a doctor gives him an informed perspective on this drug crisis, and he has been open to progressive ideas like medication-assisted treatment. He has spearheaded an initiative, largely inspired by Henke's death, called the Grand Forks Call to Action, which focuses on opioid abuse. It kicked off in May 2017, when he and other civic leaders spoke before an audience of more than two hundred locals to discuss the crisis and potential solutions. "We know addiction is a disease, and in order to save lives we must be a community that is welcoming people into the services they need," he began.

"There's been a lot of new thoughts on

how we treat addiction," affirmed Michael Dulitz, the project coordinator for the Grand Forks Public Health Department's Opiate Response program. "Nowadays individuals aren't being arrested for overdosing, which is a strong change."

Grand Forks police lieutenant Brett Johnson acknowledges that even while his department has employed new tactics to confront the NPS crisis — having received special tech training to combat the Dark Web menace — the police can't arrest their way out of this problem. The opioid deaths of Henke and others have changed perspectives of officers in the department and others in the community. "It's not just your stereotypical drug user that's using these substances," Johnson recognized. "It cuts across all societal groups, not just what you would traditionally think of as a drug user."

"We have to *educate* our way out of the problem," said Mayor Brown.

In December 2016, President Obama signed into law the 21st Century Cures Act, a wide-ranging bill that helped streamline the approval process for new drugs, provided funding for medical research, and gave $1 billion in state grants to fight the opioid epidemic. North Dakota received $2 million, which was distributed among five cities, including Grand Forks, which received $180,000. This money was, in part, used to create Michael Dulitz's position within the city's Public Health Department, and he has been implementing a number of harm-reduction tactics.

Dulitz is a former paramedic who was treating opioid overdoses on the street level in nearby Fargo as the crisis heated up. "The summer of 2015 was when I realized there was a big problem here. We were pulling [overdose victims] out of cars, where their friends were speeding away. There were a lot of questions about fentanyl, and we weren't getting a lot of answers. It was assumed to be heroin at first. And it wasn't until later that we realized it was *illicitly produced fentanyl.*"

He went on to receive a master's in public health from the University of North Dakota, in 2017, and began his position later that year, helping lead Grand Forks' progressive opioid crisis response, which includes a partnership with a local pharmacy to distribute free harm-reduction kits — which have naloxone, fentanyl test strips, plastic containers to carry needles, and condoms. These are handed out to those in need in the community. "Their availability has been spread rapidly by word of mouth," Dulitz reports. He purchased fifteen hundred fentanyl test strips from DanceSafe for a dollar each, in the process becoming an early municipal adopter of this approach.

In many regards, Grand Forks has been a model city when it comes to compassionately confronting the problem head on. Further, owing to a rules change at the North Dakota Board of Medicine that took effect at the beginning of 2018, state residents with opioid use disorders are now able to access medication-assisted treatment providers via telemedicine, a system that involves communicating with doctors in other places, using a technology similar to Skype. This allows for access to opioid addiction drugs like buprenorphine and methadone in areas with no medication-assisted treatment providers.

Another progressive change in North Dakota occurred in 2017, when the state updated its Good Samaritan law to protect people who seek medical help for overdose victims, granting them immunity from drug-possession charges. This law makes a real difference. Tanner Gerszewski, the friend whose apartment Bailey Henke died in, said he knew people in high school who didn't call in when their friend overdosed, because they thought they would go to jail.

Gerszewski himself may have been worried about this exact thing; he moved his drugs from his apartment to his van at the very moment Henke was overdosing. "I thought, 'This is a big deal, they go through and search my house, there's a death in my place, that's not good,' " Gerszewski said, though he adds that because another friend was performing CPR on Henke at the time, and they were waiting for an ambulance, Gerszewski didn't believe there was anything he could do to help the situation.

If and when the opioid scourge is contained in Grand Forks, it will leave behind a larger legacy. According to Dulitz, the response to the crisis has caused the community to rethink how it addresses other types of addiction. "Now they're even treating alcohol as an addiction and reducing stigma around it," he said. "More treatment options are available."

Laura Henke, Bailey's mother, is generous and quick to laugh. She tends to immediately agree with the person she's speaking with, to give him or her the benefit of the doubt. Hailing originally from Hallock, Minnesota — near the Canadian border, about an hour north of her current home in Grand Forks — she's the very definition of

"Minnesota nice." But despair nonetheless lurks within her since Bailey died.

Still disturbed by the events surrounding the evening he passed away, she is no longer in touch with Tanner Gerszewski, and when asked by a documentarian if she forgives Kain Schwandt — Bailey's friend, who was also with him that day — she responded, "I'd like to, I guess forgive him for Bailey, because Bailey would want him to be a better person."

Schwandt said alcoholism and drug abuse runs in his family, and admits that he was a reckless drug user when Henke was alive — and afterward. He even overdosed on a fentanyl patch about three months after Henke died, before spending about a year and a half in a Duluth, Minnesota, prison. He wasn't charged in Bailey's death, but rather pled guilty to conspiracy to possess heroin with intent to distribute. He got his GED behind bars and received early release after completing a drug treatment and behavioral program. He has stayed clean of opioids and other drugs since; the key, he imparts, is avoiding the old crowd he used to take drugs with. Instead, he is concentrating on work, building vinyl and carpet floor installations with his stepfather. "I'm just working and staying out of trouble the best

I can. And I'm on probation for another two and a half years, so that's another good motivator."

Gerszewski has a harder time putting on a brave face. He has never been able to remember everything about the night of Bailey's death, because he was so high, and even that tragedy didn't slow down his drug abuse. Still in the throes of opiate dependency on January 7, 2015, just days after Bailey died, Gerszewski saw his girlfriend, Jade Nelson, overdose on heroin — also at his apartment — though she was transported to the hospital and survived. Heroin and marijuana were found in Gerszewski's home, and he was charged with intent to distribute, for which he did about three months in jail. "Seeing Bailey die, and then having my girlfriend OD, and then doing jail time, losing my freedom, everything. . . . I just sat in jail one day and thought, 'Jesus, what am I doing? Either I'm gonna die or I need to stop, because this just isn't working.' " He has gotten clean since then, but his conscience continues to nag at him. "There's still that guilt of, 'Why did he die, and why did I survive?' I almost wish it were the other way around." He is seeing a psychologist, is on depression medication, and has made it his mission to help prevent deaths like Bailey's, spreading the word about the horrors of fentanyl.

Laura Henke and her husband, Jason Henke, have the same mission. After Bailey's death they started a scholarship at his high school in his memory. They have also been generous in talking with the media about his death, and Laura even went so far as to help me track down contact information for Bailey's friends and his hospital medical records.

Before departing the pizza parlor where we met to talk, Laura took me to the back of the restaurant, to show off a wall of scribbling above one of the booths. Hundreds of people have signed their names and written messages on the wall, forming layers upon layers of pastel Crayola marker and loud primary colors, so that the specific words have become hard to make out. But as she pointed I saw her son's name, written in huge orange letters near the top of the wall. "Bailey Henke Forever," it said. Below that, in black letters is a smaller message, which Bailey's mother added after his death. It read: "Laura Henke Forever Also!!"

ACKNOWLEDGMENTS

My thoughts are with victims and their families. I wrote this book to uncover truth, and hopefully inspire change. Thank you for reading.

This project would not have been possible without Jada Li, researcher and translator. She led me on the ground in China, from Wuhan to Shanghai, helping interview everyone from drug dealers to police, coaching me on Chinese culture and dissecting documents. She's a wizard with languages and a fantastic journalist. She put herself in harm's way, and I am in her debt.

My editor George Gibson is a legend. His wisdom, insight, elbow grease, and good sense are on every page. The book would have never launched without my visionary agent Ethan Bassoff, who saw forest where I only saw trees. More than anyone else Adam Auctor, of Bunk Police, helped me understand the rapidly evolving world of

NPS. Welcoming me to Denver and Ljubljana, he was a fantastic tutor for more than three years. The man known as Jack Sanders revisited a dark chapter of his life for my benefit. His recovery story is inspiring. My best wishes to the courageous couple Bree and Mike from East Alton, Illinois, and to Channing Lacey, who is making tough choices and good progress.

Jean-François Tremblay spent hours explaining China's complicated chemical industry to me, interspersed with delightful dry jokes. Michael Meyer was like a cool older brother taking me to the 7th St. Entry, except for China. His books are highly recommended; thanks also to his wife Frances. Hearing Danny Parrott's observations in Beijing was a blast, as was commiserating with Nathan VanderKlippe. Erika Kinetz, in Shanghai, helped me understand the Chinese synthetic drug lab landscape, and thanks also for China guidance to Christine Chiao, James Fallows, Guo Qing Yuan, Holly Williams, Jing Song, and Huan Hsu.

Eric Brown does tremendous educational work on NPS, and he graciously welcomed me into his home. RIP, Montana. Jack Brown, Grace Raulston, Leslie Cherryholmes, Alan Hunter, and Courtney Pero were also great help, as was Lee Stockton and Parkland toxicologists Ashley Haynes, Kristina Domanski, and Shannon Rickner. Still grieving from her son Bailey's passing, Laura Henke told me his story, and Kain Schwandt and Tanner Gerszewski opened up as well. Thanks to Grand Forks Police Lieutenant Brett Johnson, public health superhero Michael Dulitz, mayor Michael R. Brown, and reporter April Baumgarten, who helped me navigate Grand Forks.

Cheers to the big homie Aaron Baines for friendship and European travel companionship. In Ljubljana I spoke with knowledgeable psychonauts including Vlad, Anton (a corporate chemist by day and incredible source of information), and Sidney Picej, who increased my understanding of these new drugs and their culture. If you ever meet Sidney ask him for his American stereotypes. Thanks also to Slovenian harm reduction activists Dare Kochmur and Marko Verdenik. In Spain, Mireia Ventura, Cristina Gil, Núria Calzada, Ivan Fornis, Rafael Sacramento, and Diego Aranega from Energy Control blew my mind with their knowledge, generosity, and selfless work. Nos vemos! In Vienna, danke to

Anton Luf, Rainer Schmid, and Steve Mueller.

Mike Power wrote the first book on NPS, *Drugs 2.0,* and was generous with his time. Sam Quinones is an amazing journalist; I consult *Dreamland* frequently. Johann Hari's *Chasing the Scream* is indispensable, and Ko-Lin Chin and Sheldon X. Zhang's *The Chinese Heroin Trade* was critical to my project. *Vice* has covered NPS better than anyone; Hamilton Morris is the O.G., and Maia Szalavitz's work is invaluable. Shout out also to Keegan Hamilton and Brian McManus. Jack Schafer covered fentanyl before almost anyone, and Jeanne Whalen has done great reporting on NPS for at least a decade. Natalie Tecimer provided helpful information, including about tramadol in India. My buddy the terrific reporter Amanda Chicago Lewis tipped me off about NPS in the Dallas suburbs. Thanks to Tom Finkel for #journalism. Dark Web dealers Desifelay1000, high_as_fxck_GER, and particularly U4IA took huge risks to help me understand NPS distribution, as did others unnamable here. Thanks to William Leonard Pickard for his story.

Matt Bowden was an unparalleled resource. Martin Raithelhuber, along with his colleague Tun Nay Soe, and Roumen Sedefov helped me understand the global picture. David Nichols and John William Huffman answered countless questions about their work. Thanks also to Stefanie Jones of Drug Policy Alliance, Toby Muse, and the academics Anna Lembke, Justin Hastings, Peter Reuter, Gary Ranken, Marvin Wilson, Phil Williams, and my badass friend Bridget Coggins. DEA agents Melvin Patterson, Dennis Wichern, Elaine Cesare, James Jones, and Sharon Lindskoog were very helpful, as was Michael Felberbaum of the FDA. For geopolitical facts, figures, and context I'm in debt to Bryce Pardo, of RAND, Katherine Tobin, and Sean O'Connor of the U.S.-China Economic and Security Review Commission. From the Peterson Institute for International Economics, thanks to Gary Hufbauer, Lucy Lu, and Nicholas Lardy. My Mexico reporting was aided tremendously by Deborah Bonello, Mario Moreno, and Mike Vigil.

DanceSafe's Mitchell Gomez knows more about drugs than anyone I know, and thanks also to Missi Wooldridge, Emanuel Sferios, and Amy Raves. Ann Shulgin welcomed me to the Farm in Lafayette, and Paul Daley showed me Sasha Shulgin's lab. Two superb SoCal journalists, Nicholas Schou offered great background on Orange County LSD, while Dennis Romero has been schooling me on ecstasy and electronic music since I was knee-high to a grasshopper. Thanks to my friend Katie Bain for guiding me through life's Electric Forest, and to another friend Sarah Fenske for general awesomeness. Gracias to Andrea Gleckner; please say what's up to your brother.

Jaye Shyken is doing life-saving work in St. Louis. Thanks also to River Citians Seth Ferranti, Kosta Longmire, Jeremy Kohler, Brooke Taylor, Aisha Sultan, Jesse Bogan, Blythe Bernhard, Ricardo Franklin, Jim Delworth, Bob Duffy, and Jeff Smith. Doctors Sarah Hartz and Margaret Baum provided crucial sources and information about the fentanyl crisis. Sorry Amy Ravin that I never go to book club. Imade Nibokun and Linda Leseman did great transcription work, and thanks also to Anna Bonelli, Michael Mason, Tal Rosenberg, Emily Witt, Sarah Purkrabek, Andy Van De Voorde, Chris Walker, Kate Steilen, and Rosemary Gibson. At Grove Atlantic, my thanks to Emily Burns, Deb Seager, John Mark Boling, Julia Berner-Tobin, Amy Hundley, Erica Nuñez, Sal Destro, Gretchen Mergenthaler, and Morgan Entrekin, and to my excellentest copy editor Amy Hughes.

My father and my longtime friend Sam

Ives helped me understand fentanyl use in medical practice, and were great sounding boards. My mother inspires me in her life and work, and thanks also to Alex, Sean, Julia, and Jay for their support in myriad ways. Kudos to Kai Flanders, Jon Milde, Kevin Kuntz, Steven Kurutz, Stefan Merrill Block, and Sam Stern. Thanks to Nicole Nice for putting me up (and putting up with me). PM and LR are the most wonderful companions I could ask for.

Thanks most of all to my wife Anna, who sacrificed and helped guide this project. I'm grateful for our life together, every day.

APPENDIX:
DRUGS DISCUSSED
IN THIS BOOK

TRADITIONAL

Recreational Drugs
Marijuana / Hashish
Cocaine / Crack
Methamphetamine
MDMA (aka Ecstasy or Molly)
Psilocybin (found in Magic Mushrooms)
LSD
DMT
Mescaline
Ketamine

Opiates and Opioids
Opium
Morphine
Heroin
Oxycodone (found in OxyContin and Per-
cocet)
Hydrocodone (found in Vicodin)
Tramadol

Benzodiazepines
Valium
Xanax

Opioid Treatment Drugs and Medications
Methadone
Buprenorphine (sold as Suboxone and
    Subutex)
Naltrexone
Naloxone (sold as Narcan)

NOVEL PSYCHOACTIVE
SUBSTANCES (NPS)

Psychedelics
2C-B
N-bombs (aka 25I-NBOMe, 25B-NBOMe,
    25C-NBOMe, and others)
DOM (aka STP, "Serenity, Tranquility, and
    Peace")

Synthetic Opioids
Fentanyl
U-47700

Fentanyl Analogues
Carfentanil
Alpha-methylfentanyl (aka China White)
3-Methylfentanyl
Acetylfentanyl

Methoxyacetylfentanyl (aka MAF)
Benzoylfentanyl (aka BUF-fentanyl)

Synthetic Cathinones
4-MMC (aka Mephedrone or Meow Meow)
3-MMC (aka Ice Cream)
a-PVP (aka Flakka)
Methylone

Synthetic Cannabinoids
JWH-018
5F-ADB
AB-FUBINACA
AB-CHFUPYCA
MMB-Fubica
AMB-Chmica
5F-MDMB-2201

Fentanyl Precursors
NPP
4-ANPP
N-phenylpiperidine-4-amine / N-phenyl-
  piperidine-4-amine dihydrochloride
4-anilino-1-benzylpiperidine

Stimulants / Other
Benzylpiperazine (aka BZP)
Paramethoxyamphetamine (PMA)
Paramethoxymethamphetamine (PMMA)

Note: "Spice," "K2," and "synthetic marijuana" refer to various synthetic cannabinoid mixtures. "Bath salts" generally refer to synthetic cathinone mixtures. "Legal highs" refer to synthetic cathinones, synthetic cannabinoids, and other NPS that were previously legal to buy in stores, but now have been mostly outlawed.

NOTES

Introduction

Bailey Henke went on a road trip. Kain Schwandt, author interview, June 12, 2018.

"I'd never tried it until Bailey brought some over one day." Tanner Gerszewski, author interview, June 27, 2018.

"We had a really nice Christmas." Laura Henke, author interview, June 24, 2018.

"Fentanyl is the deadliest drug in America, CDC confirms." Nadia Kounang, "Fentanyl Is the Deadliest Drug in America, CDC Confirms," CNN.com, December 12, 2018.

As of 2017, Americans were statistically more likely to die from an opioid overdose than a car accident. Kevin Flower and Meera Senthilingam, "Odds of Dying from Accidental Opioid Overdose in the US Surpass Those of Dying in

525

Car Accident," CNN.com, January 14, 2019.

Overdose death rates among African Americans, middle-aged women. Ashley Welch, "Drug Overdose Deaths Skyrocket among Middle-Aged Women," CBS News, January 10, 2019.

And young people. Assistant US attorney James Delworth, head of the Organized Crime and Drug Enforcement Task Force for the Eastern District of Missouri, author interview, October 25, 2018.

Opioid deaths expected to increase 147 percent by 2025. Qiushi Chen, Marc R. Larochelle, Davis T. Weaver, Anna P. Lietz, Peter P. Mueller, Sarah Mercaldo, Sarah E. Wakeman, Kenneth A. Freedberg, Tiana J. Raphel, Amy B. Knudsen, Pari V. Pandharipande, and Jagpreet Chhatwal, *Journal of the American Medical Association,* "Prevention of Prescription Opioid Misuse and Projected Overdose Deaths in the United States," February 1, 2019. Author note: The rates are expected to increase 147 percent by 2025, compared to 2015 rates.

The deadliest drug in Sweden. National Operations Department, Polisen (Swedish Police Authority), *Swedish National Threat Assessment on Fentanyl Analogues and*

Other Synthetic Opioids, October 2018, https://polisen.se/siteas-sets/dokument/ovriga_rapporter/fentanyl-analogues-report-english.pdf.

"Today, we are facing the most deadly crisis in America's history." Jeff Sessions, "Attorney General Jeff Sessions Delivers Remarks at the Department of Justice Opioid Summit," Office of Public Affairs, US Department of Justice, October 25, 2018, https://www.justice.gov/opa/speech/attorney-general-jeff-sessions-delivers-remarks-department-justice-opioid-summit.

"Fentanyl is the game changer." Keegan Hamilton, "How Fentanyl Gets to the U.S. from China," *Vice News,* December 22, 2017.

China produces over 90 percent of the world's illicit fentanyl. Linda Massarella, "Schumer Wants Fentanyl to Be Part of Talks with China," *New York Post,* May 13, 2018.

"The most disruptive innovation in the history of the international drug trade." Vanda Felbab-Brown, Jonathan P. Caulkins, and Keith Humphreys, "How Synthetic Opioids Can Radically Change Global Illegal Drug Markets and Foreign

527

Policy," Brookings Institution, April 30, 2018.

"It got a bunch of my aggression out." Channing Lacey, author interview, June 12, 2018.

Ulbricht was finally arrested at a San Francisco library in 2013. Nick Bilton, *American Kingpin: The Epic Hunt for the Criminal Mastermind Behind the Silk Road* (New York: Portfolio/Penguin, 2017), 282.

"BTH King of the Dark Net!" PRxBlack [*sic*] (vendor name), "The one, the only, pdxblack from Agora (H man with super rep) has opened up a second shop on TE as pdxwhite! Finally people of TorEscrow, get some FIRE H with full-escrow!!!" Reddit.com/r/torescrow, March 9, 2014.

"Heroin wouldn't even get me past sick anymore." Bree (pseudonym), author interview, June 9, 2017.

Originally from Colombia, Ceron had come to Canada as a child. Paul Cherry, "Aspiring Montreal Crime Kingpin Charged in Connection with Fentanyl Overdoses in U.S.," *Montreal Gazette,* August 18, 2015.

Ceron's cut from a sale might be $10,000. Paul Cherry, "Aspiring Montreal Crime Kingpin Charged in Connection with Fentanyl Overdoses in U.S.," *Mon-*

treal Gazette, August 18, 2015.

A street value of $1.5 million. Sarah Volpenhein, "Oregon Man Indicted in Fatal Grand Forks Overdose Case," *Grand Forks Herald,* March 19, 2015.

Operation Denial received special recognition. Office of National Drug Control Policy, "White House Recognizes Superior Drug Interdiction Efforts," Whitehouse.gov, November 1, 2018.

"Combating the flow of fentanyl into the United States is a top priority." US Department of the Treasury, "Treasury Sanctions Chinese Fentanyl Trafficker Jian Zhang," Treasury.gov, April 27, 2018.

They did not have "solid evidence" that he broke Chinese law. Keegan Hamilton, "Exclusive: China Won't Arrest Two Fentanyl Kingpins Wanted by U.S.," *Vice News,* December 21, 2017.

Most NPS were invented in labs in Europe and the United States. "Fentanyl Becomes the Black Swan!" *Securities Times,* December 2, 2018, http://news.stcn.com/2018/1202/14700181.shtml.

"They should come out and say it." Rong-Gong Lin II, "ER Doctors: Drug-Fueled Raves Too Dangerous and Should Be Banned," *Los Angeles Times,* August

10, 2015.

"You don't see many ecstasy overdose deaths." Author interview, Emanuel Sferios, February 10, 2016.

"Molly means, like, anything now." Ashley Haynes, author interview, April 29, 2016.

"There are a seemingly infinite number of possible new chemical compounds." Elaine Cesare, author interview, June 1, 2016.

Called the synthetics industry "hydra-headed." United Nations Office on Drugs and Crime, *World Drug Report 2013* (Vienna: United Nations, May 2013), publication no. E.13.XI.6.

"Criminals are always one step ahead of law enforcement." "UN: China Synthetic Drugs Trade 'Out of Control,'" *Al-Jazeera,* June 28, 2016.

"This is an act of war." Erin Vogel-Fox, "Lawmakers Step off Capitol Hill to Explore Solutions to Opioid Crisis," Sinclair Broadcast Group, n.d.

"It's almost a form of warfare." John Fritze, "President Trump Threatens to Sue Opioid Makers, Says Crisis Is 'Warfare,'" *USA Today,* August 16, 2018.

"Where it becomes a national security emergency." Sandy Winnefeld (guest host), "Former DEA Special Agent Derek Maltz on Opioids and Transnational Crime," *Intelligence Matters* (podcast), November 6, 2018.

One

"It was our holy mission, to cure the world of its pain." Sam Quinones, *Dreamland: The True Tale of America's Opiate Epidemic* (New York: Bloomsbury, 2015), 188.

More than twice as likely to write OxyContin prescriptions. Patrick Radden Keefe, "The Family That Built an Empire of Pain," *New Yorker,* October 30, 2017.

Purdue's own study from 1999 found the rate to be 13 percent. Ibid.

"It's in 1996 that prescribing really takes off." Ibid.

"A jail sentence is a deterrent and a fine is not." Arlen Specter, "Evaluating the Propriety and Adequacy of the Oxycontin Criminal Settlement," Hearing before the Committee on the Judiciary, United States Senate, July 31, 2007, https://www.govinfo.gov/content/pkg/CHRG-110shrg40884/html/CHRG-110shrg40884.htm.

2015 study, psychiatrists at Washington

University in St. Louis. Theodore J. Cicero and Matthew S. Ellis, "Abuse-Deterrent Formulations and the Prescription Opioid Abuse Epidemic in the United States," *Jama Psychiatry* 72, no. 5 (May 2015): 424–30, doi:10.1001/jamapsychiatry.2014.3043.

2018 study at the University of California, San Francisco. Sarah G. Mars, Daniel Rosenblum, and Daniel Ciccarone, "Illicit Fentanyls in the Opioid Street Market: Desired or Imposed?" *Addiction,* December 4, 2018, https://doi.org/10.1111/add.14474.

Fentanyl doesn't have much in the way of nicknames. Laura Kurtzman, "Drug Wholesalers Drove Fentanyl's Deadly Rise, Report Concludes," UCSF News Center, December 4, 2018, https://www.ucsf.edu/news/2018/12/412466/drug-wholesalers-drove-fentanyls-deadly-rise-report-concludes.

"Sexual relations with doctors in exchange for Subsys prescriptions." Julia Lurie, "Behave More Sexually": How Big Pharma Used Strippers, Guns, and Cash to Push Opioids," *Mother Jones,* May 31, 2018.

The FDA had information about doctors prescribing Subsys. Emily Baumgaertner, "F.D.A. Did Not Intervene to Curb Risky Fentanyl Prescriptions," *New York Times,* August 2, 2018.

Congress allowed it — and even encouraged it. Scott Higham and Lenny Bernstein, "The Drug Industry's Triumph over the DEA," *Washington Post,* Oct. 15, 2017.

"Few lawmakers knew the true impact the law would have." Scott Higham and Lenny Bernstein, "Did President Obama Know Bill Would Strip DEA of Power?" *Washington Post,* October 16, 2017.

"Four more are dying from switching to heroin and fentanyl." Zachary Siegel, "The Opioid Epidemic Is Changing Too Fast for Any Solutions to Stick," *The Cut,* October 18, 2017.

"The issue of counterfeit drugs is more complex." "Over Half of U.S. States Have Now Seen Fatalities from Counterfeit Drugs Made with Fentanyl," Partnership for Safe Medicines, August 16, 2018.

[Prince] may not have realized he was taking counterfeit medication. "Prosecutor: Evidence Shows Prince Thought He Was Taking Vicodin, Not Fentanyl," CBS News, June 18, 2018.

Cocaine production is at an all-time high. Deborah Bonello, Ángela Olaya, and Seth Robbins, "GameChangers 2018: As Opioids and Cocaine Boom, the Americas Wilt," *InSight Crime,* January 9, 2019.

Fentanyl was involved in two of five cocaine overdose deaths in 2016. Holly Hedegaard, Brigham A. Bastian, James P. Trinidad, Merianne Spencer, and Margaret Warner, "Drugs Most Frequently Involved in Drug Overdose Deaths: United States, 2011–2016," *National Vital Statistics Reports* 67, no. 9 (December 12, 2018).

African Americans . . . nearly twice as likely to die from cocaine overdoses. Charles Fain Lehman, "White Lines, Black Epidemic," *American Conservative,* August 6, 2018.

In Massachusetts, cocaine used in conjunction with fentanyl. Martha Bebinger, "To Anyone Using Illicit Drugs in Mass.: 'There's a Very High Likelihood Fentanyl Could Be Present,' Official Says," *CommonHealth,* WBUR, August 24, 2018.

In Ohio, cocaine was often mixed with carfentanil. Dennis Cauchon, "STUDY: Carfentanil in cocaine caused overdose death spike in Dayton." harmreduction ohio.org.

Two

"The most prolific drug inventor of all time." James Black, "A Personal Perspective on Dr. Paul Janssen," *Journal of Medicinal Chemistry,* March 17, 2005.

"Come up with something better yourself, then." Paul Janssen, "A Personal Memoir," *Collegium Internationale Neuro-Psychopharmacologicum,* Fall 2000.

"We didn't even have a calculator." Ibid.

"I often watched him at meetings." Black, "Personal Perspective."

He tested the effectiveness of these creations. Paul Lewi, "Drug Design With Dr. Paul Janssen" (monograph), 2010.

Fentanyl came on faster, was much more powerful, and wasn't as likely to cause nausea. Dr. Samuel Ives, author interview, April 4, 2018.

"Fentanyl, . . . made it possible for the first time." Janssen, "Personal Memoir."

"Fentanyl is a good medicine but a bad drug." Andrew Cass, "United Nations Commission Takes Step to Combat Fentanyl's Deadly Rise," *News-Herald* (Ohio), March 17, 2017.

Robert Dripps . . . agreed to a compromise after being lobbied by Paul Janssen. Theodore H. Stanley, Talmage D.

Egan, and Hugo Van Aken, "A Tribute to Dr. Paul A. J. Janssen," *International Society for Anaesthetic Pharmacology* 106, no. 2 (February 2008).

"China White is a sort of fantasy for [opiate] addicts." Darryl Inaba, quoted in *US Navy Medicine* 77, January–February 1986.

"Let the fantasy roll." Alexander Shulgin and Ann Shulgin, *TiHKAL: The Continuation* (Berkeley, CA: Transform Press, 1997), 145.

"You could walk around with a shopping bag full of it." Jack Shafer, "Designer Drugs," *Science 85,* March 1985.

New discoveries leading to advancement in Parkinson's research. Claudia Wallis, "Surprising Clue to Parkinson's," *Time,* June 24, 2001.

Sweden, which lacks an analogue act. National Operations Department, Polisen (Swedish Police Authority), *Swedish National Threat Assessment on Fentanyl Analogues and Other Synthetic Opioids,* October 2018, https://polisen.se/siteassets/dokument/ovriga_rapporter/fentanyl-analogues-report-english.pdf.

Carfentanil was responsible for killing more than eleven hundred Ohio residents. "Ohio's Carfentanil Death Rate 21

Times Higher — Yes, 2000%! — Than in Other States," HarmReductionOhio.org, August 6, 2018.

"Anything goes, as long as it's not fatal if you use it the first three times." Julijan "Sidney" Picej, author interview, December 2, 2017.

"He made a few grams of the drug — millions of doses." Shafer, "Designer Drugs."

"Perhaps hundreds, . . . maybe thousands." Ibid.

"The future drugs of abuse will be synthetics rather than plant products." Gary Henderson "Designer Drugs: Past History and Future Prospects," *Journal of Forensic Sciences,* March 1988.

Three

"A kind of regional wholesaler to dealers from cities around the Northeast." Edmund Mahony, "Stalking a 'Serial Killer' Narcotic from Boston to Wichita," *Hartford Courant,* February 23, 1993.

"They want to find some of it for themselves." Evelyn Nieves, "Toxic Heroin Has Killed 12, Officials Say," *New York Times,* February 4, 1991.

"Syringes were still embedded in their

537

arms." Knight-Ridder Newspapers, "Intensive DEA Investigation Uncovers Lethal Fentanyl Drug Lab in Wichita," *Baltimore Sun,* February 17, 1993.

"The very best illicit chemist in the history of American drugmaking." Cristina Costantini, Darren Foster, and Mariana Van Zeller, "Death by Fentanyl," *Fusion,* February 1, 2016.

"An anti-drug film in which a mouse on LSD chased a cat." "Drug Wizard of Wichita," *Newsweek,* June 20, 1993.

"I read the forensic science literature religiously." Costantini, Foster, and Van Zeller, "Death by Fentanyl."

He never made any money off it. Marvin Wilson, author interview, June 22, 2017.

"No way known to medical science." Bill Mesler, "The Pentagon's 'Nonlethal' Gas," *Nation,* January 30, 2003.

"To my knowledge, no such strategy exists." Anna Edney, *Bloomberg,* "Senator Seeks Strategy to Prevent Fentanyl Terror Attacks," January 28, 2019.

A thousand or more Estonians died from fentanyl and 3-methylfentanyl. Ryan Hoskins, "What Canada Can Learn from Tiny Estonia's Huge Fentanyl Problem," *Globe and Mail* (Canada), June 17, 2016.

"The dealers realize it's easier to traffic and package fentanyl than heroin." Ibid.

2016 study showed Estonia to have the highest increase. Naomi Thomas, *CNN,* "US Has Highest Rate of Drug Overdoses, Study Says," November 12, 2018.

United Kingdom . . . buys more fentanyl from the Dark Web than any other European country. Ceylan Yeginsufeb, "Fentanyl Adds Deadly Kick to Opioid Woes in Britain," *New York Times,* February 4, 2018,

Now, because of the fentanyl analogues. National Operations Department, Polisen (Swedish Police Authority), *Swedish National Threat Assessment on Fentanyl Analogues and Other Synthetic Opioids,* October 2018, https://polisen.se/siteassets/dokument/ovriga_rapporter/fentanyl-analogues-rcport-english.pdf.

European and Eastern European countries are also starting to see fentanyls from China. Author interview, Martin Raithelhuber, January 25, 2019.

European fentanyl . . . stolen from pharmacies. Martin Raithelhuber, Author interview, January 28, 2019.

Until recent years, European fentanyl was procured . . . from Russia. Roumen Sedefov, Author interview, June 23, 2017.

Russia itself imports vast quantities of ecstasy. Mike Power, "We Went Undercover in a Chinese MDMA Factory," *Mix Mag,* May 29, 2018, https://mixmag.net/feature/we-went-undercover-in-a-chinese-mdma-factory

Synthetic cannabinoids from China. At the Chemsky lab outside Shanghai I saw untold quantities of synthetic cannabinoids, and the proprietors told me much of it was headed for Russia.

[Russia] has widespread public-health problems with . . . heroin and "bath salts." Victoria Kim, "Bath Salts Are a Big Problem in Russia, Especially for Women," *The Fix,* December 20, 2017, https://www.thefix.com/bath-salts-are-big-problem-russia-especially-women.

Russia also harbors a huge psychonaut community. Anton (pseudonym), psychonaut, author interview, April 8, 2017.

Mafia-run laboratories in Azerbaijan. William Leonard Pickard, author interview, November 19, 2018.

Phyllis Riley, doesn't believe he knew the drug was used illicitly. Phyllis Riley, author interview, November 16, 2017.

"Any competent chemist could make the substance." John Noble Wilford, "U.S. Drug Sleuths Finally Solve Mystery of the Deadly China White," *New York Times,* December 30, 1980.

"We weren't thinking of it as a new heroin." Marvin Wilson, author interview, June 22, 2017.

"The quality of 'El Diabolito.' " Costantini, Foster, and Van Zeller, "Death by Fentanyl."

"It brings more business." Ricardo Franklin, author interview, October 15, 2018.

"Most people, they want to be drooling." Jack Sanders (pseudonym), author interview, July 15, 2017.

Duragesic was approved by the FDA. "Janssen Duragesic Fentanyl Transdermal Patch Approved for Chronic Pain, One Weed After NDA Day," *Pink Sheet,* August 13, 1990.

"False or misleading." Fred Schulte, "Rival Opioid Makers Used the OxyContin Panic to Cash In," *Daily Beast/Kaiser Health News,* July 30, 2018.

Fentanyl was prescribed by doctors 6.5 million times. Drug Enforcement Administration, Diversion Control Division,

"Fentanyl," *Drug & Chemical Evaluation Section,* October 2018.

Duragesic patches . . . are manufactured in the United States . . . and Belgium. Andrew Wheatley, author interview, September 10, 2018.

Four

"We . . . have quietly acceded to a nonscientific authority." Alexander Shulgin and Ann Shulgin, "Barriers to Research," *Yearbook for Ethnomedicine and the Study of Consciousness: The Continuation,* iss. 2, 1993. (This was also published in *TiHKAL.*)

"The depths of my memory and my psyche." Alexander Shulgin and Ann Shulgin, *PiHKAL: A Chemical Love Story* (Berkeley, CA: Transform Press, 1991), 17.

"He argued to his superiors that this could be therapeutically important." Solomon Snyder, in Etienne Sauret (dir.), *Dirty Pictures,* Breaking Glass Pictures, 2010.

He coached the famous psychedelic chemist Nick Sand. Paul Daley, author interview, May 26, 2017.

Shulgin first synthesized MDMA in

1965. Shulgin's protégé Paul Daley says he has confirmed this account by way of Shulgin's notebooks.

"I feel absolutely clean inside." Shulgin and Shulgin, *PiHKAL,* 736.

"An easily controlled altered state of consciousness with emotional and sensual overtones." Alexander T. Shulgin and David E. Nichols, "Characterization of Three New Psychotomimetics," in *The Psychopharmacology of Hallucinogens* (New York: Pergamon, 1978).

Zeff . . . introduced MDMA to "countless other therapists." Shulgin and Shulgin, *PiHKAL,* 74.

The new "yuppie psychedelic." Bill Mandel, "The Yuppie Psychedelic," *San Francisco Sunday Examiner & Chronicle,* June 10, 1984.

"Premature to extrapolate the present findings to humans." Jane Leavy, "Ecstacy: The Lure and the Peril," *Washington Post,* June 1, 1985.

"Cookbooks on how to make illegal drugs." Drake Bennett, "Dr. Ecstasy," *New York Times Magazine,* January 30, 2005.

It's snorted like cocaine. Toby Muse, author interview, November 28, 2017.

"He was saddened seeing it escape."

Paul Daley, author interview, May 26, 2017.

"If MDMA hadn't been scheduled." Ann Shulgin, author interview, May 26, 2017.

Approximately one of every thirteen Americans suffers from post traumatic stress disorder. PTSD: National Center for PTSD, "How Common Is PTSD in Adults?" US Department of Veterans Affairs, ptsd.va.gov, n.d.

"They take the MDMA and have this expansiveness." Josh Dean, "How MDMA Went from Club Drug to 'Breakthrough Therapy,' " *Wall Street Journal,* October 18, 2017.

Five

Rare type of sassafras tree prized for its capacity. Mike Power, *Drugs Unlimited: The Web Revolution That's Changing How the World Gets High* (New York: Thomas Dunne Books, 2013), 119.

Known as *mreah prew phnom,* it's found. Sam Campbell, "Harvested to Make Ecstasy, Cambodia's Trees Are Felled One by One," *PRI GlobalPost,* August 30, 2009.

"Some erroneously suspected that it

was used for *yama.*" Tom Blickman, "Harvesting Trees to Make Ecstasy Drug," *Irrawaddy,* February 3, 2009.

"The illicit distilling of sassafras oil in these mountains." "Ecstasy Tabs Destroying Forest Wilderness," *Irin News,* July 20, 2008.

"There wasn't any MDMA to be had." Maia Szalavitz, "How Legal Highs and the Internet Are Transforming the Underground Drug World," *Alternet,* November 24, 2014, https://www.alternet.org/2014/11/how-legal-highs-and-internet-are-transforming-underground-drug-world/.

"I got bored." Matt Bowden, author interview, February 29, 2016.

"We are surrounded by water and have strong border controls." Eleanor Ainge Roy, "Making Meth: How New Zealand's Knack for 'P' Turned into a Home-baked Disaster," *Guardian,* July 12 2016.

[BZP] first came onto the DEA's radar in 1996. J. R. Kerr and L. S. Davis, "Benzylpiperazine in New Zealand: Brief History and Current Implications," *Journal of the Royal Society of New Zealand,* March 16, 2011, https://doi.org/10.1080/03036758.2011.557036.

"This light shined down upon this man." Maia Szalavitz, "The Drug Lord with a Social Mission," *Pacific Standard Magazine,* March 2, 2015.

"Piperazines were the first new drug to adulterate MDMA that we saw." Rainer Schmid, author interview, April 10, 2017.

[BZP was New Zealand's] second-most-popular recreational drug. Kerr and Davis, "Benzylpiperazine in New Zealand."

"I'm not actually promoting drug use." Hamilton Morris, "Hamilton Morris Meets New Zealand's Synthetic Drugs Baron," *Vice,* July 15, 2016.

"No record of any death, long-lasting injury or illness." Kerr and Davis, "Benzylpiperazine in New Zealand."

"They gave me this little packet." Szalavitz, "The Drug Lord with a Social Mission."

Six

"50mg didn't do too much." Kinetic (pseudonym), "4-Methyl Methcathinone," *Hive* (archived at Erowid.org), April 4, 2003.

"I prefer mephedrone to MDMA." Mike Power, *Drugs Unlimited: The Web Revolution That's Changing How the World Gets High* (New York: Thomas Dunne Books,

2013), 129.

"He was a very busy guy." Frank Lang-fitt, "A Chinese Chemical Company and a 'Bath Salts' Epidemic," *Morning Edition,* NPR, June 16, 2014.

Sentenced [Eric Chang] to fourteen years in prison. Author interview, Erika Kinetz, February 1, 2019.

Relatively mild punishment [for Eric Chang]. Author interview, Reiner Pungs of the International Narcotics Control Board, August 13, 2018.

"Khat is alcohol for Muslims." Andrew Lee Butters, "Is Yemen Chewing Itself to Death?" *Time,* August 25, 2009.

[Flakka] had a particularly lethal run in the Fort Lauderdale, Florida, area. "After Ravaging Florida, Street Drug Flakka Disappears," CBS News/ Associated Press, April 8, 2016.

[Flakka] more popular . . . than cocaine. David Adams and Zachary Fagenson, "Cheap, Synthetic 'Flakka' Dethroning Cocaine on Florida Drug Scene," Reuters, June 10, 2015.

Methylone . . . developed . . . as a possible antidepressant. Psychonaut Wiki, "Methylone," https://psychonautwiki.org/ wiki/Methylone

[PMA and PMMA linked to] more than

one hundred deaths in the United Kingdom. David Nutt, "The Superman Pill Deaths Are the Result of Our Illogical Drugs Policy," *Guardian,* January 5, 2015.

"It has similar effects to MDMA." Amy Raves, author interview, March 8, 2016.

"Quite simply they will now have to . . . make sure it is safe." Peter Dunne, "Drug Law Reversing Onus of Proof on Way," Beehive.govt.nz, July 16, 2012.

"New Zealand's Designer Drug Law Draws Global Interest." "New Zealand's Designer Drug Law Draws Global Interest," CBS News/Associated Press, August 2, 2013.

[Matt Bowden forced] to liquidate his company. Matthew Theunissen, "Party Pill Godfather Matt Bowden Declares Himself Bankrupt," *New Zealand Herald,* December 20, 2016.

"Fixed assets" of Bowden's company . . . sold off. "Party Pill Godfather Matt Bowden Owes $3.5m," *New Zealand Herald,* November 26, 2015.

"It is believed they have started manufacturing their own product." Helen King, "Synthetic Cannabis: The Danger Drug Overwhelming New Zealand," *Stuff,* August 3, 2017.

More than fifty New Zealand fatalities

had been tied to synthetic cannabinoids. "Govt Science Institute Testing for Synthetic Cannabis," RNZ, December 27, 2018, https://www.radionz.co.nz/news/national/379094/govt-science-institute-testing-for-synthetic-cannabis.

Seven

"That's why most people start smoking it." Mike (pseudonym), author interview, June 9, 2017.

K2 is . . . a chemical compound . . . dissolved in a solvent . . . and then sprayed onto dried plant leaves. Hamilton Morris, interviewed by Allie Conti, "Visiting the Factories in China Where Synthetic Marijuana Gets Made," *Vice,* January 19, 2016.

"These receptors don't exist so that people can smoke marijuana." David Zucchino, "Scientist's Research Produces a Dangerous High," *Los Angeles Times,* September 28, 2011.

"These compounds that Huffman made were pharmacological tools." Terrence McCoy, "How This Chemist Unwittingly Helped Spawn the Synthetic Drug Industry," *Washington Post,* August 9, 2015.

Pennsylvania State University College

of Medicine researchers. Catharine Paddock, *Medical News Today,* "Colorectal cancer: Scientists halt growth with cannabinoid compounds," February 8, 2019.

[Demi Moore's] body temperature rose dramatically, and she went into convulsions. Andrew Blankstein and Richard Winton, "911 Tape: Demi Moore Suffered Convulsions after 'Smoking Something,' " *Los Angeles Times,* January 27, 2012.

[Obama's] law "was obsolete before the ink . . . dried." Brandon Keim, "New Federal Ban on Synthetic Drugs Already Obsolete," *Wired,* July 12, 2012.

"I think if we talk to a lot of kids five, ten years from now." Courtney Pero, author interview, April 29, 2016.

Synthetic cannabinoids are turning up in oils sold for vaporizers. US Department of Justice, DEA Strategic Intelligence Section, *2018 National Drug Threat Assessment,* October 2018.

Kevin Hagen . . . said the company . . . did not find any synthetic cannabinoids. Janet Burns, "Tests of CBD Oils Reveal Three Surprise Chemicals, One Big Problem," *Leafly,* December 20, 2018, https://www.leafly.com/news/industry/ tests-of-cbd-oils-reveal-three-surprise -chemicals-one-big-problem.

"The highest-level synthetic designer drug trafficker." US Drug Enforcement Administration, "Top China-Based Global Designer Drug Trafficker Arrested in U.S.," press release, May 28, 2015.

"It's not like there's one K2 distributor." Malcolm Gay, "Synthetic Marijuana Spurs State Bans," *New York Times,* July 10, 2010.

[Synthetic-cannabinoid vendors mix batches] inside spinning cement mixers. Dennis Wichern, author interview, June 9, 2016.

"The spike that we're seeing." Paul Mueller, "Clearwater Police See Spice 'Zombies,' "WFLA.com, March 17, 2016.

***New England Journal of Medicine* report.** Axel J. Adams, Samuel D. Banister, Lisandro Irizarry, Jordan Trecki, Michael Schwartz, and Roy Gerona, " 'Zombie' Outbreak Caused by the Synthetic Cannabinoid AMB-FUBINACA in New York," *New England Journal of Medicine,* January 19, 2017.

"Even while we were trying to return." Samantha Schmidt, " 'It Is Taking People Out': More Than 70 People Overdose on K2 in a Single Day in New Haven," *Washington Post,* August 16, 2018.

Homeless are particularly at risk. Elly Yu, "Outreach Teams Counsel Users on 'Unpredictability' of K2 as Overdoses Top 3,000 for 2018," WAMU.org, December 4, 2018, https://wamu.org/story/18/12/04/as-overdoses-continue-d-c-outreach-teams-try-to-combat-k2/.

Synthetic cannabinoids . . . tainted with . . . rat poison. Tandem Media Network, "CDC: Fake Marijuana Can Contain Chemical Used in Rat Poison," *Norwalk (OH) Reflector,* December 12, 2018, http://www.norwalkreflector.com/Government/2018/12/12/Public-warned-again-about-synthetic-cannabinoids.html.

"Gee it took these people a long time." Julie Rose, "The Unlikely Clemson Chemist behind Synthetic Marijuana," WFAE.org, January 25, 2011.

2011 study of twenty-five hundred users of both synthetic cannabinoids and marijuana. Adam R. Winstock and Monica J. Barratt, "Synthetic Cannabis: A Comparison of Patterns of Use and Effect Profile with Natural Cannabis in a Large Global Sample," *Drug and Alcohol Dependence,* July 2013, https://doi.org/10.1016/j.drugalcdep.2012.12.011.

August 2016 report from the New York City Department of Health. Michelle L. Nolan, Bennett Allen, Hillary V. Kunins, and Denise Paone, "A Public Health Approach to Increased Synthetic Cannabinoid–Related Morbidity among New York City Residents, 2014–2015," *International Journal of Drug Policy* 34 (August 2016).

Eight

[LSD] has never caused someone to fatally overdose. Leah Walker, "LSD Overdose," DrugAbuse.com, October 27, 2017, https://drugabuse.com/library/lsd-overdose/; "Only a Handful of People in History Have Ever Overdosed on LSD. This Is What Happened to Them," IFLScience.com, n.d., https://www.iflscience.com/health-and-medicine/only-a-handful-of-people-in-history-have-ever-overdosed-on-lsd-this-is-what-happened-to-them/.

"A spiritual black hole" full of "white trash." Krystle Cole, *Lysergic* (N.p.: Createspace, 2014, 3rd ed.), 13.

[Gordon "Todd" Skinner and Krystle Cole] hit it off. Hamilton Morris, "Getting High on Krystle," *Vice,* September 27, 2011.

Mind-altering trips . . . expensive luxu-

ries . . . cutting-edge music system. Peter Wilkinson, "The Acid King," *Rolling Stone,* July 5, 2001.

[Kansas silos] built by the government to withstand nuclear attack. "Old War Bunker Becomes Modern Mansion," *Wired,* April 19, 2009.

"Lots of money being spent and not much happening." J. Travis, "Missile Site LSD Lab Dismantled," *Topeka Capital Journal,* November 19, 2000.

[Leary] was finally arrested in Afghanistan in 1973. Nicholas Schou, *Orange Sunshine: The Brotherhood of Eternal Love and Its Quest to Spread Peace, Love, and Acid to the World* (New York: Thomas Dunne Books, 2010), 231.

[Pickard's] much-younger fiancée, a Russian émigré named Natasha. Cole, *Lysergic,* 26.

[Pickard] anticipat[ed] the current fentanyl epidemic. William Leonard Pickard, author interview, February 24, 2017.

When tested on animals [LSD] caused them to become "restless during the narcosis." Albert Hofmann, *LSD: My Problem Child: Reflections on Sacred Drugs, Mysticism and Science* (Santa Cruz: Multidisciplinary Association for Psychedelic Studies, 2009), 44.

Stanislav Grof . . . LSD's potential benefits. Ibid, 14.

"There were no aftereffects that could be discerned." Paul Daley, author interview, May 26, 2017. Daley coedited the book *Chemical Warfare Secrets Almost Forgotten* (Santa Rosa, CA: ChemBooks, 2006), written by Dr. James S. Ketchum, the man who did most of the US Army's LSD testing.

DEA hadn't busted an acid lab since 1991. Wilkinson, "The Acid King."

[Skinner grabbed] "hundred dollar bills . . . while [Cole] lay down on the ground." Cole, *Lysergic*, 31.

Skinner . . . engaged in " 'smurfing,' or money laundering." Wilkinson, "The Acid King."

"Skinner said Pickard had tried unsuccessfully for three years." *Topeka Capital-Journal*, referenced in Cole, *Lysergic*, 139.

According to Cole, Skinner believed Pickard was responsible for having this man killed. Cole, *Lysergic*, 105.

Chemicals capable of producing between thirty-six million and sixty million doses of LSD. "Kansas LSD Lab

One of Largest in Country," Associated Press, November 22, 2000.

Ely added that he and Pickard had discussed. Mark Portell, "Pickard: 'I Investigated Drug Trafficking for Government,'" *Wamego (KS) Times,* March 20, 2003.

[Skinner and Cole] lived "like psychedelic royalty." Morris, "Getting High on Krystle."

"Dosed my house with some sort of mystery psychedelic." Cole, *Lysergic,* 168.

Hauck and Cole both pled no contest. *FindLaw,* "Skinner vs. State," https://caselaw.findlaw.com/ok-court-of-criminal-appeals/1251267.html

[Green] said [Cole] actually paid only a small fraction of her debt. Michael Mason, Chris Sandel, and Lee Roy Chapman, "Subterranean Psychonaut," *This Land,* July 28, 2013.

There is speculation that Skinner was also unofficially being punished. Michael Mason, author interview, April 17, 2017.

"90.86 pounds" of LSD they had seized. US Drug Enforcement Administration, "Pickard and Apperson Sentenced on LSD Charges," press release, DEA.gov, November 25, 2003.

Analysis by *Slate* estimated that the lab had about ten million LSD hits. Ryan Grim, "The 91-Pound Acid Trip: The Numbers Touted by the Government in Its Big LSD Bust Just Don't Add Up," *Slate,* March 14, 2005.

"As soon as they got busted, everybody just freaked out." Mitchell Gomez, author interview, March 24, 2017.

Nine

McKinney, Texas, . . . the best place to live in America. "Best Places to Live 2014," *Money,* Time.com/Money, September 19, 2014.

"Me and my friends got interested in the spiritual enlightenment that they promise." Lee Stockton (pseudonym), author interview, April 30, 2016.

The number of children affected [by N-bomb overdoses] was much higher. Eric Brown, author interview, March 29, 2016.

[Naked student found] walking along highway. Madeline Schmitt, "Three McKinney Teens Overdose on LSD within 24 Hours," CBSDFW.com, April 5, 2014. Author note: The drug in question was later determined to be not LSD but N-bombs.

"When I got there, she was in a powerful [state]." Anonymous source, author interview, April 30, 2016.

"Getting too hung up on the exact chemical." Kristina Domanski, author interview, April 29, 2016.

"It's hard to stay on top of these." Ashley Haynes, author interview, April 29, 2016.

"The dose makes the poison." Shannon Rickner, author interview, April 29, 2016.

Between 25 and 30 percent of . . . kids . . . taking these new synthetics. Grace Raulston, author interview, April 28, 2016.

"Love you more." Eric Brown, author interview, March 29, 2016.

"Originally, we didn't want to do anything *that* crazy." Jack Brown, author interview, March 29, 2016.

[Montana Brown text messages.] Shared with author by Eric Brown.

Stephen Wagner. . . . received six months in jail. Julieta Chiquillo, *The Dallas Morning News,* "Trio sentenced to prison for roles in Frisco teen's fatal drug overdose, January 13, 2015."

"He saw lots of damage and lots of dead

bodies." Dr. David Nichols, author interview, August 29, 2017.

[Hefter] funded in part by Bob Wallace. Ibid.

[Heim's experiments] with a serotonin receptor known as 5-HT2A. Ralf Heim, "Synthese und Pharmakologie potenter 5-HT2A-Rezeptoragonisten mit N-2-Methoxybenzyl-Partialstruktur," dissertation, Free University of Berlin, 2003.

"Affinity increases up to 300-fold" for the 5-HT2A receptor. Michael R. Braden, Jason C. Parrish, John C. Naylor, and David E. Nichols, "Molecular Interaction of Serotonin 5-HT2A Receptor Residues Phe339(6.51) and Phe340(6.52) with Superpotent N-Benzyl Phenethylamine Agonists," *Molecular Pharmacology* 70, no. 6 (2006).

"Everything we sell is legal." Jeanne Whalen, "In Quest for 'Legal High,' Chemists Outfox Law," *Wall Street Journal,* October 30, 2010.

"When people use this stuff chronically." Ibid.

"My laboratory had shown that rats." David Nichols, "Legal Highs: The Dark Side of Medicinal Chemistry," *Nature,* January 5, 2011.

An N-bomb drug "creates problems by

thickening the blood." Julian Morgans, "Everything We Know about NBOMe and Why It's Killing People," *Vice,* February 8, 2017.

"It was never our intention to develop drugs for people to take." David Nichols, author interview, August 30, 2017.

"Whatever helps him sleep at night." Eric Brown, author interview, September 8, 2017.

"Make it tougher for the bad guys." Katie Moisse and ABC News Medical Unit, "Chemist David Nichols Haunted by Discovery's Deadly Misuse," ABC News, January 7, 2011.

"The hallmark of experimental science is reproducibility." David Nichols, author interview, January 3, 2019.

"He published [numerous] papers on PMMA." David Nichols, author interview, January 25, 2019.

"They were already being abused." Richard Glennon, author interview, September 26, 2017.

"I did not develop these agents." Richard Glennon, author interview, January 24, 2019.

"The betterment of well people." Michael Pollan, "The Trip Treatment," *New Yorker,* February 9, 2015.

560

"Most people who have tried N-bombs." Mitchell Gomez, author interview, March 24, 2017.

Ten

During the late 2010s [the factory] was slated for demolition. Chris Naffziger, "Magic Chef Factory, under Demolition," *St. Louis Patina,* October 23, 2017.

Jack Sanders started going [to the factory]. Jack Sanders (pseudonym), author interview, July 15, 2017.

"Third wave" of the opioid epidemic. Centers for Disease Control and Prevention, "Opioid Overdose: Understanding the Epidemic," CDC.gov, August 30, 2017.

Another record-setting year is projected for the region. Blythe Bernhard, "First It Was Painkillers, Then Heroin. Now It's Fentanyl Driving Record Overdose Deaths in St. Louis Area," *St. Louis Post-Dispatch,* November 26, 2018.

"There really is no pure heroin in St. Louis anymore." Ibid.

"It really became a problem for us around 2014." Ricardo Franklin, author interview, October 15, 2018.

"Fentanyl has taken over." Bernhard,

"First It Was Painkillers."

"It was my first time ever relapsing straight to fentanyl." Bree (pseudonym), author interview, June 9, 2017.

"We pretty much lost everything to that drug." Mike (pseudonym), author interview, June 9, 2017.

"This change is evidenced by fentanyl being sold as fentanyl." US Department of Justice, DEA Strategic Intelligence Section, *2017 National Drug Threat Assessment,* DEA.gov, October 1, 2017.

Eleven

He sells magic mushrooms, DMT, and 25I-NBOMe. high_as_fxck_GER (Dark Web vendor name), author interview, July 18, 2017.

"It is like morphine." French Connection support staff, author interview, July 18, 2017.

"We are not normal criminals." Anonymous Majestic Garden user, author interview, July 1, 2017.

"Your kind of making me leery with all your digging." U4IA (Dark Web vendor name), author interview, July 19, 2017.

A Weiku representative told the *New York Times* that fentanyl wasn't per-

mitted to be sold. Sui-Lee Wee and Javier C. Hernández, "Despite Trump's Pleas, China's Online Opioid Bazaar Is Booming," *New York Times,* November 8, 2017.

Properly preparing a fentanyl analogue nasal spray. Moderator of online fentanyl forum, author interview, October 2, 2017.

"I don't care about ethics. I'm a drug dealer." Desifclay1000 (Dark Web vendor name), author interview, July 19, 2017.

United States announced it was withdrawing from an international postal agreement. "Trump Pulls US out of UN Postal Scheme on China Price Concerns," *Guardian,* October 17, 2018.

400 million international packages arrive in the United States every year. Richard Cowan, "China's Illegal Opioids Enter U.S. Through Postal Service Gaps: Probe," Reuters, January 24, 2018.

China is the starting point for most of these packages. Erika Kinetz, author interview, September 29, 2017.

"China doesn't deny that shipments to the U.S. happen." Gerry Shih, "China: U.S. Should Curb Demand for Opioids, Not Blame Us," Associated Press, December 28, 2017.

US Senate subcommittee report. US Senate Permanent Subcommittee on Investigations, Committee on Homeland Security and Governmental Affairs, "Combatting the Opioid Crisis: Exploiting Vulnerabilities in International Mail," staff report, January 23, 2018.

"We have our people in the postal companies." GN (vendor name), interviewed by researcher Jada Li, July 30, 2017.

New synthetic-drugs dealer who said he and his associates "lie to customs all the time." Erika Kinetz, author interview, September 29, 2017.

Twelve

They used a complicated code, one that didn't even sound like English. Jack Sanders (pseudonym), author interview, July 15, 2017.

Mexicans or Mexican Americans who had come up Interstate 44 from Texas. St. Louis County drug enforcement detective Ricardo Franklin confirms that the majority of the synthetic opioids used in the St. Louis region originate in Mexico. They're brought over the border, often in Texas, and then up I-44. Ricardo Franklin, author interview, October 15, 2018.

More than 90 percent of heroin in America comes from Mexico. Joshua Partlow, "U.S. Has Been Quietly Helping Mexico with New, High-Tech Ways to Fight Opium," *Washington Post,* April 15, 2018.

Xalisco [cells] fanned out around the United States. Sam Quinones, *Dreamland: The True Tale of America's Opiate Epidemic* (New York: Bloomsbury, 2015), 100, 166.

"Guys from Xalisco had figured out that what white people." Ibid, 45.

US heroin deaths hovered around two thousand annually for decades. DEA agent Dennis Wichern, author interview, December 16, 2016.

[US heroin deaths reached] sixteen thousand by 2017. National Institute on Drug Abuse, "Overdose Death Rates," August 2018, https://www.drugabuse.gov/related-topics/trends-statistics/overdose-death-rates.

Jalisco Nueva Generation was reportedly the first [cartel] to sell fentanyl. Michael O'Brien, "Fentanyl Changed the Opioid Epidemic. Now It's Getting Worse," *Rolling Stone,* August 31, 2018.

Fentanyl is "the most profitable drug the Mexican cartels are trafficking."

Scott Stewart, "Mexico's Cartels Find Another Game Changer in Fentanyl," Stratfor, August 3, 2017.

"The cartels realize that fentanyl is much more profitable." Nick Miroff, "Mexican Traffickers Making New York a Hub for Lucrative — and Deadly — Fentanyl," *Washington Post,* November 13, 2017.

"The only way to have money." Sean Penn, "El Chapo Speaks," *Rolling Stone,* January 10, 2016.

Sinaloa earned millions per day [in Canada]. Andrew Russell, "El Chapo's Sinaloa Cartel Made Nearly $3M a Day in Canada, Former DEA Agent Claims," *Global News* (Canada), January 9, 2019.

Thirty-three thousand people were killed in Mexico in 2018. Reporting by Delphine Schrank; Editing by Cynthia Osterman, *Reuters,* "Murders in Mexico rise by a third in 2018 to new record," January 21, 2019.

Sinaloa was distributing more [fentanyl] than any other cartel. Mike Vigil, author interview, November 13, 2018.

Fentanyl operation inside a building of the Azcapotzalco municipal government. Carlos Jiménez, "Hallan Narcolaboratorio en CDMX," *Diario Contra Rep-*

lica, December 27, 2018, https://www
.contrareplica.mx/nota-hallan-narcolabor
atorio-en-cdmx2018131259.

El Chapo's legal defense "may be funded in part with profits from fentanyl sales." Miroff, "Mexican Traffickers Making New York a Hub."

"The Chinese role is that of a facilitator." Joshua Philipp, "China Is Fueling a Drug War Against the US," *Epoch Times,* December 18, 2015.

"Six customs officials became ill." US Drug Enforcement Administration, "Counterfeit Prescription Pills Containing Fentanyls: A Global Threat," intelligence brief, DEA.gov, July, 2016.

"It's near impossible to stop these drugs." Phil Williams, author interview, August 31, 2017.

"Those that control Mexico's ports are in the best position." Stewart, "Mexico's Cartels Find Another Game Changer in Fentanyl."

Sinaloa cartel has laundered vast amounts of drug money in the city's banks. Bryan Harris, "Mexican Drug Cartels Expand into Hong Kong to Launder Money, Source Chemicals for Ice," *South China Morning Post,* April 7, 2015.

It was the shipment of a much-larger

item through Hong Kong. Jermyn Chow and Joyce Lim, *The Straights Times,* "SAF armoured vehicles seized in Hong Kong port, Mindef expects shipment to return to Singapore 'expeditiously'," November 28, 2016.

"These shipments were going on for years and years." Author interview, Jean-Francois Tremblay, September 6, 2017.

Top five "transnational organized crime threats." Office of the Attorney General, "Attorney General Sessions Announces New Measures to Fight Transnational Organized Crime," Justice.gov, October 15, 2018.

"It's easier to sidestep into fentanyl." Deborah Bonello, author interview, November 14, 2018.

"Fentanyl can be produced anywhere a laboratory can be set up." Stewart, "Mexico's Cartels Find Another Game Changer in Fentanyl."

Fentanyl is cut with many different powders. Taís Regina Fiorentin, Alex Krotulski, David M. Martin, Thom Browne, Jeremy Triplett, Trisha Conti, and Barry Kerr Logan, *Journal of Forensic Sciences,* "Detection of Cutting Agents in Drug-Positive Seized Exhibits within the United States," November 28, 2018.

There isn't much indication yet that they [cartels] are involved with NPS. Mario Moreno, author interview, January 1, 2019.

A meth-overdose crisis has begun accelerating again in the United States. Drew Kann, *CNN,* "While America wages war on opioids, meth makes its comeback," November 6, 2018

Some of these schemes involve cryptocurrency. Peter J. Brown, "US Says Drug Gangs Moving Money via China Crypto Channels," *Asia Times,* December 28, 2018.

The resulting dollars are "washed" in the Los Angeles fashion district. Peter Kouretsos, "Dragon on the Border: Mexican and Chinese Transnational Criminal Networks and Implications for the United States," *Small Wars Journal,* n.d.

Money-laundering schemes are used in Canada as well. Kathy Tomlinson and Xiao Xu, "B.C. Vows Crackdown after Globe Investigation Reveals Money-Laundering Scheme," *Globe and Mail* (Canada), February 16, 2018.

[Fentanyl] "disrupted the Vancouver-area real estate market." Sam Cooper, Stewart Bell, and Andrew Russell, "Fentanyl Kings in Canada Allegedly Linked to

Powerful Chinese Gang, the Big Circle Boys," *Global News* (Canada), November 27, 2018.

Thirteen

Most fentanyl analogues used in America . . . originate from mail shipments from China. DEA Strategic Intelligence Section, dea.gov, "2018 National Drug Threat Assessment," October, 2018.

Fentanyl seized at the US border with Mexico averages about 7 percent purity. Mike Gallagher, "Seizures of Deadly Fentanyl Soaring," *Albuquerque Journal,* June 5, 2018.

"With any enterprise that is getting into another line of business." Mike Vigil, author interview, January 2, 2019.

[Experts doubt] a wall would help abate the opioid crisis. Francie Diep, "How Drugs Pour into the U.S. from Mexico," *Pacific Standard,* January 11, 2019.

Secret, elaborately engineered underground passages. Ron Nixon, "By Land, Sea or Catapult: How Smugglers Get Drugs across the Border," *New York Times,* July 25, 2017.

El Chapo masterminded the first such tunnel. Christopher Woody, " 'A Candy

Store for Smugglers': Step inside the Million-Dollar Drug Tunnels That 'Riddle' the US–Mexico Border," *Business Insider,* April 3, 2016.

Customs officials seized only about 1 kilogram of fentanyl in 2013. US Customs and Border Protection, "CBP Border Security Report Fiscal Year 2017," CBP.gov, December 5, 2017. https://www.cbp.gov/sites/default/files/assets/documents/2017-Dec/cbp-border-security-report-fy2017.pdf.

Thirty thousand [fake] oxycodone pills in a vehicle outside Tempe. Sam Hoyle (with wire reports), "DEA Seizes 30K Fentanyl Pills during Enforcement Operation in Tempe," AZCentral.com, August 18, 2017.

In January, 2019, 115 kg of fentanyl was seized. Mike Brest, *The Daily Caller,* "Largest Fentanyl drug bust in history made as truck tried crossing the southern border," January 30, 2019.

"We're the main stopping point for the majority of Sinaloa cartel drugs." Nicole Garcia, "The Human Toll of the Fentanyl Epidemic," KSAZ-TV, November 13, 2018.

"Law enforcement is set up to find volume." Deborah Bonello, author interview,

November 14, 2018.

"If state troopers are running interdiction." Ricardo Franklin, author interview, October 15, 2018.

They are subdivided further and farmed out. Nick Miroff, "Mexican Traffickers Making New York a Hub for Lucrative — and Deadly — Fentanyl," *Washington Post,* November 13, 2017.

"They're in sleepy towns." Ken Serrano, "Drug Cartel in NJ: Sinaloa Traffickers Now Live among Us," *Asbury Park (NJ) Press,* December 3, 2017.

"They know that if they kill people." Miroff, "Mexican Traffickers Making New York a Hub."

"Places like West Virginia have these relatively new distribution gangs." Mario Moreno, author interview, November 16, 2018.

"It's not like they're in a laboratory." Garcia, "The Human Toll of the Fentanyl Epidemic."

"It's like playing Russian roulette." James Delworth, author interview, October 25, 2018.

Mallinckrodt Pharmaceuticals, one of America's largest oxycodone manufacturers. Reuters, "FDA Declines to Approve Reformulated Mallinckrodt Opioid," *St. Louis Post-Dispatch,* December 12, 2018.

"There's been this very severe fragmentation." Deborah Bonello, author interview, November 14, 2018.

"The Sinaloa cartel has expanded to over forty countries." Mike Vigil, author interview, November 13, 2018.

White powder heroin . . . black tar heroin. Mark Stringer, Missouri Department of Mental Health, Division of Alcohol and Drug Abuse, "Heroin-Related Deaths in Missouri," January 2011.

Fentanyl is often clearly labeled as such [in San Francisco]. Christine Vestal, "Some Drug Users in Western U.S. Seek Out Deadly Fentanyl. Here's Why," PewTrusts.org, January 7, 2019.

[Western states] showing "significant increases" in synthetic-opioid deaths. Centers for Disease Control and Prevention, "New Data Show Growing Complexity of Drug Overdose Deaths in America," CDC.gov, December 21, 2018.

"Heroin has a much smaller using population than prescription pills." Mario Moreno, author interview, November 16, 2018.

Investigative study on the Mexican fentanyl trade by *InSight Crime*. Steven

Dudley. *InSight Crime.* "Fentanyl: Summary & Major Findings," February 12, 2019.

Fourteen

Seafood dishes spiked with ground-up poppy pods. Barbara Demick, "In China, Poppy Seedpod Is a Spice Too Hot to Handle," *Los Angeles Times,* October 21, 2013.

Twenty-eight hundred tons of opium per year by the British East India Company. Julia Lovell, *The Opium War: Drugs, Dreams, and the Making of Modern China* (New York: Overlook Press, 2011), 23.

"The Opium War is seen in China as the original sin of Western imperialism." John Pomfret, "What a Previous Trade War with China Might Teach Us," *Washington Post,* August 9, 2018.

"In a short period of three years, China wiped out the scourge of opium." Information Office of the State Council of the People's Republic of China, "Narcotics Control in China," Embassy of the People's Republic of China in the United States, June 2000.

North Korea . . . trafficked [meth] to

subsidize its regime. Brendon Hong, "Kim Jong-un Breaking Bad: The Secret World of North Korean Meth," *Daily Beast,* February 7, 2016.

[Meth in] garden hoses, handbags, lamps, aquarium pebbles. Dan Levin, "In China, Illegal Drugs Are Sold Online in an Unbridled Market," *New York Times,* June 21, 2015.

"The villagers would brandish replica AK-47s." Associated Press in Beijing, "China Deploys 3,000 Police, Speedboats and Helicopters in Village Drug Raid," *Guardian,* January 3, 2014.

"*Ti naodai zou* (walking about with your head in your hands)." Ko-lin Chin and Sheldon X. Zhang, *The Chinese Heroin Trade: Cross-Border Drug Trafficking in Southeast Asia and Beyond* (New York: New York University Press, 2015), 14.

"On the day of the execution." Sheldon X. Zhang and Ko-lin Chin, "A People's War: China's Struggle to Contain its Illicit Drug Problem," Foreign Policy at Brookings, 2016.

Raging bonfires . . . and officials posing like action movie stars. "Lhasa Destroys 1055.17 Kilograms of Drugs," *Xinhua News,* June 26, 2013, http://www.gov.cn/

jrzg/2013-06/26/content_2434786.htm.

Day Against Drugs stamp. "International Anti-Drug Day Commemorative Stamp Issue," *Xinhua News,* June 26, 2017, http://www.gov.cn/xinwen/2017-06/26/content_5205600.htm#1.

"Let us ask, where is your conscience?" "Lin Zexu (1785–1850) Patriotic Official Fights the Opium Trade," ShanghaiDaily.com, January 20, 2012.

People who are suspected to be addicted are . . . forced to register . . . and subsequently tracked. Anna Lembke and Niushen Zhang, "A Qualitative Study of Treatment-Seeking Heroin Users in Contemporary China," *Addiction Science and Clinical Practice,* October 19, 2015.

An alarm is triggered whenever they use their ID. Chen Min, Chinese drug-rehab employee, author interview, July 6, 2017.

Rehab centers . . . labor camps. Chin and Zhang, *The Chinese Heroin Trade,* 207–11.

"At least in the US we know that detox isn't treatment." Anna Lembke, author interview, July 28, 2017.

Chinese chemical companies selling drugs for illicit purposes to Western

customers. Author research, and data compiled in the spring of 2018 from searches of Chinese e-commerce websites by: *Bloomberg News,* with assistance by Rachel Chang, Dandan Li, Adrian Leung, and Hannah Dormido, "China's Fentanyl Crackdown 'Almost Impossible' Despite Trump Promise," *Bloomberg,* December 3, 2018.

"Many manufacturers of fentanyl and other NPS are legitimate companies." Sean O'Connor, "Fentanyl: China's Deadly Export to the United States," US–China Economic and Security Review Commission, staff research report, February 1, 2017.

"Some of the pictures of these Chinese labs are sickening." Dennis Wichern, author interview, June 9, 2016.

"The purity is usually high." Participant in online fentanyl forum, author interview, July 7, 2017.

"They are clean." Desifelay1000 (Dark Web vendor name), author interview, July 19, 2017.

"Unlike their counterparts in Latin America." Zhang and Chin, "A People's War."

Triads have been involved in the international meth trade. Bryan Harris,

577

"Hong Kong Triads Supply Meth Ingredients to Mexican Drug Cartels," *South China Morning Post,* January 12, 2014.

"They're a shadow of their former selves." Justin Hastings, author interview, March 11, 2018.

Cartels basically nonexistent. Chin and Zhang, *The Chinese Heroin Trade,* 78.

Big Circle Boys . . . allegedly smuggled massive amounts of fentanyl from China. Sam Cooper, Stewart Bell, and Andrew Russell, "Fentanyl Kings in Canada Allegedly Linked to Powerful Chinese Gang, the Big Circle Boys," *Global News* (Canada), November 27, 2018, https://globalnews.ca/news/4658158/fentanyl-kingpins-canada-big-circle-boys/.

Big Circle Boys sprang from the Cultural Revolution. Ibid.

"The sophistication and complexity of the Big Circle Boys' structure." P. Wang, "Vicious Circles: Gang Legacy of the Cultural Revolution," *Jane's Intelligence Review,* August, 2011.

"China has a deep, visceral understanding of how an Opium War." Markos Kounalakis, "China Is Using Fentanyl in a Chemical War Against America," *Miami Herald,* November 2, 2017.

Some observers have called attention.

Joshua Philipp, "China Is Fueling a Drug War Against the US," *Epoch Times,* December 18, 2015.

US Army Special Operations Command white paper report. United States Army Special Operations Command, "Counter-Unconventional Warfare, White Paper."

"Whereas China has gone to war with other drugs that have a demand in China." Matt Hadro, "Smith Bill Aims to Combat Deadly Threat of Chinese Fentanyl," Office of US Congressman Chris Smith, ChrisSmith.house.gov, October 26, 2018.

Fifteen

That is not true, according to Andrew Wheatley. Andrew Wheatley, author interview, September 10, 2018.

Illicit drugs . . . are for sale on ChemicalBook.com. Chemical Book: Mefentanyl, https://www.chemicalbook.com/ChemicalProductProperty_EN_CB8117 6407.htm. (Accessed February 12, 2019.)

"Take the largest one." Dowson Li, author interview, January 4, 2018.

"China has been an incredible partner." Associated Press, "Tom Price: China an

'Incredible Partner' in Controlling Synthetic Opioid Production," STATNews.com, August 21, 2017.

China has scheduled hundreds of new drugs. *Bloomberg News,* with assistance by: Rachel Chang, Dandan Li, Adrian Leung, and Hannah Dormido, "China's Fentanyl Crackdown 'Almost Impossible' Despite Trump Promise," *Bloomberg,* December 3, 2018.

"For the first time, China is expressing some responsibility." Katherine Tobin, author interview, April 3, 2019.]

In 2016 . . . China appeared to promise to crack down. Sean O'Connor, "Fentanyl Flows from China: An Update since 2017," US–China Economic and Security Review Commission, staff research report, November 26, 2018.

"China can develop human intelligence." Zhuang Pinghui, *South China Morning Post,* "What China needs to do to stem the flow of fentanyl to the US," December 20, 2018.

The indictments "mark a major milestone in our battle to stop deadly fentanyl." Office of the Deputy Attorney General, "Justice Department Announces First Ever Indictments Against Designated Chinese Manufacturers of Deadly Fentanyl and Other Opiate Substances," Justice.gov, October 17, 2017.

[China] did "not have solid evidence to show that they have violated Chinese law." Keegan Hamilton, "Exclusive: China Won't Arrest Two Fentanyl Kingpins Wanted by U.S.," *Vice News,* December 21, 2017.

China's Narcotics Control Commission said it regularly tips off the US government. Zhao Yusha, "China–US Jointly Fight Drugs," *Global Times,* August 29, 2018.

[After] US tip . . . Chinese police in Hebei province began investigating. Ibid.

Zhang . . . earned comparisons to *Breaking Bad*'s Walter White. Julia Hollingsworth, *South China Morning Post,* "Former chemistry professor sentenced to life for making and exporting narcotics." April 14, 2017.

"Bo had luxury products like a Mercedes Benz." rongbiz.com, n.d., http://www.rongbiz.com/info/show-htm-itemid-365987.html. (Accessed February 12, 2019.)

Prosecutors gave the accused "a taste of their own medicine." Ruan Zhanjiang, Zhou Yan, and Yang Yingjie, "The Country's First Defendants in the Fentanyl Drug Trafficking Case Were Sentenced to Life Imprisonment," News.CNR.cn, February 20, 2016.

Sixteen

[China's] legitimate chemical industry . . . created $100 billion in profits in 2016. Bryce Pardo, "Evolution of the U.S. Overdose Crisis: Understanding China's Role in the Production and Supply of Synthetic Opioids," testimony presented before the House Foreign Affairs Subcommittee on Africa, Global Health, Global Human Rights, and International Organizations, September 6, 2018.

"Almost any chemical that you want can be made in China." Jean-François Tremblay, author interview, September 6, 2017.

[China's exports] seen as critical to the country's continued growth. Stella Qiu and Elias Glenn, "China to Increase Export Tax Rebates on 397 Products," Reuters, September 7, 2018.

Inspections remain sporadic. Sean O'Connor, "Fentanyl: China's Deadly Export to the United States," US–China Economic and Security Review Commission, staff research report, February 1, 2017.

"Instances of Chinese law enforcement and drug regulators delaying visa approvals." Ibid.

"Lack of coordination and competing regulatory oversight." Pardo, "Evolution of the U.S. Overdose Crisis."

" 'Semi-legitimate' producers." O'Connor, "Meth Precursor Chemicals from China."

"As long as, in China, you can produce chemicals without serious supervision." Sui-Lee Wee and Javier C. Hernández, "Despite Trump's Pleas, China's Online Opioid Bazaar Is Booming," *New York Times,* November 8, 2017.

"It's highly potent, showing activity in sub-milligram dosages." "5F-MDMB-2201," Drugs-Forum.com, May 4, 2017.

"You couldn't really protect the IP." Matt Bowden, author interview, February 29, 2016.

They closed the [psychonaut] forum to outsiders. Anton (pseudonym), psychonaut, author interview, April 8, 2017.

"So long as the cartels can obtain the necessary chemicals." Scott Stewart, "The Chinese Connection to the Flood of

Mexican Fentanyl," Stratfor, November 9, 2017.

Seventeen

Founded in 1999, Yuancheng employs about 650 people and has branch offices all over China. Ye Chuan Fa, author interview, February 10, 2019.

"To quote the people around him." "Ye Chuan Fa: Hot Spring 'New Generation,' " *Wuhan Morning News,* 2007.

Chen Li . . . goes by Abel, because it is "an English name." Chen Li, author interview, October 20, 2017.

"Below 10 kg is express delivery, above 10 kg by air." Chen Li, author interview, October 17, 2017.

"Food additives officially." Alisa (sales name), author interview, October 18, 2017.

These fentanyl precursors were available "for export only." Kay, author interview, September 30, 2017.

"My friend we sold this product in large quantities." Ian.Dang (Skype name), author interview, October 11, 2017.

"Ye Chuan Fa dresses exceptionally plainly." Jean-François Tremblay, "Central China Gets in Gear," *Chemical &*

Engineering News, April 26, 2004.

"They had all sorts of businesses." Jean-François Tremblay, author interview, December 12, 2017.

Ye was born in Wuhan in 1953, the son of parents who were factory workers. Ye Chuan Fa, author interview, February 10, 2019.

"Everything was in demand: watches, stereos, leather." "Ye Chuan Fa: Hot Spring 'New Generation,' " *Wuhan Morning News,* 2007.

"As insurance against a crackdown on the rich." Jean-François Tremblay, "Central China Gets in Gear," *Chemical & Engineering News,* April 26, 2004.

"People who have eaten at Jia Ye." He Jianbao, "Wuhan Yuancheng: Stepping onto the New Economic Stage," *Changjiang Daily,* April 21, 2006.

"The biggest opportunities in China." Jean-François Tremblay, author interview, December 12, 2017.

News account [about stolen trade secrets]. "A Pharmaceutical Company in Hubei Had Their Core Technology Stolen, Intellectual Property Department Stepped in for Rights Advocacy," Roll.Sohu.com, February 7, 2013, http://roll.sohu.com/20130207/n365778075.shtml. (Accessed

February 12, 2019.)

Jia Lun didn't have natural hot springs. "The Boss of Jia Lun Is a Liar," Tieba. Baidu.com, September 4, 2008, http:// tieba.baidu.com/f?kz=474206659.

Eighteen

NPP is reacted with a compound called aniline. Siegfried, "Synthesis of Fentanyl," Erowid.org, August 2004, https:// erowid.org/archive/rhodium/chemistry/ fentanyl.html.

About a thousand people died in cities including Chicago and Philadelphia. "Feds Count More Than 1,000 Dead from Illegal Fentanyl," Associated Press, July 24, 2008.

"I am not aware of any other product." Martin Raithelhuber, author interview, June 13, 2017.

"The U.S. doesn't import fentanyl." Melvin Patterson, author interview, July 30, 2018.

"There was little scrutiny on their manufacture." Bryce Pardo, "Evolution of the U.S. Overdose Crisis: Understanding China's Role in the Production and Supply of Synthetic Opioids," Testimony presented before the House Foreign Affairs Subcommittee on Africa, Global Health, Global Human Rights, and International Organizations, September 6, 2018.

In 2013 [Yuancheng] "achieved 300 million platform transactions." Yuancheng recruitment advertisement, June 26, 2015, http://www.deyi.com/thread-6295546-1-1 .html. (Accessed February 12, 2019.)

"In 2015, the export volume reached 2 billion." Company introduction, Yuan Cheng Group, n.d., http://www.ychemade .com/about.html. (Accessed February 12, 2019.)

Yuancheng has established "good business relations." Company profile, Hubei Yuancheng Saichuang Technology Co., Ltd., n.d., http://www.hbycgroup.com/ about.html. (Accessed February 12, 2019.)

Ye Chuan Fa himself admitted as much. Ye Chuan Fa, author interview, February 10, 2019.

"A precursor in the synthesis of fentanyl and related opioids." "Wuhan Hengwo Scien-Tech [*sic*] Co., Ltd.," products, n.d., http://www.global .chinaomp.com/space.php?do=product& userid=wuhanhengwoscientechco.%2Cltd (Accessed February 12, 2019.)

"Most the NPP and 4-npp are sold from my company." Anonymous Yuancheng saleswoman, author interview, October 3, 2017.

"Our company is the only manufacture of this product in China." Chen Li, author interview, January 29, 2019.

Documents attached to the letter indicated. Jeanne Whalen, "U.S. Seeks Curb on Chemicals Used to Make Fentanyl, a Powerful Opioid," *Wall Street Journal,* October 14, 2016.

"Exporting governments have to send pre-export notifications." Reiner Pungs, author interview, July 31, 2018.

Ten legal shipments of NPP and twelve of 4-ANPP. Reiner Pungs, author interview, February 6, 2019.

"Double-western route from China to the United States." Chen Li, author interview, October 20, 2017.

"You won't get in trouble." Anonymous Yuancheng saleswoman, author interview, October 3, 2017.

"Economic Construction Leading Enterprise" award. "This Company Won the Hubei Province Economic Construction Leading Enterprise, 2011," https://club.1688.com/article/27315168.htm, December 27, 2011.

[Yuancheng] wa also certified . . . an official "New and High Technology Enterprise" *(NHTE) in 2011.* A database at http://www.innocom.gov.cn contains the list of applications and certifications for NHTEs. (Accessed February 12, 2019.)

[Yuancheng] chosen . . . as one of Hubei Province's top 10 "innovation companies." Wuhan Yuancheng Gongchuang Technology Co., Ltd., " 'Top 10 Innovative Companies' Won by Hubei Yuancheng Pharmaceutical Co.," http://www.yccreate.com/en/News/2012/1017/107740.html, October 17, 2012. (Accessed February 12, 2019.)

In 2016 [Yuancheng] was a finalist in a contest honoring Wuhan's best entrepreneurs. Hubei Yuancheng Saichuang Technology Co., Ltd, "Wuhan City Top Ten Entrepreneur Contest Organising Committee came to our company for a visit," http://www.hbycgroup.com/news_detail/id/78.html, December 18, 2016. (Accessed February 12, 2019.)

"If you're a chemical company." Lucy Lu, author interview, February 21, 2018.

[Yuancheng has] 180 "self-developed products" and more than fifty patents. "Hubei Yuancheng Saichuang Technology Co., Ltd.: Company Profile," n.d., http://

589

company.zhaopin.com/CC621388322 .htm. (Accessed February 12, 2019.)

"Since China's new Enterprise Income Tax Law took effect." Jake Liddle, "Tax Incentives for High-Tech Companies in China," China Briefing from Dezan Shira & Associates, china-briefing.com, September 29, 2015.

Beginning in 2012, Yuancheng was sponsored for three years by an initiative called the Torch Program. "2012 National Torch Program Key NHTE list," www.innocom.gov.cn, October 19, 2012. Archived by Wayback Machine: https://web .archive.org/web/20141004033505/http:// www.innocom.gov.cn/gxjsqyrdw/xxtg/ 201211/ 54da1e194fe943dfa19af6a589 d27d82.shtml. (Accessed February 12, 2019.)

Torch Program which is run by China's Ministry of Science and Technology. Joel R. Campbell, *Issues in Technology Innovation,* "Becoming a Techno-Industrial Power: Chinese Science and Technology Policy," brookings.edu, April 2013.

"In size, scale and commercial results China's Torch Program." Steve Blank, "China's Torch Program: The Glow That Can Light the World," *Huffington Post,*

April 12, 2013.

Yuancheng has also been the beneficiary of the Spark program. Ministry of Science and Technology of the People's Republic of China, "Notice on the Publicity of the National Spark Program Project Selected in the "Twelfth Five-Year Plan" Rural Science and Technology Plan Preparation Project Library," Attachement #2, Entry 1104, March 6, 2012. (Accessed February 12, 2019.)

Spark Program . . . "aimed at popularizing modern technology in rural areas." Editor: Yangtze Yan, Source: Xinhua, "Rural technology 'Spark Program' covers over 90% counties," http://www.gov.cn/english/2006-10/15/content_413723.htm, October 15, 2006.

The Innovation Fund has "channeled 3.5 billion yuan of investment." Zhao Yang, "China, on Its Way to Innovation," http://english.cri.cn/12954/2015/03/12/1261s869790.htm, March 12, 2015.

[Innovation Fund] granted Yuangcheng an award of 500,000 yuan. Innovation Fund for Technology Based Firms, "2012 Project Announcement," July 6, 2012. Archived by Wayback Machine: https://web.archive.org/web/20150803235439/http://www.innofund.gov.cn/2/sdfed/201402/

37c8787020694ada8263469e631a527f
.shtml. (Accessed February 12, 2019.)

[Yuancheng] won 50,000 yuan for a particular patent. Science and Technology Department of Hubei Province, "Xiaonan District hosted a district wide technology innovation reward ceremony," http://www.hbstd.gov.cn/sjb/kjyw/dfkj/24363.htm, April 24, 2013. (Accessed February 12, 2019.)

Some of Yuancheng's sub-companies list an address in a special industrial zone. "Company Profile," Zhuzhou Yuancheng Hezhong Technology Development Co., Ltd., http://steroidfactory.sell.everychina.com/aboutus.html. (Accessed February 11, 2019.)

"China has been very generous in building these industrial parks." Gary Hufbauer, author interview, February 21, 2018.

"The high-tech zones have become a major engine to China's economic growth." Xinhua, "More High-Tech Zones in China," Europe.ChinaDaily.com.cn, March 27, 2017.

"I think the government, when they approve the company's application for the subsidies." Lucy Lu, author interview, February 21, 2018.

[5A] located in an economic development zone. Official website of Hubei, China, "Wuhan Livika Technology Co., Ltd," http://en.hubei.gov.cn/business/enterprises/201607/t20160721_869598.shtml, July 21, 2016.

[5A] claimed to have received certification as an NHTE, but this could not be confirmed. Author note: Though I could not verify that 5A was certified as an official NHTE, a webpage devoted to its parent company found at http://livika.lookchem.com/About.html, reads as follows: "5A Pharmatech Co.,Ltd . . . is honored as the high-tech enterprise which engaged in researching, developing, manufacturing and exporting advanced pharmaceutical intermediates and Active Pharmaceutical Ingredients (API), high-tech electronic materials and other fine chemicals."

"This is horrifying." Esmé E. Deprez, Li Hui, and Ken Wills, "Deadly Chinese Fentanyl Is Creating a New Era of Drug Kingpins," *Bloomberg,* May 22, 2018.

One of these employees is Cuiying Liu. US Department of the Treasury, "Treasury Sanctions Chinese Fentanyl Trafficker Jian Zhang," Treasury.gov, April 27, 2018.

[Dezhou Yanling] lists a woman named Cuiying Liu as its legal representative. "Dezhou Yanling Biological Technology Co., Ltd.," n.d., http://www.11467.com/dezhou/co/57907.htm. (Accessed August 8, 2018.)

[Dezhou Yanling] company materials cite its award-winning. YanlingMijiu, "Historical Events," n.d., http://www.dzylsw.com/lsdsj.asp. (Accessed February 12, 2019.)

Nineteen

Difficult to find out which household drugs come from China. Rosemary Gibson and Janardan Prasad Singh, *China Rx: Exposing the Risks of America's Dependence on China for Medicine* (Amherst: Prometheus Books, 2018), 28.

In 2017 Chinese companies received thirty-eight approvals from the US FDA. Huileng Tan, "China's Pharmaceutical Industry Is Poised for Major Growth," CNBC, April 19 2018.

"It's not whether they are going to." Sui-Lee Wee, "Made in China: New and Potentially Lifesaving Drugs," *New York Times,* Jan. 3, 2018.

[Fentanyls and precursors get VAT re-

bates.] Chinese State Taxation Administration, http://hd.chinatax.gov.cn/fagui/action/InitChukou.do.

In September 2018, China announced it would raise VAT rebates. Stella Qiu and Elias Glenn, "China to Increase Export Tax Rebates on 397 Products," Reuters, September 7, 2018, https://www.reuters.com/article/us-china-economy-tax/china-to-increase-export-tax-rebates-on-397-products-idUSKCN1LN12F.

[VAT rebates have] had "a large and significant positive impact." Piyush Chandra and Cheryl Long, "VAT Rebates and Export Performance in China: Firm-Level Evidence," *Journal of Public Economics* 102 (June 2013).

In 2012, the US Department of Commerce announced. John Richardson, "US Targets China VAT Rebates," ICIS, June 24, 2012, https://www.icis.com/asian-chemical-connections/2012/06/us-targets-china-vat-rebates-1/.

"Even small variations in these rebates can have a big impact." Simon J. Evenett, Johannes Fritz, and Yang Chun Jing, "Beyond Dollar Exchange-Rate Targeting: China's Crisis-Era Export Management Regime," *Oxford Review of Economic Policy* 28, no. 2 (July 1, 2012).

Only five [Chinese companies] are permitted to [sell medical fentanyl.] "Fentanyl Goes Viral!" *China Fund News,* December 2, 2018, http://westdollar.com/sbdm/finance/news/1353,20181202997330043.html.

Fentanyl is a dominant painkiller [in Chinese hospitals]. "Fentanyl Becomes the Black Swan!" *Securities Times,* December 2, 2018, http://news.stcn.com/2018/1202/14700181.shtml.

Renfu Pharmaceutical [exports fentanyl to] the Philippines, Turkey, Sri Lanka, and Ecuador. Ibid.

"Illegally processed and smuggled by underground factories." "Fentanyl Goes Viral!"

Only three types of fentanyls are legally permitted to be manufactured in China. Qi Peas, "Renfu Medicine: No Fentanyl Exports to the United States," *Shanghai Securities News,* December 3, 2018, http://news.cnstock.com/paper,2018-12-03,1092044.htm.

Ye Chuan Fa said his company takes advantage of VAT rebates. Ye Chuan Fa, author interview, February 10, 2019.

"If China had a subsidy on lead." Bryce Pardo, author interview, November 21, 2018.

"As with many of China's policies, the aid in fentanyls export is myopic." Justin Hastings, author interview, March 11, 2018.

"The primary incentive, particularly for local-level Chinese government officials." Katherine Tobin, author interview, December 14, 2018.

"My feeling is that it's just like a race." Nathan Vanderklippe, "China, Claiming Success on Fentanyl, Admits It Is Being Outrun by Criminal Chemists," *Globe and Mail* (Canada), June 19, 2017.

"For them to shut down an entire legal pharmaceutical company." Lenny Bernstein and Katie Zezima, "U.S.–China Fentanyl Pact Is Not Expected to Produce Immediate Results," *Washington Post,* December 3, 2018.

Chinese FDA is once again being reorganized. Bryce Pardo, "Evolution of the U.S. Overdose Crisis."

[Chinese FDA will be absorbed into] the State Administration for Market Regulation. "China's New State Administration for Market Regulation: What to Know and What to Expect," Ropes & Gray, April 3, 2018, https://www.ropesgray.com/en/newsroom/alerts/2018/04/Chinas-New-State-Market-Regulatory-Administration

-What-to-Know-and-What-to-Expect.

"If the Chinese government pursued drug smugglers." Nicholas Kristof, "The Dangerous Naïveté of Trump and Xi," *New York Times,* November 17, 2018.

"They just didn't see what was in it for them." Dan Levin, "In China, Illegal Drugs Are Sold Online in an Unbridled Market," *New York Times,* June 21, 2015.

Mexico's government "was hesitant to press China." Jeanne Whalen and Brian Spegele, "The Chinese Connection Fueling America's Fentanyl Crisis," *Wall Street Journal,* June 23, 2016.

"The drugs . . . exploit the differences in drug policing in different countries." You Yan, Deng Yi, and Zhao Min, Lu Zhou City, "Third Generation Drugs — New Psychoactive Substances," Na Xi district branch police department, February 2017.

Being convicted of drugs sales . . . could get a public official executed. Justin Hastings, author interview, August 9, 2017.

Twenty

Wuhan is . . . the "capital of petrochemical equipment and fine chemicals in

598

China." Official website of Hubei, China, "Wuhan Livika Technology Co., Ltd," http://en.hubei.gov.cn/business/enterprises/201607/t20160721_869598.shtml, July 21, 2016.

Ye Chuan Fa still owns the building. Ye Chuan Fa, author interview, February 10, 2019.

That number had risen to forty-one. Ibid.

"We ourselves only do sales." Ibid.

It has a thirty-thousand-square-meter plant, built to "GMP standard." Zhuhai Shuangbojie Technology Co., Ltd, n.d., http://www.trademetro.net/exporter-supplier-sell-96671/Zhuhai-Shuangbojie-Technology-Co-Ltd.html.

"To be honest, it's not GMP." Julie (sales name), author interview, December 13, 2017.

The company's ads promise. Yuancheng recruitment advertisement, June 26, 2015, http://www.deyi.com/thread-6295546-1-1.html.

"I don't know buyers usage." Sean (sales name), author interview, Oct 11, 2017.

"NPP is a sensitive products. Why you buy it?" Anonymous Yuancheng saleswoman, author interview, October 3, 2017.

Yuancheng posted a notice on one of its websites. Wuhan Yuancheng Gongchuang Technology Co., Ltd. "Effective, January 27, 2018, All products can only be sold to companies or institutions, and not to private clients," January 27, 2018, http://www.ycgcbio.com/news/show23253.html.

Sub-Saharan African plant . . . naturally produced tramadol. Tim Wogan, "Painkiller Found in Plants May Not Be Natural after All," *Chemistry World,* September 18, 2014, https://www.chemistryworld.com/news/painkiller-found-in-plants-may-not-be-natural-after-all/7757.article.]

One hundred kilograms of [Indian] fentanyl . . . reportedly being prepared for shipment to a Mexican cartel. Srinath Rao, "Seized Opioid Was Bound for Mexico, Key Accused a Known Narcotics Offender: Mumbai Police," *Indian Express,* December 29, 2018, https://indianexpress.com/article/cities/mumbai/ seized-opioid-was-bound-for-mexico-key-accused-a-known-narcotics-offender-mumbai-police-5514410/.

[India] producing large quantities of synthetic cannabinoids. Yudhijit Bhattacharjee, "How Synthetic Drugs Get into Your Joint," *Daily Beast,* May 28, 2017.

India has trailed when it comes to scheduling NPSs and fentanyl precursors. Natalie Tecimer, "Tramadol: The Dangerous Opioid from India," *Diplomat,* January 19, 2018.

"We recommend another stuff that similar to NPP or 4-ANPP." Kay, author interview, January 12, 2018.

"Can these two products replace 4-ANPP?" Author interview, Chen Li, January 9, 2018.

"It's very hot . . . it sells a lot." Sean (sales name), author interview, January 28, 2019

Yuancheng now had "overseas warehouses." Author interview, Chen Li, January 29, 2019.

Sixteen different known [fentanyl] precursor chemicals. Sean O'Connor, "Fentanyl: China's Deadly Export to the United States," US–China Economic and Security Review Commission, staff research report, February 1, 2017.

Twenty-One

Nixon . . . said the target of his drug war was hippies and blacks. Dan Baum, "Legalize It All: How to Win the War on Drugs," *Harper's,* April 2016.

"In terms of taking down kingpins." Ioan Grillo, "El Chapo Puts the Drug War on Trial," *New York Times,* November 15, 2018.

"See, if you look at the Drug War from a purely economic point of view." Milton Friedman, from a 1991 television interview, "Friedman & Szasz on Liberty and Drugs," on *America's Drug Forum;* transcript archived at: https://www.ukcia .org/research/argue/milton.htm.

"We have a regulatory system that's designed for plant-based drugs." Bryce Pardo, author interview, November 21, 2018.

"I know there's still ecstasy out there, but we don't see it near in the amount." Dennis Wichern, author interview, June 9, 2016.

"They serve you in your car." Paul Solotaroff, "El Chapo: Inside the Hunt for Mexico's Most Notorious Kingpin," *Rolling Stone,* August 11, 2017.

"The people that are dealing this are street gang members." Jeremy Gorner, "More Than 30 Arrested in Sweep Targeting Fentanyl and Heroin Laced with Fentanyl," *Chicago Tribune,* September 23, 2016.

"Chicago's street gangs have likely been

more inclined to involve themselves." author interview, Sharon Lindskoog, August 16, 2018.

"The Chicago epidemic is affecting 45- to 65-year-old men." Tanveer Ali and Sam Charles, "A 4-Block Radius on the West Side Is at the Heart of Chicago's Opioid Epidemic," *Chicago Sun-Times,* May 25, 2018.

"There's nothing unique about how we work these." James Jones, author interview, November 1, 2016.

"Everything that we do makes a dent." Matt Masterson, "More Than 50 Charged after West Side Narcotics Raids," News .WTWW.com, June 13, 2018.

"With the addition of fentanyl from China." Evan Garcia, "Chicago's Top DEA Official Retiring after 30 Years," News.WTWW.com, December 20, 2017.

In 2017, Chicago EMS crews administered naloxone ninety-six hundred times. Chris Coffey and Katy Smyser, "Chicago-Area Paramedics Reviving Opioid Overdose Victims in Record Numbers," NBCChicago.com, November 10, 2018.

"At HHS and across this administration." Kimberly Leonard, "HHS Secretary Alex Azar Commits to Approaching

Opioid Epidemic as a 'Medical Challenge' Rather Than Moral Failing," *Washington Examiner,* March 1, 2018.

"These aren't two distinct sets of people." Julia Lurie (text), "Finding a Fix: Embedded with the Suburban Cops Confronting the Opioid Epidemic," *Mother Jones,* January–February 2018 issue.

Criminal justice reform legislation. Osita Nwanevu, "The Improbable Success of a Criminal-Justice-Reform Bill under Trump," *New Yorker,* December 17, 2018.

States . . . seek to impose tougher sentences on fentanyl dealers. Mike Hellgren, "New Initiative Targets Fentanyl Dealers with Harsher Punishments," CBS Baltimore, December 12, 2018, https:// baltimore.cbslocal.com/2018/12/12/ maryland-u-s-attorney-announces-new -initiative-to-get-fentanyl-off-the-streets/.

Twenty-Two

"Now is the first time in history." Hamilton Morris, "Synthetic Drug Revolution: Vice on HBO," Episode 5, YouTube video, 3:35, posted by Vice, April 10, 2015.

"When I have two grams of weed." Ben Westhoff, "Small Town Police Are on the

Hunt for Electric Forest Fans," *Westword,* June 26, 2015.

"People trust us." Ben Westhoff, "We're Still a Long Way from Being Realistic about Drug Use at Festivals," *Westword,* June 27, 2015.

"DanceSafe was actually participating at the festival as a nonprofit information booth." Carrie Lombardi, author interview, June 26, 2015.

"Promoters feel their hands are tied due to the Rave Act." Author interview, Emanuel Sferios, February 10, 2016.

"Fan safety is our highest priority." Jennifer Forkish, author interview, August 14, 2014.

Project #OpenTalk. Stefanie Jones, "DPA and Insomniac Partner on a New Harm Reduction Effort: Project #OpenTalk," DrugPolicyAlliance.org, October 26, 2016.

"While progress has been made." Stefanie Jones, author interview, March 7, 2018.

"One was a young girl, and she looked really frightened." Adam Auctor (pseudonym), author interview, April 11, 2016.

Formal study conducted by DanceSafe. Sarah Saleemi, Steven J. Pennybaker, Missi Wooldridge, and Matthew W. Johnson, "Who Is 'Molly'? MDMA Adulterants by Product Name and the Impact of Harm-Reduction Services at Raves," *Journal of Psychopharmacology,* July 10, 2017.

"I don't recall the last time we seized pure MDMA." Courtney Pero, author interview, April 29, 2016.

"People were dropping like flies." Adam Auctor (pseudonym), author interview, September 17, 2018.

2017 study carried out at a supervised-injection site in Vancouver. Matt Meuse, "Insite Fentanyl Test Reduces Overdoses, Study Finds," CBC News, May 15, 2017.

2018 study released by Brown University. Mollie Rappe, "Fentanyl Test Strips Prove Useful in Preventing Overdoses," News.Brown.edu, October 18, 2018.

"Drug users are far more rational." Zachary Siegel, "The Opioid Epidemic Is Changing Too Fast for Any Solutions to Stick," *The Cut,* October 18, 2017.

"We cannot guarantee that the strips will always have 100 percent accuracy." Elinore F. McCance-Katz, "For Beating the Opioid Crisis, America Has Better Weapons Than Fentanyl Test Strips," Blog.SAMHSA.gov, October 3, 2018, https://blog.samhsa.gov/2018/10/03/

for-beating-the-opioid-crisis-america-has -better-weapons-than-fentanyl-test-strips. **"We know that pill testing won't work."** Olivia Willis, "Drug Experts Say Yes. Many Politicians Say No. What's the Evidence for Pill Testing?" ABC.net.au, December 20, 2018.

Twenty-Three

Those engaged in drug manufacturing [in Slovenia] are still subject to incarceration. "Slovenia Country Drug Report 2018," European Monitoring Centre for Drugs and Drug Addiction, n.d., http:// www.emcdda.europa.eu/countries/drug -reports/2018/slovenia/drug-laws-and -drug-law-offences_en.
"That cost six times more than my car." Adam Auctor (pseudonym), author interview, April 8, 2017.
Picej explained how he went from high school dropout. Julijan "Sidney" Picej, author interview, April 9, 2017.
"During the pig studies." Expert Committee on Drug Dependence, "3-Methylmethcathinone (3-MMC) Critical Review Report," World Health Organization report, November, 2016.
"I get addicted to everything." Vlad

(pseudonym), author interview, April 10, 2017.

"Ice cream" . . . can become habit forming. Dare Kochmur, author interview, April 11, 2017.

Twenty-Four

Russian harm-reduction organization, the Andrey Rylkov Foundation . . . ordered to pay a fine. Niko Vorobjov, "Russia Is Punishing People for Helping Drug Users," *Vice,* December 11, 2018.

[Switzerland heroin-prescription program] led to drops in deaths, drug-dealing, and crime. Johann Hari, *Chasing the Scream: The First and Last Days of the War on Drugs* (New York: Bloomsbury, 2015), 221.

Heroin use by people under forty has fallen dramatically [in the Netherlands]. Thijs Roes, "Only in the Netherlands Do Addicts Complain about Free Government Heroin," *Vice News,* May 6, 2014.

Only after doctors were forced to stop [administering heroin]. Hari, *Chasing the Scream,* 38.

Energy Control's . . . budget. Núria Calzada, author interview, July 31, 2017.

[Cristina Gil] is equally at home. Cristina Gil, author interview, April 14, 2017.

"As long as the overall purity and information is increasing, it's a benefit." Rafael Sacramento, author interview, April 14, 2017.

Pure-ecstasy supply has rebounded. Mike Power, "We Went Undercover in a Chinese MDMA Factory," *Mix Mag,* May 29, 2018, https://mixmag.net/feature/we-went-undercover-in-a-chinese-mdma-factory.

"One of the reasons is that we have several drug-checking services around the country." Mireia Ventura, author interview, February 22, 2017.

"If you overemphasize the negative effects, they don't believe you." Steve Mueller, author interview, April 10, 2017.

The relevant English authorities received the information too. "Superman Ecstasy Pills: Drugs Expert Says Government Failed to Act on Warning, *Telegraph* (UK), January 7, 2015.

"I've been to other festivals in Canada." Ben Westhoff, "Can This Man Clean up EDM? 'They Find All Kinds of Things in Those Pills,' " *Guardian,* April 19, 2017.

"I think a lot of kids are going to take drugs no matter what we say." Ryan

Raddon (aka Kaskade), author interview, March 27, 2017.

K2 menace . . . significantly reduced. Grace Raulston, author interview, April 28, 2016.

"The biggest thing we're fighting now is education." Courtney Pero, author interview, April 29, 2016.

Twenty-Five

BBC investigation into [opioids]. Owen Amos, "Why Opioids Are Such an American Problem," BBC News, October 25, 2017.

"Making it harder for people to get pain medication legally." Richard A. Friedman, "Ordering Five Million Deaths Online," *New York Times,* April 4, 2018.

A flurry of new regulations . . . are going into effect. John W. Rusher, "Monitoring Programs, State Regulations Help Physicians Prescribe Opioids Responsibly," *AAP News,* December 26, 2018.

In Colorado, some doctors require their patients to take special classes. Shelley Neth, author interview, June 5, 2018. An employee at the UC Health Family Medicine Center in Fort Collins, Colorado, confirmed the requirements described by Neth.

"I am uncomfortable with this approach." Shelley Neth, author interview, June 5, 2018.

"All we're doing is reviving them, we're not curing them." Corky Siemaszko, "Ohio Sheriff Says His Officers Won't Carry Narcan," NBCNews.com, July 7, 2017.

"I know it is not uncommon for users." Brett Johnson, author interview, June 25, 2018.

"I would set up free drug-purity testing sites." Todd Zwillich (host), "A Crisis of Ignorance: A Controversial View of the American Opioid Crisis," *Takeaway,* WNYCStudios.org, November 6, 2017.

[Safe-injection sites] found to provide dramatic societal benefits. Jessica Williams, "Safe Injection Spaces Save Lives and Money, but Will They Make It in America?" IRETA, June 1, 2017, https://ireta.org/resources/safe-injection-spaces-save-lives-and-money-but-will-they-make-it-in-america/.

"In an undisclosed location in the US." Maia Szalavitz, "There's Been a Secret Safe Injection Site in the US for Three Years," Tonic.Vice.com, August 10 2017.

A planned [Safe-injection site] in Phil-adelphia. Bobby Allyn, "Former Gov. Ed Rendell Says 'Arrest Me First' for Backing Supervised Injection Facility," WHYY .org, October 2, 2018.

"Heroin is illegal. Will the police allow illegal drug use?" Lisa DuFour, "I Lost My Son to a Drug Overdose: Say No to Safe Injection Sites," *Seattle Times,* March 17, 2017.

Some twelve thousand used syringes were collected. "La Nueva Sala Baluard Abrirá en Perecamps entre Primavera y Verano de 2017," *La Vanguardia,* July 12, 2016.

"The target group here is problematic users." Diego Arànega, author interview, April 13, 2017.

2017 study [on substitution therapy]. Madeline Morr, "Methadone Maintenance Treatment Reduces Mortality in Opioid-Dependent Patients," Clinical Advisor.com, May 3, 2017.

HIV diagnoses "attributed to injecting" have plummeted in Spain. "Spain Country Drug Report 2018," European Monitoring Centre for Drugs and Drug Addiction, n.d., http://www.emcdda .europa.eu/countries/drug-reports/2018/ spain_en.

"The consumption room is the best tool I have." Jann Schumacher, "The Swiss Four Pillar Drug Policy," Just.ee, March 7, 2016.

"By moving people from the streets inside." Dare Kochmur, author interview, April 11, 2017.

Officials in some states have marshaled resources. Lisa Gillespie, "Kentucky Will Soon Lead Nation in Syringe Exchanges, but Work Isn't Done," WFPL, April 11, 2018.

[Canadian government provided] supervised-injection sites with an exemption. Jace Larson and Scott Sherman, "Here's What It's Like in a Facility Where Drug Users Are Allowed to Shoot Up," NBC 26, April 11, 2018.

Philadelphia. . . . had the highest opioid death rate of any major U.S. city. Kayla Dwyer, *The Morning Call,* "Former Pennsylvania governor Ed Rendell says come 'arrest me' over this program," February 7, 2019.

"They can come and arrest me first." Allyn, "Former Gov. Ed Rendell Says 'Arrest Me First.' "

Centers for Disease Control and Prevention attributed [life-expectancy drop] in part to fentanyl. Rachael Rettner, "US Life Expectancy Dropped in 2017. Drug Overdose Deaths Are a Big Reason Why," *Live Science,* November 29, 2018.

Fentanyl driving down life expectancy in regions of Canada. Nicole Ireland, "Life Expectancy in Canada May Be Decreasing as Opioid Crisis Rages On," CBC, October 23, 2018.

"It could be an indication." Mario Moreno, author interview, November 16, 2018.

Rhode Island's strategy. Erick Trickey, "How the Smallest State Is Defeating America's Biggest Addiction Crisis," *Politico,* August 25, 2018.

[Ohio] overdose death rate drop dramatically in some areas. Abby Goodnough, "This City's Overdose Deaths Have Plunged. Can Others Learn From It?" *New York Times,* November 25, 2018.

"Data indicates that women run a higher risk of drug craving." Ashley Welch, "Drug Overdose Deaths Skyrocket among Middle-Aged Women," CBS News,

January 10, 2019.

"There's money for in-patient stabilization." Jaye Shyken, author interview, June 6, 2017.

Studies have given medication-assisted treatment credit for reducing overdose deaths. National Institutes of Health, "Methadone and Buprenorphine Reduce Risk of Death after Opioid Overdose," news release, June 19, 2018.

[Buprenorphine] had traditionally been difficult for doctors to prescribe. Susan Svrluga, "The Drug Suboxone Could Combat the Heroin Epidemic. So Why Is It So Hard to Get?" *Washington Post,* January 13, 2015.

Some treatment providers . . . stress the importance of abstinence-based recovery. James Legge, "Drug Addicts Need a Clean Break," *Guardian,* June 5, 2012.

Hazelden . . . in 2012 began providing medication-assisted treatment. Martin D. Seppala, *Integrating the Twelve Steps with Medication-Assisted Treatment for Opioid Use Disorder* (Center City, MN: Hazeldon Publishing, 2012), https://www.hazelden.org/OA_HTML/item/ 376138 ?Integrating-the-Twelve-Steps-with -Medication-Assisted-Treatment-for

-Opioid-Use-Disorder-Set-of-3&src
_url=itemquest.

Spiritual approach . . . has been recognized in academic literature. Marc Galanter, Helen Dermatis, Gregory Bunt, Caroline Williams, Manuel Trujillo, and Paul Steinke, "Assessment of Spirituality and Its Relevance to Addiction Treatment," *Journal of Substance Abuse Treatment,* June 16, 2006.

"We have this whole infrastructure set up." Christine Vestal, "These Pills Could Be Next U.S. Drug Epidemic, Public Health Officials Say," Pew: *Stateline,* July 18, 2018, https://www.pewtrusts.org/en/research-and-analysis/blogs/stateline/2018/07/18/these-pills-could-be-next-us-drug-epidemic-public-health-officials-say.

"Bailey's death shocked us to our core." Michael R. Brown, author interview, June 27, 2018.

"We know addiction is a disease." "Grand Forks Call to Action" and "Call to Action" video, GrandForks.gov, May 25, 2017, http://www.grandforksgov.com/government/city-leadership/mayor-s-office/call-to-action.

"There's been a lot of new thoughts on how we treat addiction." Michael Dulitz, author interview, June 22, 2018.

"It's not just your stereotypical drug user." Brett Johnson, author interview, June 25, 2018.

Tanner Gerszewski . . . at the very moment Henke was overdosing. Tanner Gerszewski, author interview, June 27, 2018.

"I'd like to, I guess forgive him." "Opial Pain: The Fatal Fentanyl: From China to American Small Town," Daily Video News, *Voice of America China,* February 28, 2018, https://www.voachinese.com/a/opioid-20180227/4273229.html.

"I'm just working and staying out of trouble the best I can." Kain Schwandt, author interview, June 12, 2018.

ABOUT THE AUTHOR

Ben Westhoff is an award-winning investigative reporter who has covered stories ranging from Los Angeles gangsta rap to Native American tribal disputes to government corruption. He is the author of two previous books: *Original Gangstas* about the birth of West Coast rap, and *Dirty South* about the southern rappers who re-invented hip-hop. He has written at length about culture, drugs, and corruption in the *Wall Street Journal, Rolling Stone,* the *Guardian, Village Voice, Vice, Oxford American,* and elsewhere.

The employees of Thorndike Press hope you have enjoyed this Large Print book. All our Thorndike, Wheeler, and Kennebec Large Print titles are designed for easy reading, and all our books are made to last. Other Thorndike Press Large Print books are available at your library, through selected bookstores, or directly from us.

For information about titles, please call:
(800) 223-1244

or visit our website at:
gale.com/thorndike

To share your comments, please write:
Publisher
Thorndike Press
10 Water St., Suite 310
Waterville, ME 04901